WILMA MANKILLER

*How One Woman United the Cherokee Nation
and Helped Change the Face of America*

D. J. HERDA

TWODOT®

GUILFORD, CONNECTICUT
HELENA, MONTANA

A · TWODOT® · BOOK

An imprint and registered trademark of The Rowman & Littlefield Publishing Group, Inc.
4501 Forbes Blvd., Ste. 200
Lanham, MD 20706
www.rowman.com

Distributed by NATIONAL BOOK NETWORK

British Library Cataloguing in Publication Information available

Library of Congress Cataloging-in-Publication Data

Names: Herda, D. J., 1948- author.
Title: Wilma Mankiller : how one woman united the Cherokee Nation and
  helped change the face of America / D.J. Herda.
Other titles: How one woman united the Cherokee Nation and helped change
  the face of America /
Description: Helena, Montana : TwoDot, 2021. | Summary: "This book
  chronicles the life of Wilma Pearl Mankiller, the first woman ever
  elected to be chief of the Cherokee Nation"—Provided by publisher.
Identifiers: LCCN 2021032031 (print) | LCCN 2021032032 (ebook) | ISBN
  9781493050611 (hardcover) | ISBN 9781493050628 (epub)
Subjects: LCSH: Mankiller, Wilma, 1945-2010. | Cherokee women—Biography. |
  Cherokee Indians—Kings and rulers—Biography. | Cherokee
  Indians—Social conditions. | Indian leadership—North America. |
  Cherokee women—North America—Politics and government.
Classification: LCC E99.C5 M3334 2021 (print) | LCC E99.C5 (ebook) | DDC
  973.04/975570092 [B]—dc23
LC record available at https://lccn.loc.gov/2021032031
LC ebook record available at https://lccn.loc.gov/2021032032

∞™ The paper used in this publication meets the minimum requirements of American National Standard for Information Sciences—Permanence of Paper for Printed Library Materials, ANSI/NISO Z39.48-1992.

Contents

Introduction

A Bridge Too Far

IT IS 1956. FROM SECTION C, ROW 14, SEAT 1 OF THE COLONY THEATER on the south side of Chicago, a young boy watches great men wearing white hats defeat less-than-great men wearing war paint and feathers.

The cowboys of the Old West, the *real* West, the one that Hollywood gave us before most of us even knew there *was* an Old West (Hollywood rarely exaggerates or obfuscates or otherwise paints an unrealistic portrait of life, remember), those very same cowboys always win in the end. That's because they stand for Truth and Justice and the American Way of Life, and they always win in the end.

They are America's heroes.

Luckily for Americans everywhere, their archenemies and nemeses throughout history have been easy enough to pick out: They are dark of skin and wear a lot of Ultrasuede. They race through trees while carrying ponderous primitive weapons that never once snag on a bush or shrub. They eat raw meat and plunder, rape, and pillage those who are different than they. They live in tents and dance around in frenetic circles, half-crazed beneath the silvery light of the moon, and they always lose in the end. They stand for savagery and brutality and unbridled ignorance, and they always lose in the end.

They are America's villains.

Life is filled with ironies and misconceptions. That the "noble savage" could be anything less than a wretched throwback to primordial time is preposterous. Hollywood tells us so. Not only Hollywood but also literature. Who other than Natty Bumppo himself could have shaped a nation besieged by prairie-dwellers utterly devoid of spirituality and scruples? Who but Davy Crockett could have carved a swath through red-skinned savages to open the West to civilized Americans? Who but Daniel Boone could have rid the landscape of deer-slayers and scalp-takers and returned morality and internal fortitude to a peace-loving people?

But spirituality, scruples, morality, and fortitude are not the first character traits that come to mind when perusing the history of humankind. In fact, they are among the last.

Unfold the history of *great* men and women, however, and examine the lives of some of humanity's brightest thinkers and wildest achievers, and those concepts are right there at the forefront. They *are* the mark of greatness, and they belong to no one race as much as they do to everyone.

Enter, stage right: Wilma Mankiller.

Accidentally. Arbitrarily. Coincidentally. Unmistakably.

For nearly half a century, she had not been in the vanguard but had *been* the vanguard, on the cutting edge, engulfed in social reform, devoted to spirituality, mired in scruples. She had struggled with the cookie-cutter image of the American Redskin, the *Injun*, the typically ignorant brave and the ever-complacent squaw, all her life. With the patience of Job and the persistence of the ages, she had endured while she had endeared. She was nobody's idea of a Native American, and she was everybody's.

And when she came reluctantly to Political America, she came complete with her own instruction booklet written among the strange words of her own language. Charley. Irene. Oakes. Indian Center. Alcatraz Island. Forced Occupation.

These are mere words to most people. These are more than words to others. These words to Mankiller marked what life was all about. They were some of life's most valuable lessons—the inspirations that drove humanity forward. These were to a young girl growing up in abject poverty and near-hopelessness life's most cherished inspirations.

To a woman named Mankiller, the world held, as it will forever, the promise of a better tomorrow. She could afford the luxury of clinging to the notion. She had been there, walked the walk, talked the talk, and accomplished what needed to be done when the world needed to see it happen. And damn the consequences.

If Honest Abe and Mary Todd Lincoln had had a daughter, she would have been a Mankiller. If George and Martha Washington had had a daughter, she would have been a Mankiller. If anyone throughout history had had a daughter—not just a daughter but one destined to pick up the struggle heaped upon the shoulders of humanity, to bear the brunt of every American's mistakes, to revel in the glory of everyone's victories and no one's defeats—she would have been a Mankiller.

She would have been Wilma.

As in Pearl.

As in Wilma Pearl Mankiller.

And the story has just begun.

Unveiling the Past

In a wire-fenced plot of land in south-central Wisconsin, 1980, a construction company petitions county administrators to allow it to create a new upper-middle-income residential development. There is a market for homes in affluent Dane County, and there is money to be made—lots of money. But the area has been designated an Indian burial ground for years, a sacred plot, and thus immune from development.

The construction company that has bid on the property files a motion for a review to release the land for development. The county executive contacts the Winnebago Nation and asks for formal clarification, and the deputy chief dispatches a medicine man to examine the grounds.

The medicine man, named Running Wolf, arrives at precisely 1:02 p.m. on Thursday, October 2, and begins walking through the leaves that have started falling from the oak and maple and hickory trees towering overhead. The clouds roll in on a blanket of mist. And the dew—the humidity or dampness or light drizzle so faint it is barely perceptible—filters its way down to earth.

Stretched out before Running Wolf, large rolling hills dot the grounds, and before long, the medicine man walks to the edge of one of the earthen swells and stops. He closes his eyes and lowers his head, mumbling something incoherent to the young journalist who had received word of the investigation and rushed out to witness the event.

Running Wolf raises his head, opens his eyes, and looks to his left before taking several steps in that direction and stopping suddenly at the edge of another rolling mound.

"Burial mound," he says softly, so softly that the journalist has to ask him to repeat the words. Running Wolf complies and takes several more steps, stopping intermittently to brush aside the musty leaves from the tall grass underfoot. He pauses once more, draws upon his thoughts, glances skyward, and finally peers back down at the earth. He reaches beneath his jacket and extracts a pouch of packaged tobacco and a booklet of rolling papers from his shirt pocket and begins to roll a cigarette. He offers the tobacco and papers to the journalist, who declines politely before thinking better of it. He takes the pouch, waves off the papers, and pulls a spent pipe from his slicker before filling the instrument to the brim and handing the tobacco back to the man. He extracts a pouch of his own pipe tobacco and holds it out to the Native American. "Cherry blend," the journalist comments.

The Indian nods, looks down at his own pouch, and laments simply, "Cheap." He dumps his own tobacco back into his pouch and finishes rolling the butt with the journalist's blend. Lighting up, he draws several times into his cheeks before inhaling deeply.

"I used to smoke this when I was in college," the journalist tells him. "The smell drove the girls crazy."

Running Wolf smiles. "I never smoked in college. Tobacco to us is sacred," he says. "It offers us a link to the spirits. It offers us a bridge to the past."

The journalist holds a lighter over the bowl of his pipe and sucks sharply against the bit. The tobacco begins to glow, and the smoke filters skyward. It fills his cheeks and feels pleasant, comforting, and then the journalist puckers his lips and blows out a plume of white-gray mist that snakes its way up toward the treetops.

"And what do the spirits tell you?" the journalist asks.

"These are hallowed grounds," he whispers, his gravel-worn voice unwavering in its decisiveness, "and must not be disturbed."

ONE

Pure Pearl

WILMA PEARL ENTERED THE WORLD A MANKILLER ON NOVEMBER 18, 1945, in the W. W. Hastings Indian Hospital at Tahlequah, Oklahoma, the very heart of the sprawling Cherokee Nation. It was an uneventful birth so far as they go, similar to the one her father, Charley, had experienced in *his* father's home, a small frame house not very far from where his daughter was born. Charley had made his debut thirty-one years earlier on November 15, 1914. It was the year of the outbreak of World War I and seven years after Oklahoma had become America's forty-sixth state.

Charley Mankiller was raised in a strict Cherokee environment by his aunt, following his mother's death when he was two. He had been educated in the Sequoyah Training School, a mandatory boarding facility where American Indians were forbidden to speak their Native tongues and were punished for even the slightest infraction. The school, appropriately enough, had been founded as an asylum in 1871 to provide housing for children orphaned by the Civil War, a conflict that had been fought partly in the Cherokee Nation with Cherokees serving in both the Union and the Confederate armies. Blue and gray knew no family allegiances, regardless of race.

At the war's end, the state expanded the facility into a sanctuary for Indian people who experienced mental or physical problems so severe they couldn't function in society without continuing professional help. In 1914, Cherokee chief W. C. Rogers sold the facility and forty acres of land to the federal government, which designated its use as a federal institution under the control of the Secretary of the Interior for "the

Indian orphans of Oklahoma of the restricted class." That meant for Native people of one-half Indian heritage or more. Congress passed an act in 1925 officially changing the name of the school to the Sequoyah Orphan Training School in honor of the red man credited with developing the Cherokees' written language, the first one in Native American history.

Despite the school's rich history, Charley didn't like it. In fact, he didn't like schools in general. He couldn't understand how leaving home and family and being immersed in a society that tried to strip him of everything he had ever learned or believed in could be of any use to him in the future. It was as if the first ten or twelve years of his life—going off alone into the woods, fending for himself, and learning from the tribal elders the difference between right and wrong—had all been wasted. His childhood experiences apparently amounted to nothing, offered him little of value, and were worth a pittance in return. His entire young life had been squandered on foolishness. Or so he was taught.

He *did* like the fact that the Sequoyah School had its own orchard, a sprawling garden, and plenty of farm animals from chickens and cows to mules and horses. He especially liked the fact that he was given responsibility for their care. That brought him a measure of pride, instilling in him a sense of trust, one of the few areas in his life where he felt as though he still maintained some control.

Charley also liked the fact that, while many of the personnel at the school were nothing short of vicious toward the students, one man—the head of the school, Superintendent Jack Brown (who was himself part Cherokee)—treated Charley well. Brown was a history and literature buff, and he went out of his way to tutor the boy in those subjects. In time, the young Cherokee student discovered a whole new world opened up to him through the white man's books. Charley learned to love reading, a gift he would later pass on to his children.

But many of his other teachers didn't care much about their students. They worked at Sequoyah not so much to educate their charges as to achieve a common goal. They were there to do a specific job—to reeducate the Indian "savage" in the ways of the white man—and they attacked their task with demonic determination.

The concept behind Indian boarding schools, which at the time were located nearly exclusively on Indian lands in the south-central United States, was simple. The institutions, both government-run and church-sponsored, were designed to wean Native American children of their bond to tribal living and to acclimatize them to the world of whiteness. They were to force the children to abandon their Native heritage, history, and language and cleanse them of their ethnic culture.

"The boarding-school concept," Wilma Mankiller recalled in her autobiography, "was simply another way for the federal government to deal with what its officials always called 'the Indian problem.' After first trying to wipe us all off the face of the earth with violence, they attempted to isolate us on reservations or, in the case of many people such as the Cherokees, place us in an area that the government called Indian Territory. All the while, they systematically conjured up policies to kill our culture."[1]

It was a concept that, in the case of Charley Mankiller, was destined to fail.

Even as a young boy, Charley was headstrong and proud. He learned to read and write well enough to understand the white man's language. He acquired the skills to perform basic math, recite some poetry, and grapple with the concept of "civilization" and what that meant in white America. He learned to function and thrive in another man's world. He absorbed, in fact, virtually everything his educators threw at him, every single thing they *wanted* him to learn except one. He never learned to turn his back on his heritage.

"I am thankful that even though my father was raised in such a boarding-school environment, he did not buy into everything that was being taught," Charley Mankiller's daughter wrote decades later. "Fortunately, he came from a strong family, and because of his traditional upbringing, the school was not successful in alienating him from his culture. He was a confident man and, to my knowledge, he never felt intimidated in the non-Indian world—a world he came to know even better after he met my mother."[2]

Wilma's mother, Clara Irene Sitton (Irene), was born to Robert Bailey and Pearl Halady Sitton in Adair County, Oklahoma, on

September 18, 1921. The prodigy of hardworking Dutch-Irish-American plains people, Irene's genealogy was composed mostly of Sittons and Gillespies, whose ethnic backgrounds were predominantly Dutch and Irish. Although she had no Indian blood in her, she was familiar with the Cherokee way of life, having lived among their people while attending school with Cherokee children.

Irene's ancestry extended back to North Carolina, where her lineage included some of the first iron-makers in the New World. It also included some less-than-desirable forbearers. The family still speculates that it is related to Charles Arthur Floyd, the rural Okie Dust Bowl–era bandit better known as "Pretty Boy" Floyd, one of the day's most notorious gangsters and the FBI's Public Enemy Number One. The Sittons had come from the same county in northern Georgia as Floyd and his kinfolk.

The Gillespies, on the other hand, were talented if less notorious contributors to society. Many of them worked as skilled craftsmen who turned out well-regarded long rifles, some of which had been used against the very Cherokee and other Indian tribes of the region from which sprang future generations of Gillespies.

Wilma's maternal grandfather was born in 1874, nine years after the end of the Civil War. He was, according to family accounts, tall and distinguished-looking—a family trait. He was a farmer by vocation and died, as had her great-grandfather, at the relatively young age of fifty-eight, right in the midst of the Great Depression.

According to legend, he had been skinning rabbits before going to the barn to harness two mules to the plow. The animals smelled the blood on his hands, spooked, and bolted, crushing the man against the side of the stall. He suffered severe internal injuries from which he never recovered.

Wilma's maternal grandmother was born in 1884 and lived until 1973, most of those years without a mother, who died when the woman was young. Wilma's grandmother went to live with her half-sister, Ida Mae Seism Jordan, in Washington County, Arkansas. In 1903, when she was nineteen years old, "Grandma Sitton" left her home in Arkansas to visit friends. Arriving at the Wauhillau community in Indian Territory, she soon caught the eye of Wilma's grandfather. At twenty-nine, Robert Sitton was a confirmed bachelor, but the vivacious if diminutive young Ida Mae captured his heart. After a brief courtship, they were married that same year and soon began a family. Wilma recalled, "My grandparents set up housekeeping near Wauhillau, where my grandfather's parents, William and Sarah Sitton, lived. Wauhillau was a thriving new settlement made up of Cherokee people and white pioneers, many of whom had come from Georgia about the same time as the Sittons in 1891."[3]

After a few years, Wilma's grandparents packed their belongings in a wagon and a two-seated buggy and moved to a small farm they had purchased near the eastern Oklahoma town of Titanic, "presumably named after the famous British transatlantic liner that had sunk on her maiden voyage in 1912."[4] The town even boasted one resident who had survived the sinking of the ship. Helen Churchill Candee, a nearby Guthrie resident, shared Lifeboat No. 6 with the "Unsinkable" Molly Brown. Her only injury throughout the horrific affair was a fractured ankle that left her on crutches for a year.

Shortly after acquiring their new farmland, Wilma's grandparents began clearing the fields for planting. Except for their oldest daughter, Sadie, who had stayed with her grandparents in Wauhillau, they sent their children to the one-room schoolhouse in Titanic. In all, Wilma's grandparents had seven children—three sons and four daughters—born between 1904 and 1921.

Following several more moves, including a stop at the town of Foraker in Osage County, Oklahoma, where Wilma's grandfather got a job working for the railroad, the Sitton family relocated once more, this time to Adair County. Grandma Sitton was determined to raise her family in the fresh country air, so she was delighted when they found a farm for sale not far from the community of Rock Mountain, where Wilma's mother, Irene, the youngest of the clan, was born.

Predictably, work on the farm was backbreaking physical labor. But Wilma's grandmother was up to every task. "I have heard it said that there was not a job on the farm my grandmother would not tackle, including plowing the fields. Folks described her as being spunky. Some years after my grandfather died and her children were raised, she sold her farm and moved into the town of Stilwell to run a boardinghouse."[5]

Wilma's mother, Irene, met Charley when she was quite young. The two had grown up in the twenties and thirties, living and playing together in the same rural community for most of their lives. Whenever their paths crossed, it was often with predictable results: Charley teased the petulant white girl mercilessly, and she struck back in kind—occasionally literally. Once, Irene recalled, her future husband had upset her so much that she threw a pie at him. Irene never did reflect upon the accuracy of her aim.

But any of the childhood aggravations that Irene had felt toward Charley soon turned to affection and—wooed by the young man's undeniable good looks and confidence—she eventually convinced her parents to allow him to court her. Not long after, the two were married. She was a mere girl of fifteen, and he was barely twenty-one, not unusually young for that era. Charley went to work, earning enough money to support the family—just barely—by raising strawberries and peanuts for cash crops, picking berries and green beans for extra money, and traveling to nearby Colorado during the harvest season to cut broomcorn, a plant with long, stiff stalks used to make brooms.

Irene's mother—just as with most respectable mothers everywhere—had been against the marriage of her daughter to Charley from the start. Charley had been raised in an Indian boarding school and had a reputation for "getting around." Irene had led the relatively sheltered life of a God-fearing country girl. "Mommy Dearest" considered the consummation a disaster in the making that couldn't possibly last.

But Irene and Charley were in love, as often happens even in rural America, and the young girl finally agreed to become Charley's wife. They exchanged their vows at the First Baptist Church in the sleepy little hamlet of Mulberry in Adair County. The local minister performed the Christian ceremony on March 6, 1937. Relations between Wilma's grandparents and the newlyweds remained strained for the next several years.

By the time Wilma entered the world in 1945, Irene had already adapted to the Cherokee culture in which she had found herself immersed. She spoke some Cherokee—enough to get by, although nowhere near as fluently as did Charley, who was bilingual.

Not even the name Mankiller fazed Wilma's mother, for as strange as it sounds to some white people, it was revered within the Native American community. It was a title bestowed upon the bravest of warriors whose job was to protect the tribe from hostile neighbors and marauding renegades. Besides, the name must have seemed pretty tame compared to other popular Cherokee surnames in the area—monikers such as Thirsty, Hummingbird, Wolf, Beaver, Squirrel, Soap, Canoe, Gourd, Fourkiller, Sixkiller, and Walkingstick. Author Gerald Hausman explains:

> *The name of honor was received after a person had attained some kind of special distinction in the tribe. This would occur through the performance of an act of great character, or it could be given by a secret society. The second name marked a moment of excellence in a person's life and was not a hereditary position. Hereditary names, such as that of an Iroquois chief, were passed down successively to whoever filled the position for as long as there were people to fill it.[6]*

Wilma learned as she matured that the coveted name *Mankiller* could be spelled different ways. One version is the literal *Asgaya*, meaning "man," combined with the personal-name suffix *dihi*, or "killer." Another is *Outacity*, an honorary title that also means "Man-killer." Cherokee historians and genealogists believe that Mankiller is a military title, but Wilma learned there was another kind of Mankiller in her tribal past. In the Cherokee medicinal and conjuring tradition, Mankillers were known to attack other people to avenge wrongs that had been perpetrated against themselves or others whom they served. An enforcer of right, this type of Mankiller could alter things for better or worse and could change people's minds, make an illness worse on a whim, or even shoot a deadly invisible arrow into the body of an enemy.

As Wilma discovered her family's heritage, she learned that many distinguished leaders from the past had held the title of Mankiller, differentiated by the towns in which they lived. In the eighteenth century, for example, there was the Mankiller of Tellico, the Mankiller of Estatoe, and the Mankiller of Keowee. One prominent warrior and tribal leader, Outacity, or "Man-killer," apparently joined a delegation of Cherokees visiting London in 1762, fourteen years before the American War for Independence began, to address the troubled reign of King George III.

Even though the Mankiller name had been honored for centuries, Wilma was forced to endure occasional derision because of it. Many people were visibly shaken when she was introduced to them as Wilma Mankiller, thinking it a fierce- and even threatening-sounding name. Wilma reflected upon the problems her name created early in her life:

Some people are startled when I am introduced to them as Wilma Mankiller. . . . Many find it amusing and make nervous jokes, and there are still those times when people display their ignorance. For example, I was invited in December of 1992 to attend President-elect Bill Clinton's historic economic summit meeting in Little Rock, Arkansas, just about a month prior to his inaugural. The Wall Street Journal, *one of America's most respected newspapers, made a rather unfortunate remark about my surname that is best described as a cheap shot.*

"Our favorite name on the summit list, we have to admit," stated the Journal *editorial, "is Chief Wilma Mankiller, representing the Cherokee Nation, though we hope not a feminist economic priority."*

Tim Giago, publisher of Indian Country Today, *a Native American newspaper, quickly fired back at the* Journal. *"The fact that this powerful lady has been featured in several major magazines . . . has appeared on countless television shows, and has been given tons of coverage in major, national newspapers, appears to have escaped the closed minds at the* Journal. *One has to ask if they ever get out into the real world."*

Fortunately, most people I come across in my travels, especially members of the media, are more sensitive and generally more aware than that editorial writer. When someone unknowingly or out of ignorance makes a snide comment about my name, I often resort to humor. I look the person in the eye and say with a straight face that Mankiller is actually a well-earned nickname. That usually shuts the person up.[7]

Nevertheless, there were times in her childhood when Wilma endured a lot of teasing about her name. On many occasions, she wished she could disappear before the class roll call was taken and everyone laughed. Her parents admonished her to be proud of the family name. In time, she found that most people had come to accept her name, many of them saying that it was only appropriate and perhaps a bit ironic that the first female chief should be referred to as *Mankiller*.

As she aged, Wilma displayed her pride in her lineage, often saying that her family moniker was "a strong name. I am proud of my name— very proud. And I am proud of the long line of men and women who have also been called Mankiller. I hope to honor my ancestors by keeping the name alive."[8]

Born into the Mankiller household on Sunday, November 18, 1945, Wilma was the sixth child of eleven in the family. She entered the world at the W. W. Hastings Indian Hospital in Tahlequah, Oklahoma. It was the tail end of autumn, a few months after the surrender of the Japanese to the Americans and the conclusion of World War II. If her father had not fallen off a log while cutting trees for railroad ties, she often mused, "I would not have been born. But his leg injuries prevented him from enlisting in the military service and going off to war. So instead of fighting, he stayed around home, and three of us were born in or around that time."[9]

Three brothers and two sisters had been born before her. Louis Donald entered the world in 1937, Frieda Marie in 1938, Robert Charles in 1940, Frances Kay in 1942, and John David in 1943. Following Wilma came Linda Jean in 1949, Richard Colson in 1951, Vanessa Lou in 1953, James Ray in 1956, and the final Mankiller to join the clam, William Edward in 1961. The last two children were the only ones born in California. So, of the eleven children born to her parents, she often said, the wrens and crickets who, according to legend, smile warmly at the birth of each female, were happy on five of the occasions.

As she grew up, nearly everyone called Wilma by her middle name, Pearl. She had been named Wilma after the wife of her father's uncle and Pearl after her mother's mother. Wilma is a short form of the Dutch name Wilhelmina. The name Pearl comes, of course, from the speck of sand inside the oyster that becomes an aggravation to the mollusk and is eventually covered with smooth layers of shell material that often develop into an object of gem quality. It is not a scientific fact that eluded the girl: "Not that I consider myself a precious treasure," she often kidded. "I don't mean to say that. But the whole notion of an irritant developing into something of worth is appealing to me."[10]

One of Wilma Pearl's earliest memories was of sitting on a trunk in the family house at Mankiller Flats in the Rocky Mountain community. They had only recently moved there, and the young girl was overjoyed. She recalled the moment clearly:

> *My folks had rented from other people until 1948, when we settled there on the family land. That house was built by Charley, my father. He built it himself. His uncle, Looney Gourd, helped him with the construction. So did my oldest brother, Don. My mother now lives on the site of that house. We eventually rented that original family house to some of our cousins. After that, other people lived there. Then there was a fire and the house burned down. But back when I was just a small girl, that house was the first real family home I can recall. Thinking back to those times, I remember it as a little bitty house with too many people living there—and more still to come.*[11]

The four-room building had been constructed of rough lumber and featured bare plank floors and walls. It was covered by a tin roof. In the winter, their only heat came from a woodstove, which also provided them with the ability to cook. The home had no electricity, so the family lighted the rooms with candles and coal-oil lamps.

The sparsely furnished home had an outhouse for a bathroom. The washing machine ran by employing a gasoline motor connected to the spindle that turned an agitator, and the clothing iron ran off natural gas. For all their bathing and cooking needs, they hauled water from the spring a quarter mile from the house. That spring also served as a refrigerator for some of their food, which they kept in a box submerged in the icy water.

"To this day," Wilma wrote in her autobiography, "I prefer to use wood for heating my home. The smell of the fire is familiar. And I still love the sound of rain. When I hear it, I remember the sound it made when it fell on our old tin roof. That's a pleasant memory for me."[12]

Other memories were not quite so pleasant. The family was not well off when it came to money. "Dirt poor" is how she often described her early existence. Like many of the people in Adair County, they lived life on the "bottom rung of the . . . ladder."[13]

Yet, despite all the hardships, none of that seemed especially important at the time, Wilma recalled—understandably so.

By the late 1940s, much of the Cherokee population had already been mixed-blood for decades. These included many successful, prominent, and high-profile people, leading to the mistaken notion that *all* Cherokees had become happily assimilated into the mainstream of white Anglo-Saxon American life. In reality, there were more full-blood, half-blood, and other mixed-blood Cherokees still living traditional lives. That means they lived in extreme poverty in Cherokee communities, as did the Mankiller clan, scattered throughout the hills. Most of those settlements didn't appear on any maps. Many of them were not visible from the road to travelers passing through the area. Each community was made up of families living on their individual government allotments of land.

These people congregated for various events at community centers, churches, schools, or at one of the tribal ceremonial grounds where they held dances. Sometimes the Mankiller family attended services at Echota Baptist Church. On other occasions, they went to the church in Rocky Mountain. But they were never, according to Wilma, regular church-goers, nor did they attend Sunday school or learn a great deal about Christianity.

Sometimes they attended ceremonial dances. On such occasions, people brought plenty of food and, of course, even more children with whom young Wilma ran and played, accompanied by laughter often well into the night. The dances were held outside, sometimes lasting into the next morning. Wilma recalled:

It gave me such a good feeling to go to the ceremonial dances. We had such a great time. But I also recall that we were always secretive about going to the ceremonial dance grounds or even about going to some other Cherokees' houses for parties with fiddles and poker games. My sister told me we had to keep it a secret because some folks thought such things were sinful. I thought that was odd. Later, I figured maybe she was right. Perhaps some of our non-Indian neighbors would not approve of music making or especially of a ceremonial dance.

Most people we knew spoke Cherokee in their homes and as their first language. There were Cherokee-language Baptist churches. A significant number of folks spoke only Cherokee and no English. In our home, both languages were used, often interchangeably. Cherokee was spoken almost exclusively whenever we visited other native people or when they came to see us. My mother, even though she is white, learned to speak passable conversational Cherokee. When it was just the family, we mostly used English except for simple phrases such as the Cherokee for "Pass the salt" or "I need some water." As children, we certainly understood Cherokee, but because we had a white mother, we never became as fluent in the language as our father and other kinfolk.[14]

In the small communities of eastern Oklahoma, Native people raised extensive vegetable gardens and harvested plant foods from the woods, including wild onions, greens, mushrooms, and berries. Hunting and fishing helped fill the people's plates, and those who could afford them raised cattle and hogs. The Mankiller family was so large that they had to supplement their diet with wild game. Occasionally, Charley or Wilma's older brother Don would be fortunate enough to kill a groundhog or a wild pig. Wilma wrote:

The younger boys also went hunting. In those early days, we ate a lot of squirrel. Squirrels are small, so you have to have several to make a meal for a family. My mother would bread the squirrels lightly and fry them like chicken. They tasted a little like chicken. She made gravy from the drippings. Sometimes we had squirrel soup and dumplings, or soup made from quail or other birds. We gathered greens such as dandelions and poke. There were walnuts and hickory nuts, as well as blackberries, mulberries, and wild grapes. We fished and ate our fill of perch, crawfish, catfish, and frogs. Mom canned jars of tomatoes, beans, and corn from our vegetable garden, and stored food underground or in the shed. In some years, we also grew strawberries or peanuts which we sold for cash. Even though we were poor, I cannot remember ever being hungry as a little girl. Somehow, we always had food on our table.[15]

She recalled in particular how they used to barter with neighbors for those things they didn't raise or collect themselves, creating a sense of community that, she said, "extended beyond my family."[16]

Employment for rural Cherokees was mostly sporadic and anything but easy. In Adair County, many Native people cut wood to sell while others worked on migrant seasonal harvest crews. For the Mankillers, life consisted of a rugged, rigorous battle, a constant struggle to earn enough money to meet the family's minimal cash needs. Wilma's parents and older brothers and sisters had to scrape a living out of the stony hardscrabble that passed for soil. Don, the eldest, quit school after the eighth grade so he could help his parents support the family.

The older kids often accompanied their parents to cut and peel timber for use as railroad ties or utility poles. Most of the time, Wilma stayed home. One of the times when she didn't, she picked up a soda-pop bottle that she had found and took a swig. What she had expected to be a sweet treat turned out to be kerosene. Her parents had to rush her to the hospital emergency room in Tahlequah. Another time, Wilma's sister Frances sliced her knee so severely while cutting ties that she had to be raced thirty miles over bad roads for emergency care.

Typical of life in rural America following the Great Depression, few people had reliable transportation. That meant the opportunities for holding "regular jobs" were few. Wilma recalled:

Besides cutting railroad ties, my father and Don went to Colorado each year to help bring in the broomcorn and generate enough money to buy shoes and some other basics for all the kids. Broomcorn was an important material for making brooms, but it was also used in shipbuilding enterprises. The corn was harvested and put into a machine that crushed it and made it into bales. The bales were hauled by truck from the farms around Campo, Colorado, in the southeastern corner of the state.[17]

The Cherokee workers often traveled to Campo together, the lucky ones by car or on buses provided by the farm owners. They were joined by Hispanics and a few whites, but mostly the field hands were Native people. Charley and Don worked seven days a week, beginning at dawn and ending at dusk, along with a crew of more than twenty other men. The work was backbreaking, the men halting only long enough to swig dippers of water and wring out their sweaty neckerchiefs. But they never complained. The crews worked straight through until noon, at which time they broke for lunch. Women from the farms carried food out to the fields and set it onto quickly arranged tables. The workers rushed through their meals to have a few minutes to rest up in the shade before going back out into the fields. For their efforts, they received from nine to ten dollars a day—a princely sum at the time.

Unfortunately for Wilma, the timing of the broomcorn harvest didn't align with her school classes, which in Oklahoma began in early August so that the children could be through with school in May to help with the local harvests. She recalled:

When school started, my father and brother were still in Colorado, so we had to begin classes without shoes for the new year. But before too long, Dad and Don would come home with some money in their pockets. Then they bought everyone shoes and warm coats before the cold weather set in. It was a very exciting time for all of us. Getting new leather shoes was pretty special. Most of our clothing was hand-me-downs or was made of flour sacks. Our flour came in huge sacks, so my mother used that cloth to make our clothes—both underwear and some of our outerwear. I recall that those sacks had roses or other floral prints on them. Even though, as the old saying goes, it is hard to make a silk purse from a sow's ear, the designs made our clothes look a little better.[18]

There were no school buses back then, so the children had to walk three miles to and from Rocky Mountain School. Occasionally, Wilma recalled, her brother Bob snuck off to hunt or just to laze around in the woods all day, joining his siblings on their return journey home. "Once when Bob skipped school . . .," she remembered, "he was bitten on the hand by a rattlesnake. By the time he returned home, his entire arm and shoulder were profoundly swollen."[19] Fortunately, their parents rushed him to the doctor in time to save him, and he suffered no additional effects.

The schoolhouse where the Mankiller children attended classes from first through fifth grades was a little, whitewashed, wood-frame building. Charley had helped to roof it. It had one large general room, a kitchen, and two classrooms large enough to hold sixty students comfortably. Well, to *hold* them, at any rate.

The teachers, Wilma wrote, "were different than any I had known before entering school. They wore lipstick, and they spoke and dressed differently than the rest of the women in our community. . . . Most days, the teachers had a big pot of beans on for lunch. Oftentimes, the families from the area would have pie suppers and auctions at the schoolhouse to raise money for Christmas or other events."[20]

One of the advantages of being poor when you're young is that you don't often recognize the affliction. Wilma never knew her family was "poor" until one day when a well-to-do little girl saw her flour-sack underwear while Wilma was in the outhouse. "She ran and told some other girls, and they all teased me about it. That was really the first time I had any inkling that we were different."[21]

Even at that, the warmth and love the Mankillers showed their children made up for their lack of material possessions. Wilma's parents had a strong relationship and never seemed to hide their love. "They were visibly affectionate with one another, hugging and holding hands. One time, when we were all going for a ride in our old car, Mom raced to beat us children so she could sit in the front seat right beside Dad."[22]

Whenever the family piled into their old, black 1949 Ford, Charley helped pass the time by telling scary stories as they drove the back roads through the woods. Often, the tales had a pointed moral, like the time he had run into some low-hanging branches on which an owl had alighted. The bird flew away, leaving blood on the windshield.

"We were terrified by the story," Wilma recalled.

Owls are ominous birds to some Cherokees. It is believed that certain persons can change themselves into owls and travel through the night doing evil to others. One time, Dad told us, someone in our area shot an owl with a silver bullet. The next day, mysteriously, the person learned that his most bitter enemy had been found shot to death.

My father's stories were important to all of us. Our main forms of entertainment were storytelling and visiting. Either we went to see other families, or folks visited us. Mostly we saw other Cherokee people.[23]

Not surprisingly, Cherokees were the people with whom young Wilma identified the most. Whenever white folks came to their house, she felt so shy and embarrassed that she often ran outside into the woods or hid upstairs in the attic. Her wariness, she believed, developed when, as a little girl, she was walking to school with her sister.

Some well-dressed white ladies occasionally would drive up in their big cars. They came to bring us clothes and offer us rides to school. I suppose they felt it was their Christian duty to pick us up and take us to school. One time when we got inside their car, those ladies looked at us with sad expressions and said, "Bless your little hearts." It was not the words that got to me, but the way they said them, along with the looks on their faces. Were they being sympathetic because we had to walk? Was it because of our social situation? Was it the way we were dressed? After that, we called those women the "Bless Your Heart" ladies. Even as a child, I could tell if someone was being condescending or patronizing to me because I was Indian.[24]

Sometimes, the family drove on weekends to the town of Stilwell, the seat of Adair County, so they could spend time with Irene's Uncle Tom Sitton and his wife, Maud. It was not a long drive, and Stilwell was a lot larger than Rocky Mountain. "Those were good trips," Wilma recalled, "because we usually ended up getting a dime to go to the movies or buy candy."[25] Every May, Stilwell hosted a strawberry festival that drew visitors from around the state to eat berries and celebrate the harvest, and the entire Mankiller family looked forward to the event.

When the Mankillers weren't traveling to Stilwell to visit relatives, Wilma's great-aunt came to see them. She brought clothes and other gifts for the children. She was one white woman Wilma didn't shy away from, most likely because she was family and worked so hard at befriending the children. She had married Charley's Uncle George, and the two lived in a sprawling brick residence in Tahlequah near the old Cherokee Female Seminary. When the Mankiller allotments had been parceled out at the turn of the century, Uncle George's ancestors received land near Bartlesville, the headquarters of Phillips Petroleum Company. When oil was later discovered on his property, George's life changed forever.

Despite her acceptance of Maud, Wilma felt much more comfortable around the family's Cherokee relatives, possibly because they saw them more often and shared common interests and histories. One woman Wilma grew particularly close to was her father's half-sister, Jensie Hummingbird. Small, birdlike, with hair so black "it looked blue in the sunlight," she wore cotton housedresses that she made herself. Since she didn't drive, the Mankillers most often initiated their visits. Even though she spoke no English, everyone managed to communicate; above all, the message she conveyed to the children was that she loved every one of them. Jensie, like many members of the Mankiller family, had some severe health problems and suffered for most of her adult life with diabetes and arthritis.

Another of Wilma's favorite relatives, Maude Wolf, grew up with Charley. Even though they were cousins, the children called her Aunt Maude. An imposingly tall, thin, attractive woman with prominent cheekbones and excellent posture, she loved to work outdoors. She enjoyed playing the traditional Cherokee game of stickball and helping her husband, Jim, maintain the ceremonial grounds. She also took long walks in the woods, during which she gathered the "gifts of nature" that she used to prepare a meal.

Lacking formal education, Aunt Maude had wisdom beyond school-books. Her husband was a strict Cherokee traditionalist, Indian doctor, and ceremonial dance leader. Maude and Jim had nine children, but because they lived a fair distance from Rocky Mountain, they didn't go to school with the Mankiller clan. Jim spoke no English, but Wilma recalled him as a "thoughtful and powerful presence with a crazy sense of humor."[26]

On their visits, the children usually played outdoor games such as hide-and-seek, or they ran through the woods playing tag. Charley often warned them about staying out too late and told them to be particularly watchful for mountain lions and bobcats. Wilma's parents most often played cards with their hosts, sometimes all night. On those occasions, the adults laid quilts on the floor for the children who invariably slept soundly, exhausted from a day and night spent outside among the trees, plants, and animals.

No doubt, Wilma's favorite relative was her father's Aunt Maggie Gourd. Wilma's dad had lived with her for a while when he was growing up. She lived only a mile and a half from the Mankillers, so they visited her often. Wilma recalled:

She had a striking, intelligent face and wore her very dark hair pulled back. Aunt Maggie had a nice wood-frame house—three big rooms and a porch. She also had good furniture, probably purchased when she had a much bigger ranch. Family legend has it that she married a much younger man, Looney Gourd, who sold a lot of her assets little by little until she owned very few cattle or goods. We traded farm goods and produce with Aunt Maggie. My brother Johnny and I walked to her house with eggs to swap for fresh milk. If we were lucky, Aunt Maggie had a story to tell us. I didn't know it at the time, but Aunt Maggie told stories in the old Cherokee tradition. Some of those tales were frightening and others were not, but all of her stories taught us a lesson of some kind.[27]

Wilma's brother Johnny was only two years older than she and strikingly dissimilar in appearance. While the girl had brown hair and hazel eyes, Johnny had brown eyes and raven-black hair. He was built like their father—sturdy with broad shoulders. Growing up, Johnny almost always wore overalls.

Since Johnny and Wilma were often asked to watch over their younger siblings while the older ones worked outside the home, their Aunt Maggie impressed upon them the importance of taking that job seriously. She told them a story about a young Cherokee man and woman who took their baby into the woods. When they stopped to make camp, they spread a blanket on the ground and put the baby down to nap. While the infant dozed, the parents crept away so as not to disturb the child. They built a fire, and when it was going well and their campsite was prepared, they returned to the blanket for the baby only to find the infant gone. Only the blanket remained. They searched everywhere but never found the child.

When the children asked what had happened to the infant, Aunt Maggie told them that the Little People, *Yunwi Tsunsdi*, who live in the woods wherever Cherokees live, had come across the baby. Believing it had been abandoned, they took it to raise as one of their own. Aunt Maggie's story did the trick. Johnny and Wilma made a solemn vow to keep a very close watch over their brothers and sisters from that day on to prevent the Little People from carrying them away. Wilma wrote in her autobiography:

Stories of Little People have always been among the favorites of Cherokee children. The Little People look like Cherokees but are small, only about three feet tall. They speak our language. Cherokees always describe them "secondhand." It is said that if one sees the Little People and tells about it, that person will surely die. If anything is found in the forest, Cherokees assume that it belongs to the Little People. If a Cherokee woman goes out to gather hickory nuts in the fall and happens on a woven basket left by another gatherer, she can pick it up and say out loud, "Little People, I am taking this basket." Then it is hers to keep. That is her right.

Others say that the Little People assist the Cherokee "Indian doctors," those who are sometimes called medicine men. It is also said that the Little People watch out for small children in the woods, like the baby in Aunt Maggie's story. But mostly, Little People are known to be mischievous.[28]

Wilma, fascinated by the rich tableau of Aunt Maggie's stories, relished each and every one of them, particularly those telling of the old days of territorial times. She spoke of outlaws and gunmen and vigilantes and hidden treasure. She relayed accounts of famous bank robbers such as Cherokee Bill and Ned Christie, who had hidden their stolen gold all around the Rocky Mountain community. To protect their loot, the bandits went to Indian doctors, or medicine men, to ask them to make powerful medicine to safeguard their booty. Presumably, that's the reason so little of all their treasure was ever recovered.

Beyond the excitement of listening to Aunt Maggie's stories, Wilma enjoyed the physical challenges sometimes associated with merely getting to her home, which she said often proved to be an "adventure."

One time Johnny and I were walking to Aunt Maggie's when a coach-whip snake dropped from a tree on the path in front of us. The snake was four or five feet long with a brown tail. Such snakes are called coachwhips because they look as if they are made of braided leather like the small whips coachmen used to drive horses. It must have stirred our imaginations, because even now when recalling that incident, it seems to me that the snake deliberately jumped down at us. The snake was so infuriated at missing its mark that it chased us. Afraid to look back, we ran as fast as we could. When we finally stopped, out of breath, we were still afraid that the snake would catch up to us and whip us to death. That was what we had heard could happen. We kept going straight to our house and never turned our heads once.

Another time on our way to Aunt Maggie's house, Johnny was carrying eggs. We decided to take a shortcut across a pasture when out of nowhere came a bull charging after us. Johnny fell down and broke every single egg. He scrambled to his feet, and we made it to the safety of a fence just in time. We never could decide which was more frightening—the charging bull or the fury of our parents over those smashed eggs.[29]

Despite such hidden hazards—or possibly because of them—Wilma always loved being outdoors. She cherished the smells of the open air and the sights of the rocks and trees, the plants and animals. Most of all, she loved springtime.

Our place had a lot of dogwood and redbud trees. There were also dozens of different kinds of flowers. I guess my whole family loved the outdoors. My mother could name every tree, bush, flower, and edible plant we encountered in the woods. My father must have known somehow that I would love flowers because the Cherokee name he gave me is a-ji-luhsgi, *which means "flower." I have always loved the small purple and yellow flowers that grow unattended in the woods near my house. I would sometimes examine every detail of the tiny petals.*[30]

Growing up for an outdoors-loving young girl meant bonding with nature. Sharing her adventures with friends and neighbors became part of her heritage. She couldn't realize it at the time, but those bonds were soon to come to an end.

Although Wilma remembered the early years of her childhood with fondness and a sense of security, the financial burden of caring for a large family on a limited and unstable income finally forced her father to take drastic steps.

In 1956, Charley, driven to provide a better life for his steadily expanding family, agreed to move them from Oklahoma to California as part of an ambitious Bureau of Indian Affairs (BIA) resettlement program. It was initiated by the same bureaucrats who had previously "relocated" Japanese Americans during World War II. The program, yet another misguided experiment in social engineering, transplanted rural Native Americans into industrial cities scattered across the country. The BIA trumpeted its efforts as a wonderful opportunity for Indian families to get great jobs, obtain a good education for their kids, and, once and for all, leave poverty behind. The Indian Relocation Act of 1956 (also known as Public Law 959 or the Adult Vocational Training Program) encouraged Native Americans to leave Indian reservations, acquire skills, and assimilate into the general population. As part of the Indian termination policy of that era that removed the legal tribal status of numerous groups, it played a significant role in increasing the population of Indians in urban America in the coming years.

At a time when the US government was decreasing subsidies to Indians living on reservations, the Relocation Act offered to pay moving expenses and provide some vocational training for those who were willing to leave the reservations for certain government-designated cities where employment opportunities were thought to be more favorable. The assistance consisted of relocation transportation, moving household goods, a daily stipend for both the time of relocation and up to four weeks after, and funds to purchase tools and equipment for apprentice workers. Additional benefits included medical insurance for workers and their dependents, grants to buy work clothing, subsidies to buy household goods and furniture, tuition cost reimbursement for vocational night-school training, and, in some cases, funds to help buy a home.[31]

It all sounded too good to be true. And it was. The program's ultimate goal had nothing to do with providing increased opportunities for oppressed Native Americans but instead was designed to weaken reservation ties and diffuse whatever political power the tribes had once held.

The move was, in its goals, similar to the 1838 relocation of the Cherokee Nation from its ancestral grounds in the Southeast when federal troops under President Andrew Jackson ripped Indian families from their homes in the Carolinas, Tennessee, and Georgia. Acting under the vigilant eye of the US Army, the emigrants were forced to march to new reservations scattered throughout the Southwest. Wilma's great-grandfather was among the more than sixteen *thousand* Native Americans and African slaves uprooted and forced to make the journey on foot. Harsh weather, hunger, disease, and abuse from both US soldiers and private profiteers along the way decimated the marchers, resulting in the deaths of at least four thousand of them.

The infamous "Trail of Tears" resulted in the relocation of nearly twelve thousand men, women, and children who survived the brutal journey only to become wards of the state for decades to come.[32]

By the time the Civil War ground to a halt in 1865, whatever good fortune and prosperity that remained for the Cherokee Nation had ended with it. Because of where they lived, the North viewed the Cherokees, many of whom had not taken a side in the conflict, as defeated Southern sympathizers. Poverty replaced affluence as the government began stripping land from the Cherokees to make room for other tribes that had also been forced to leave their native lands for Indian Territory.

Shortly after the turn of the century, the federal government succeeded in dismantling the Cherokees' tribal government, blunting the Cherokee Constitution, and dividing their tribal lands into individual allotments.[33] The Mankiller family, like many others, had received its share of land in the wooded Oklahoma hills.

But by 1956, a weak regional economy had targeted the Mankillers for relocation. It was the perfect impetus to move local tribes off their native lands so the government could open up their property to resettlement by rambunctious whites. By relocating the Indians to reservations scattered across the country, the BIA hoped to reclaim their lands, which contained some of the richest deposits of coal and oil in the nation. They planned on selling those lands to large corporations for development.

So, with a fistful of government assurances and a heart filled with hope, Charley Mankiller packed up his family and moved them west to the Bay Area, where he was told he would have the best chance of finding success and *meaningful employment.*

Although relocation was voluntary—unlike the implementation of so many other federal Indian programs—the BIA acted with impunity in coercing Native American participation. At least one piece of relocation propaganda appealed directly to Indian parents: "If you won't do this much for yourself, at least do it for the sake of your children."[34] Charley believed their move to Daly City, California, in October 1956 was the best thing for everyone. And so did many other families.

In a Native American community that was staunchly pro-family, the government's appeals fell on receptive ears. Many families took part in the relocation process for what they viewed to be a last-ditch effort to keep their families together. Wilma wrote:

We were not forced to do anything, but that did not matter—not to me. Not when the time came for our family to leave Mankiller Flats. Not when we had to say farewell to the land that had been our family's home for generations, and move far away to a strange place. It was then that I came to know in some small way what it was like for our ancestors [in the 1800s] when the government troops made them give up their houses and property. It was a time for me to be sad.[35]

If the promises the government made to the people had been true, things might not have been so bad. But when the families began arriving in their new host cities, most discovered the tragic realities of a program that was systemically slanted toward menial labor. If good jobs and advanced salaries were available, they weren't available to Cherokee families.

So, the government program promised the Mankiller family funds, employment, and better housing as an inducement to relocate west. Instead of enforcing relocation through the use of guns and bayonets as in the past, this new and *improved* BIA promoted resettlement through brochures featuring staged photographs of "smiling Indians in 'happy homes' in the big cities."[36]

Wilma recalled that some BIA people came to their home to talk to their father about the specific elements of the program. They said the government wanted to "get out of the Indian business," and one of the ways to do that was by helping individuals and families relocate to larger cities.

Dad listened to their pitch. . . . I think Dad initially was opposed to our leaving Oklahoma and our land. As a boy, he had been taken from his home against his will to attend Sequoyah Boarding School. He did not want to leave his community and people again. But he talked it over with some Cherokee friends, and eventually he decided it would be a good idea to move. He must have honestly believed that in a distant city he could provide a better life for his children, with all the modern amenities.

I never liked the idea of our moving away. I can still remember hiding in a bedroom in our house of rough-hewn lumber, listening while my father, mother, and oldest brother talked in the adjoining room about the benefits and drawbacks of relocating our family. We younger children tried to listen through the door. We were terrified. They were talking about possible destinations. They spoke of places we had barely heard of—Chicago, New York, Detroit, Oakland, and San Francisco. California seemed to be their favorite. Finally my parents chose San Francisco because Grandma Sitton, my mother's mom, had moved to California in 1943. A widow when she left Oklahoma, she had remarried and settled in Riverbank, a community in the farm belt about ninety miles east of San Francisco.[37]

As the family began making preparations for the move, the children had difficulty envisioning California. They had been as far as Muskogee to attend the fair on a school field trip and had traveled to nearby Stilwell and Tahlequah, but that was the extent of their world. It was a universe comprising a ten-mile radius from the family home at Mankiller Flats. Charley and Don had worked the fields of Colorado cutting broomcorn, and Irene had been to Arkansas to see her sister. Beyond that, the world was a mysterious entity somewhere "out there."

Wilma recalled her mother's particular reluctance to move: "My mother was scared about leaving, and hated the idea of moving to California. She really opposed it at first, more than anyone else. But finally, knowing she would be living close to her mother [Grandma Sitton], she was convinced to go along with my father, believing that life might be better for us all."[38]

Despite Irene's acceptance, neither Wilma nor her sister Frances was prepared to leave. They asked if they could remain behind to stay with friends, but their parents insisted they come. Then the girls toyed with the notion of running away, but they never got around to actually doing it. As moving day came closer, Wilma and her sister kept hoping that something would happen, some kind of miracle that would allow them to remain behind instead of trekking off to a faraway land.

But miracles were in short supply in those days, even for the Mankiller family. In October 1956, the day arrived for their departure for California. It was a day that would remain branded in Wilma Pearl's memory forever.

There were nine of us kids then. It was before the last two were born. My oldest sister, Frieda, was attending Sequoyah High School and did not move with us. My folks had sold off everything, including the old car. We all piled in a neighbor's car, and he drove us to Stilwell so we could catch the train headed west to California. As we drove away, I looked at our house, the store, my school. I took last looks. I wanted to remember it all. I tried to memorize the shapes of the trees, the calls of animals and birds from the forest. All of us looked out the windows. We did not want to forget anything.

When we got to Stilwell, Dad took us to a restaurant, and we had bowls of chili. We were not a very happy crew—two adults and eight children leaving everything behind for an unknown place. Just getting aboard the train was terrifying for the smaller children. It was a new experience. We settled in all over the place. Some of the children were more comfortable sleeping on the floor, others stayed on the seats or beneath them. My youngest baby sister was marking the back of a seat with a crayon. We were a wild bunch. We must have looked like a darker version of the Joad family from John Steinbeck's novel, The Grapes of Wrath.

My mother was still scared about the move. Dad was also worried, but he was excited about the chance for a better life for all of us. As we got settled on the train, he turned to my mother and said, "I don't think I will ever be back until I come home in a coffin." As it turned out, Dad was right. The next time he came home was more than fourteen years later when he was buried in his native land.[39]

As soon as the family had settled aboard the train, Frances began to cry. The conductor came along and asked if anything was wrong. She couldn't reply. Wilma remembered that she cried, too—all of them did—as the train wound its way north. The family changed trains in Kansas City and continued on their way. Finally, after two interminably long days and nights, they reached California, passing through Riverbank, where Wilma's grandmother lived. The family pressed on until they reached the city by the bay.

Charley had vouchers that BIA officials had given him for groceries and rent, but when they arrived, he discovered there were no apartments available, so the government picked up the tab for a two-week stay at an old hotel "in a notorious district of San Francisco called the Tenderloin." During the night, the neighborhood sparkled with lots of neon lights, gaudy pimps and their prostitutes, and howling laughter in the streets. "But in the morning," Wilma recalled, "we saw broken glass on the streets, people sleeping in doorways, and hard-faced men wandering around. The hotel was not much better than the streets."[40]

Wilma found the city noises, especially at night, unnerving. The family had gotten on the train two days earlier to the sounds of roosters, dogs, and cats; coyotes, bobcats, and owls; crickets, ducks, and other animals scurrying through the woods or flying overhead. She knew the sounds of nature. But these new sounds—these screeching sounds of traffic and other things—were foreign to her. Worst of all were the police and ambulance sirens. "That very first night in the big city," she recalled, "we were all huddled under the covers, and we heard sirens outside in the streets. We had never heard sirens before. I thought it was some sort of wild creature screaming. The sirens reminded me of wolves."[41]

Even their mother seemed confused. When the family got up and went out for their first breakfast in their new hometown, they didn't recognize anything on the menu. At home in Oklahoma, they had biscuits and gravy every morning. After scanning the offerings, Irene found the only thing that came with gravy was a hot roast-beef sandwich, so that's what everyone ordered—roast-beef sandwiches with gravy.

As the days scrambled by, Charley fell into the habit of rising early to go out to look for work and a house, both things the BIA had promised would be plentiful. While the family awaited his return, Wilma and her siblings explored the hotel. One day, she and her brother Richard were standing by the stairway when they saw some people come down the hall and stop. "All of a sudden," she recalled years later, "a box in the wall opened up. People got inside. Then the box closed and the people disappeared! After a minute or two the box suddenly opened again and a new bunch of people came out. Of course, we had never seen an elevator before. All we knew was that we were not about to get inside that box. We used the stairs."[42]

It was a lesson in acculturation she would have preferred to miss. As she recalled years later, "It seemed the only option available to us, so we went into the [relocation] program. We moved from a rural, isolated and insulated community to an urban, ghetto area. It was frightening and a difficult period of adjustment for us. . . . It was culture we didn't know anything about: roller skates, bicycles, and telephones."[43]

To Wilma Mankiller, it soon became apparent that the relocation program "simply doesn't work . . . with people who are interested in retaining their own sense of identity and culture."[44]

After a couple of weeks had passed, the BIA finally managed to locate a permanent place for the family to live. It was a flat in a working-class neighborhood in San Francisco's old Potrero Hill District. Wilma described it as quite small and crowded but the best location for them. The rope factory where her father was able to get a job was nearby. For his labors, he was paid the grand sum of forty-eight dollars a week. Wilma recalled, "There was no way, even then, that a man could support a big family in San Francisco on that salary. That is why my big brother Don also worked in the factory, making ropes. He and my father walked to the factory every day and worked long, hard hours. Even with both of them bringing home paychecks, we had a tough time, and our family was growing. My brother James Ray was born while we lived in the Potrero Hill District."[45]

Wilma didn't like city living, and she hated school. The other kids seemed to be way ahead of the Mankiller clan in academic and social abilities. While the siblings managed to keep pace in reading only because of what their folks had already taught them, their classmates were much more advanced in mathematics and language skills.

So, at the ripe old age of eleven, Wilma had embarked upon her junior high school years in a brand-new school in a brand-new city in a distinctively different educational system, and she was miserable. She missed the family farm and hated the school where the white kids teased her for her long black hair, her Native American features, and her name.

In the fifth grade, she suddenly realized how different everyone else in her class found her. Whenever the teacher called her name during the morning roll call, the other students laughed. Mankiller hadn't been a strange name back in Adair County, but it was quite an oddity in San Francisco. The other kids also teased her about the way she talked and dressed. She and her sister sat up late each evening reading aloud to one another to rid themselves of their Okie accents, trying to emulate how the other kids at school talked. They also reminisced about life back at Mankiller Flats, trying to recall where a specific tree was located and how everything looked when they'd left. Wilma recollected, "I still had many problems trying to make such a major adjustment. We simply were not prepared for the move. As a result, I was never truly comfortable in the schools of California. I had to find comfort and solace elsewhere."[46]

Hardly alone in her feelings, Wilma met numerous Native people from different tribes, all of whom were from remote communities. All, too, realized that the "better life" the BIA had promised them turned out to be incarceration in a rough, tough urban ghetto. Many people were unable to find jobs, and those who did usually ended up with only marginal employment. Many Native people endured a great deal of poverty, emotional suffering, substance abuse, and poor health because they had left their homelands, families, and communities—their safety nets—behind. Children were especially vulnerable without the traditional support of the extended family typical of most Native people.

Before long, urban Indian families began banding together, building Indian centers, holding picnics and powwows, and forming their own communities amid the larger urban populations. Yet there was always that persistent longing to return home. "I was as distant from myself as the moon from the earth," is how James Welch, a Native writer, described the sense of alienation he experienced in an urban setting.[47]

The BIA's termination and relocation policies of the 1950s had failed to solve the "Indian problem," and their promises never materialized. Alone and in a strange land, Charley Mankiller and his family soon learned that little had changed over the previous century in the way the government dealt with its Native American population. By the time Charley came to that realization, it was too late. There was little hope within him then but to hang on and try to survive; there was even less hope within Wilma, her four sisters, and her three brothers beyond what the promises of a new education held for them. Perhaps that, Charley rationalized, was what all the sunshiny, breezy talk the BIA had been showering upon the nation's Native American families was all about. Education leading to a better, more fulfilling, more hopeful future for the next generation of Cherokees. He could only hope.

Years later, as Wilma recalled in her autobiography, *Mankiller: A Chief and Her People,*

> *I experienced my own Trail of Tears when I was a young girl. No one pointed a gun at me or at members of my family. No show of force was used. It was not necessary. Nevertheless, the United States government, through the Bureau of Indian Affairs, was again trying to settle the "Indian problem" by removal. I learned through this ordeal about the fear and anguish that occur when you give up your home, your community, and everything you have ever known to move far away to a strange place. I cried for days, not unlike the children who had stumbled down the Trail of Tears so many years before. I wept tears . . . tears from my history, from my tribe's past. They were Cherokee tears.*[48]

Even after the Mankillers had "moved up" and into their small, cramped apartment, the family continued its struggle to adapt to the sprawling size of the city they now called home. As the book *Beloved Women* described the situation, "They may as well have landed on another planet."[49]

For young Wilma Mankiller, her entire life had changed overnight. She was no longer part of a broader Cherokee community. She was not engulfed by the pure, blissful conformities of everyday living. Now, the family had to adapt to the sound of sirens in the street, people crowding along busy avenues, tall buildings looming overhead, paved roads, concrete sidewalks, and buses. The clean, pristine air that Wilma had once taken for granted was suddenly little more than a fading memory.

Life had grown overnight to become intolerably complicated. For Wilma, the transition was nearly impossible. She and her siblings were the proverbial hicks in the big city. A neighboring family of Mexican immigrants took the Mankillers under their wing and taught them how to use a telephone. They showed them how to open a bank account and write a check. They taught Wilma how to roller-skate and ride a bike.

Regardless, the girl still found herself trying to cope with the mysteries of television, neon lights, and elevators. It was a total culture shock. More than that, it was a young girl from Mankiller Flats trying to survive beyond her mixed emotions of depression and fear, anger and hate. She felt disappointment in her parents—especially in her father, the man whom she had viewed throughout her life as her Knight in Shining Armor, her Brave on the Swift White Steed. Her hero.

Suddenly she saw him for the first time as a facilitator: He had sold the family down the river for a chance to live in a white man's world, to live the good life, to grab a piece of the Great American Dream. She saw for the first time what that meant to her brothers and sisters, and she saw what it meant to her. She saw it firsthand. She saw it, and she hated it.

She recalled in her autobiography an ancient Cherokee legend:

[The Wolves] were after [the Rabbit] at once, but he ran for a hollow stump and climbed up on the inside. When the Wolves got there, one of them put his head inside to look up, but the Rabbit spit into his eye so that the Wolf had to pull his head out again. The [other Wolves] were afraid to try, and they went away with the Rabbit still in the stump.

She related the story to herself, writing, "After my family relocated in San Francisco, where the screams of sirens echoed off warehouse walls, I was very much like Rabbit, who found himself surrounded by Wolves.

But unlike the clever Rabbit of the Cherokee myth, I had no song or dance to distract the Wolves in my life. Nor was there a hollow stump for me to crawl inside. There were not even a few blades of long grass for cover."

Indeed, the Wolves had surrounded her, but her pursuers were not of the four-legged or multi-fanged or fur-covered variety. They were of a species all their own. The girl was plagued by the anxiety, doubt, and fear that crept up to the city like the thick bay fog cradled along the shores. The muffled voices were more terrible than any beast's howls. "I could not spit in my demons' eyes to make them leave. It was impossible to escape them. It was impossible to avoid them."[50]

Unaccustomed to being surrounded by so many different people who rejected her strange clothing and even stranger accent, she found herself alone with no place to hide.

In those early days, when we were all trying to figure out how to get along, there was no real sanctuary for me. We were so far from Mankiller Flats and the wooded land I knew and loved. We might as well have been on the far side of the moon.

I was sad and lonesome most of the time. Having to grapple with the worries and pressures of big-city life and contend with the ordeals of adolescence were not pleasant experiences for a Cherokee girl from the Oklahoma outland. I knew only the country and country ways. I suffered from incurable homesickness aggravated by what felt like a permanent case of the blues. I thought my despair would never go away. Everything seemed hopeless.[51]

For the girl with the funny-sounding name from the small rural farm in Oklahoma, nothing could make her adapt and adjust to her new environment—not even roller-skating and bike riding. Nothing could diminish the pain that washed over her morning, noon, and night. The only thing that helped to lessen the agony even for an hour or two came from books. Wilma Mankiller became a voracious reader.

As far back as she could recall, books had surrounded her. Thanks especially to her father, storytelling and reading went hand-in-hand with the traditions of her Cherokee upbringing. A love for books and reading was one of the best gifts Charley Mankiller had ever given his children.

But as time ground on, not even the books could mend the heartaches the young girl suffered. She thought once more about running away, but where would she go? She considered returning to her tribal land in Oklahoma and telling others that she had been orphaned, but who would believe her? She even contemplated suicide. But none of those options seemed to offer her the solution she was looking for: a return to the peace and happiness she had once known as a young girl growing up in the Indian country of northeastern Oklahoma.

After living in San Francisco for little more than a year, Charley and Don pooled the money they had saved from work, and the family was able to make a down payment on a small house. They moved from the crowded flat in the Potrero Hill District into a new home in Daly City just south of San Francisco on the southern peninsula in San Mateo County. Daly City had come into being as a result of the earthquake and fire of 1906, when many San Franciscans fled to John Daly's dairy ranch for survival. The area grew into a residential oasis that mushroomed during the boom years after World War II, when it became one of California's fifty most populous communities.

"Our new residence looked as if it had come straight out of a cookie-cutter mold," Wilma wrote.

There were three small bedrooms, a full basement, and not many frills. My sisters and I shared bunk beds. I would describe it as modest, just like the hundreds of other ticky-tacky houses in endless rows that climbed up and down the landlocked hills flanked by the Pacific Ocean and San Francisco Bay.

For our family as a whole, the move to Daly City was a good one. It represented a marked improvement over our first dwelling. We were moving up in the world. At about that same time, my father started to become active at the San Francisco Indian Center, where we met and spent time with other native people living in the area. That had a positive impact on the family. But for me, nothing had changed. I still loathed being in California, and I particularly despised school.[52]

Wilma felt uncomfortable, stigmatized, and alienated from the other students, most of whom treated her as if she'd come from outer space. Insecure to the point of pathologic, she crossed the street to walk on the other side if she spied someone she knew coming toward her. She lowered her eyes when passing people of authority. The least little remark or glance in her direction left her mortified. The matter was made worse when someone tried teaching her something that should have been second nature, like how to use a telephone. She was convinced that any twelve-year-old who had to be taught how to pick up a phone, listen for a tone, and then dial a number must have appeared to others to be an idiot.

As time rolled on and Wilma prepared to enter the seventh grade, she found herself growing increasingly depressed. A new class meant new classmates, and new classmates meant new opportunities for ridicule. The Mankiller kids were still being teased unmercifully about their Oklahoma accents. Wilma and her sister Linda had made some progress with their nightly reading sessions, but no matter how hard they tried to sound like everybody else, it just didn't work.

And then, literally overnight, Wilma began experiencing the mysterious and frightening physiological changes taking place inside a young Cherokee woman, creating even more fear and anxiety. Wilma was at last experiencing the problems a girl faces when approaching the beginnings of womanhood. Besides dealing with that, she had also recently sprouted like a weed so that she had nearly reached her full adult height. People who saw her assumed she was much older than twelve, so she soon began hating her body, hating her height, hating everything to do with herself and her life. She still dreaded school. She still despised and feared her teachers. She especially still detested the other students.

But, most of all, she abhorred the city. It was a time of tremendous confusion for the young Indian girl.

"I was silently crying out for attention, but nobody heard me," she wrote.

My dad was constantly busy trying to earn a living while, at the same time, attempting to deal with his own frustrations with the city. . . . My mother was doing her best to help all of us with our problems while she kept us fed and clothed. Then, on top of everything, my oldest brother, Don, announced that he was going to get married. He had met a nice young Choctaw woman named LaVena. . . . They had fallen in love. Everyone was pleased with the news, but there were long discussions about Don leaving home with his bride and how that loss of income would affect the rest of the family.[53]

Don had been living with the family in California from the beginning, working odd jobs and doing whatever he could to contribute to their financial welfare. With the latest familial drama playing out, young Wilma felt even further isolated and abandoned, more frightened and insecure than ever. Don had been her most trusted sibling. Before long, she would have *no one* left to talk to or confide in.

There was no doubt about it. She decided she would have to leave home. And *soon*.

Wilma's Grandmother Sitton lived on a ranch in nearby Riverbank. The girl had gotten to know her grandmother better after the family's move to the Golden State, and she at least felt comfortable with her. She also felt that her grandmother would not hesitate to take her in.

"I liked Riverbank," Wilma wrote years later, "because Oklahoma families who had come out during the Dust-Bowl period were living in the area. I felt more comfortable around them."[54]

The young Indian girl decided the time was right. She had saved some money from babysitting, and her younger sister Linda—her "co-conspirator" in crime—donated her own money to the cause. A few days later, Wilma Mankiller found herself on a one-way bus headed for Riverbank. When she arrived at the ranch, her grandmother greeted her warmly, hugged her, listened to her granddaughter's plight, and gave her something to eat only moments before picking up the telephone hanging on the kitchen wall and dialing the number she knew by heart.

"Wilma Pearl's here," the woman said into the mouthpiece as the young girl's eyes exploded in fear. "You'd better come get her."

Wilma was stunned, betrayed, devastated. Charley Mankiller drove out and took his daughter back to their home in Daly City later that afternoon. And that, as they say, was that. Or, at least, it might have been. But for Wilma Mankiller, the word "surrender" had little basis in reality—and never would have.

Within weeks, Wilma hit the trail again, once more to her grandmother's ranch and once more with the same results. She ran away a third time . . . and a fourth . . . and a *fifth*. She always headed straight for Riverbank. And her father always drove out and picked her up to bring her back home. Things, everyone agreed, were getting out of hand.

"My parents could not control me," Wilma wrote. "Eventually, they decided that I had become incorrigible. They saw that I truly did not want to live in the city. I wanted no part of it. So they gave in and let me stay with my grandmother."[55]

By that time, Grandma Sitton had sold the ranch and moved in with Wilma's Uncle Floyd and Aunt Frauline, who owned a dairy farm north of Riverbank near the town of Escalon. Within minutes of arriving, Wilma ran afoul of the couple's four precocious children, Tommy, Mary Louise, and twins Eddie and Teddie. All competitive by nature, the children squabbled openly and fought outright for dominance. "When I arrived," Wilma wrote, "it took only the slightest agitation to provoke me. I was highly sensitive and self-conscious."[56]

After one violent squabble in which Wilma punched cousin Teddie so hard in the jaw that he nearly passed out, talk turned to sending the girl back to live with her parents. After that, the fighting eventually eased, the conflicts fading as the children settled into a more comfortable level of antagonism, and the amount of drama in the family's life decreased.

Time passed, and young Wilma found herself growing closer to her grandmother, a strict disciplinarian but a warm and accepting woman. At a critical point in her granddaughter's emotional development, Sitton taught Wilma to take stock of herself and to appreciate all the best qualities she had residing within her. Sitton built up the girl's confidence and made her feel more secure about the person she was—inside and out. In the process, she helped a young Indian girl accept the skin into which she had been born and learn to confront her problems coolly and logically—something that Wilma might never have discovered but for her grandmother's gentle encouragement.

It paid off. Before long, Wilma Mankiller found herself immersed in farmwork and enjoying every minute of it—most of it, at any rate. She looked forward to pitching in and doing physical chores and even helped her aunt deliver a calf during a particularly delicate birthing. In her free time, she enjoyed going off with the other children to explore neighboring fields or to go skinny-dipping in the creeks.

Even school to the young teen began to lose some of its tarnished facade. She made a few new friends and came to place at least *some* level of trust in her teachers. She even got to the point where, when the teacher called out "Mankiller," she no longer cringed at how the other students reacted.

Meanwhile, life on the farm looked even brighter than it had before. During Wilma's first full year there, she began to formulate much of her adolescent thinking. Her admiration for her grandmother, for the woman's internal fortitude and the strength she showed during times of adversity, coursed through her veins. Although the older woman was short in stature, she was solidly built both inside and out—opinionated, sturdy, and independent. A religious woman, Sitton sang "Rock of Ages" at the beginning of each new day and taught young Wilma how to plant and tend vegetables, raise chickens, and pick peaches at the height of their ripeness. She also taught her granddaughter how to bury the grudge she had been holding against her father, seeing him in a different light.

And it worked.

"Grandmother Sitton and my father—two of the people I most admired as a young woman—valued hard work," Wilma wrote. "I believe it was their examples more than anything else that contributed to my own work ethic."[57]

When the year Wilma spent with her grandmother on the farm finally came to a close, the girl felt ready to return to the Bay Area and the city life she had hated, although not to Daly City. While she was gone, her brother Don and his girlfriend had married and set up a home of their own near Candlestick Park. With Don no longer contributing to the family coffers, the Mankillers were forced to move to a more affordable home in an area of southeastern San Francisco known as Hunter's Point.

Named for Robert E. Hunter, an adventure-seeking forty-niner and California pioneer who had planned to build a thriving community there, Hunter's Point was eventually developed by the US Navy as a shipyard and dry dock. It flourished as a point of disembarkation for the Pacific Theater during World War II and continued to thrive as the seat of the country's West Coast shipping industry for years.

At the war's end, thousands of Japanese Americans who had been uprooted as potential security threats after the Japanese attack on Pearl Harbor began funneling back into the Bay Area, setting up "Little Tokyo" neighborhoods throughout the region. They were met by a sprawling delegation of poor blacks and whites who had already migrated to the Bay Area from Oklahoma, Texas, and other south-central states that had been the hardest hit by the Dust Bowl and the Great Depression. Tough economic times settled over the area like the fog over San Francisco Bay. To make matters worse, the navy soon closed its facility there, leaving Hunter's Point—the one-time dream community with the classy-sounding name—high and dry. It didn't take long for the area to hit the skids.

Jobs dried up, and mortgages went unpaid. Bank foreclosures soared. Welfare rolls swelled to record-breaking numbers. Hunter's Point fell into financial chaos, a giant, bubbling cauldron of ghetto life where humanity struggled daily to survive.

But as financial woes beset the nation, one person seemed to go unaffected. At home in her new community, Wilma's perceptions of the world around her began changing to match her vantage point. People still held jobs—some of them, at least. Most of the higher-paying positions, including those of police officers, teachers, politicians, and lawyers, belonged to whites. A few whites, along with a sprinkling of recent Asian and Samoan immigrants, called Hunter's Point home, but the most significant number of residents in the area were black.

Black Americans soon began exerting their influence on the young Cherokee girl. While white teens were swooning to the sounds of the Beach Boys, Pat Boone, and Elvis on the radio, Wilma and her friends were grooving to the gritty earthiness of Etta James, Dinah Washington, Sarah Vaughan, and B.B. King. When Mankiller got together with her black friends, they played records, put on makeup, fixed their hair, and danced as if they were at the center of the universe, as if at some debutante's cotillion or coming-out party.

"Even today, more than thirty years later," Mankiller wrote in her autobiography of her years in Hunter's Point, "the sisterly company of black women is especially enjoyable to me."[58]

Thrown together for their mutual support, the entire Mankiller family soon felt at home with people from various ethnic groups in what outsiders had nicknamed "Harlem West." Wilma's mother befriended a Filipina neighbor, who shared with her tips about surviving on a limited budget. Wilma's father developed several close friendships with black and Chicano neighbors and coworkers.

The house in which the Mankillers lived proved to be surprisingly comfortable. Although it was small, it was clean and—unlike some of the other places they had lived—free of rats. Wilma felt safe and secure inside. Outside, however, was another matter, as she recalled.

There was a great deal of animosity between the black youths and Samoan youths of Hunter's Point. Sometimes it seemed like a war zone when rival gangs clashed on the streets. Now and then there were enormous battles. Upstairs, in the bedroom I shared with my sister Linda, we could gaze out the window at the beauty of the sky and water, or we could lower our eyes to the streets where the gangs fought furiously.

I was taught invaluable lessons on those mean streets. They were part of our continuing education in the world of urban poverty and violence.[59]

As in any war zone, Hunter's Point grew into a hotbed of sociopolitical turmoil. The neighborhood broiled beneath constant unrest. Parents struggled to keep their children off the streets, out of the gangs, and away from drugs, often unsuccessfully. An overwhelming sense of negative energy pervaded the atmosphere: People spent lifetimes living one long, hot, dull, lazy day after another, hoping eventually to stumble upon a better way of life—all the while realizing that it would never come. Yesterday was the same as today, which would be the same as tomorrow. In Hunter's Point, little of consequence changed.

The Mankiller family discovered just how bad things were outside their front door late one evening when, after eating dinner, Wilma began to choke so violently that her father rushed to the telephone to call an ambulance. After giving the dispatcher their address, the officer told him that *no one* would go into Hunter's Point after dark. Her father finally had to reach down into her throat to dislodge a bone by himself.

Despite the harshness of her environment, Wilma believed that living in Hunter's Point had given her an insight into cultures she would otherwise never have known. Years later, in 1991, she recalled seeing the film *Boyz in the Hood* and being struck by just how familiar the families in the movie seemed to her, "even though more than thirty years had passed since I had lived in a similar place."[60]

Hunter's Point also taught Wilma something about the will to survive. Every day she spent there awakened in her one undeniable fact: *Winners never quit.* Even though the residents shared inextricable problems and overwhelming frustrations, the tough ones—particularly, as Wilma observed, the *women*—never gave up.

"They are mothers not only of their own children but of the entire community," she wrote of her experiences years later.

> *Poverty is not just a word to describe a social condition, it is the hard reality of everyday life. It takes a certain tenacity, a toughness, to continue on when there is an ever-present worry about whether the old car will work, and if it does, whether there will be gas money; digging through piles of old clothes at St. Vincent de Paul's to find clothing for the children to wear to school without being ridiculed; wondering if there will be enough to eat. But always, there is hope that the children will receive a good education and have a better life.*[61]

Charley Mankiller shared that hope. By 1960, he had quit his job at the rope factory and begun work as a longshoreman on the docks. When that paycheck proved insufficient to provide for himself, his wife, and their eleven children, he took up playing poker in the evenings to subsidize his income. He was pretty good at it. He won more than he lost. And that was just enough to keep the family poor.

But happy.

The Mother and the Corn

Selu lives with her husband, Kanati, and their two sons. Each day, she leaves the house and returns with a basket filled with ripe corn that she presents to the family for sustenance. The boys wonder where the corn comes from and one day decide to follow. When they see her enter a small building, they sneak up and spy on her through the window.

They watch as their mother sets her basket down on the ground and begins to shake. Soon, ears of ripe corn start sprouting from her body and falling to the earth. Thinking their mother possessed, they decide she must be destroyed.

Reading her sons' minds, Selu tells the boys that, if they put her to death, they will need to follow her instructions precisely so that they may continue to have corn for nourishment.

"After you kill me, you must clear two acres of ground in front of our house. Drag my body in a circle seven times. Then, you must stay up all night and watch."

The boys naturally got the instructions wrong, clearing *seven* acres of ground and dragging her body in a circle *twice*. Where Selu's blood touched the earth, corn began to grow.

Because of the boys' carelessness in listening to their mother's words, corn no longer sprouted freely but had to be planted and tended every spring of every year forever.

Two

Every Inch a Mankiller

As Wilma grew toward womanhood, she never forgot her roots. Her people had been the very backbone of her life, the center of her universe. She returned to visit the family farm every summer as an adult, mostly to see her grandmother but also to pitch in with the chores. Often, her brothers and sisters accompanied her, and the entire family periodically tended the crops of nearby truck farmers or picked fruit from local orchards to earn extra money for the younger children's clothing for school. Wilma recounted those days:

> *We worked alongside some white people in the fields, and my mistrust of whites certainly did not apply to them. The people whom some Californians derisively called Okies or Arkies were great friends— hardworking people, close to the land, and quick to share what little they had with others who had even less. The farm work was demanding, but those were summers of freedom.*
>
> *We swam in the canals, went to drive-in movies, and sipped cherry Cokes or limeades at the local Dairy Queen. Sometimes we headed to the nearby town of Modesto to cruise the streets. Later, Modesto was the setting for* American Graffiti, *the film about teenage life in small-town America directed by George Lucas, a native son.*[1]

Even after she grew up and married, Wilma looked forward to her visits with her grandmother. When Pearl Sitton announced in her mid-eighties that she was preparing to take a husband for the third time, Wilma—instead of expressing shock—volunteered to help her prepare for the big day. She dyed her grandmother's hair black (Sitton believed that made her look younger) and helped dress her for the ceremony so that the woman might look her youthful best. The wedding itself was a simple affair held at the office of the justice of the peace in Reno, Nevada.

Although long on years, Grandma Sitton was still young at heart. She walked with a quick, sure gait filled with the elemental joys she had learned from canning fruits and vegetables, caring for her chickens, and working in the garden. And, of course, she never stopped singing those hymns until the day she died.

"I am inspired whenever I think about her and all those good times we had," her granddaughter wrote years later.[2]

In time, during her days of traveling between the Sitton farm and her family home in the Bay Area, Wilma Pearl emerged as the ethereal butterfly from its eternal cocoon, her confidence restored and her self-image reenergized. She had her grandmother to thank for that, she knew. But, perhaps the most significant single influence on her young life came about as a result of a discovery she made one day while walking the streets of San Francisco.

It was called "The Center." Officially, its name was the Indian Center of San Francisco, and it provided a place for Native Americans to go to for help, camaraderie, and entertainment. It was a place for Indians from all tribes to call their home away from home. Everyone who went there shared at least some life experiences; some shared nearly all.

The Center had something for everyone. It was a safe house, a shelter in a sea of violent storms, a haven even if someone only wanted to hang out. A lauded sanctuary, it "was the heart of a vibrant tribal community," as Wilma described it.[3]

The Center provided entertainment and various social and cultural outlets for the area's youths; it offered the elders a place to hold powwows and discuss matters of importance with BIA officials. It was there that Mankiller grew increasingly interested in politics, fascinated in particular by the machinations of civil rights and how they affected her own Native people, not to mention her family and herself.

Located upstairs in an old frame building on Sixteenth Street on the periphery of the rough-and-turbulent Mission District, the Indian Center became Wilma's own sanctuary. It would be her safe place for many years to come. "At last," she recalled in reflection, "the mythical Rabbit had finally found a hollow stump the Wolves were not able to penetrate."[4]

Before long, the Center grew to be even more influential to Wilma than the two high schools she had attended. During her teens, her parents helped her transfer from an inner-city school dominated by violence and gang warfare to another public school with a mostly Asian student body that offered a more peaceful environment. Even at that, changing schools was not without its trauma. Just about the time she had managed to gain confidence and self-esteem at one school, she found herself starting all over again at another. She was never able to make plans or set meaningful goals for her future. Even as Wilma grew well into her teenage years, she had no idea what she wanted to do once she finished school and found herself treading the cold, choppy seas of the real world.

But at the Indian Center—that was different. There, she could count on a place of constancy where she could share her feelings and frustrations with kids from similar backgrounds. And that was a first since the family had moved to California!

At the Center, Wilma found a warm, accepting environment, no matter what she felt like doing. Hang out and watch TV? No problem. Socialize through various organized events? She felt welcomed to join in. Dance, compete in sports, or even work occasionally behind the snack bar to earn a little extra money? At the Center, the world proved to be Wilma Mankiller's oyster.

And she wasn't alone. Even the adults enjoyed the facilities, taking advantage of bingo and the intertribal powwows that were an everyday part of life. Her parents went to meetings there to air their discontent regarding their issues with the BIA. Wilma and her friends often hopped a city bus and headed for the Indian Center the way teenagers today jump into a car and flock to the malls.

The Center proved to be a godsend for Wilma's family. Even her father, who had recently quit work as a longshoreman and taken a job as a shop steward and union organizer with a local spice manufacturing company, felt the security of belonging there. Besides his union activities, he had become active in various Indian Center projects, such as a push for a free health clinic for Indians living in the Bay Area. In an all-out effort to heighten public awareness, he went so far as to appear on a television panel debating the advantages of having such an urban clinic. Her own father! She recalled her dad's take-charge attitude with pride.

When he believed in something, he worked around the clock to get the job done. He was always dragging home somebody he had met, someone who was down on his luck and needed a meal and a place to stay. It was a tight fit, but we made room. My dad never gave up on people. I think my father's tenacity is a characteristic I inherited. Once I set my mind to do something, I never give up. I was raised in a household where no one ever said to me, "You can't do this because you're a woman, [or an] Indian, or poor." No one told me there were limitations. Of course, I would not have listened to them if they had. . . .

The exception would have been my father. I always listened to him, even if I did not agree with what he had to say. From the time I was a little girl, we discussed all the topics of the day. Our very best debates concerned politics. Sometimes those conversations would get a bit heated. After my political awakening as a teenager, I became aligned with the party of Franklin Roosevelt, Harry Truman, and a rising young star of the sixties—John F. Kennedy. My father, on the other hand, was a registered Republican, which was not unusual among older members of the Five Tribes, especially the Cherokees. Folks who know our people's past can usually figure out why so many of the older Cherokees belonged to the Republican Party. The story goes that a historian once asked an Oklahoma Cherokee why so few of the old-timers became Democrats. The Cherokee supposedly replied, "Do you think we would help the party that damned ol' Andy Jackson belonged to?" For the elders, the choice was obvious—Republicans were the lesser of two evils.[5]

Despite his political differences with his daughter, Charley Mankiller and Wilma thrived on their political discussions. Once they had found the Center, they quickly realized how many other families were in the same situation as they. Indian families throughout the Bay Area had come to realize that the BIA's promises were nothing more than empty shells. Everyone reached the same conclusion nearly at once: The government's relocation program was a flop. Instead of making their lives better, all it did was rob the people of their positive outlook on life by usurping their sense of place.

That was the main reason the Indian Center was so important to the tribes. It was always there for them. It was a constant. During the turmoil and anguish of the 1960s, it was the first place toward which everyone turned for solace.

Never was the Center more critical in the lives of the Mankiller family than in 1960. Wilma's brother Bob had recently joined the National Guard. He had boxed semiprofessionally for a while, and he'd held various odd jobs. Floundering, he never seemed to have any concrete plans for his future. Charley wanted him to settle down and find a good-paying job. But Bob had other ideas. He and his pal Louie Cole, a quarter Choctaw, decided to leave the city. Louie was nineteen, and Wilma had a crush on him. He was her first "real boyfriend." She recalled what happened when he and Bob took off one morning, intent on making money for a grubstake so they could go off on an adventure to explore the world.

Bob and Louie had been gone for two or three weeks and were up the coast in Washington State when they found work as apple pickers. The boys lived in sharecroppers' cabins near the orchards. When they got up early in the morning, it was still cold and dark outside, so they would start a fire in a wood stove using a little kerosene to get the flames going. One morning, my brother was still groggy with sleep when he lit the fire. Instead of the kerosene, he mistakenly picked up a can of gasoline. The cabin exploded in flames. The door was locked with a dead bolt, so by the time the boys got outside, they were severely burned. Louie was burned over much of his body, but Bob was in far worse condition.

My parents, my brother Don and my oldest sister, Frieda, who still lived in Oklahoma, traveled to Washington to be with Bob. The doctor told them that if Bob lived for seven days, he would probably survive. Among Cherokees, the number seven is considered sacred. We have seven clans, our sacred fire is kindled from seven types of wood, and there are seven directions—north, south, east, west, up, down, and "where one is at." We thought maybe the seven days would bring luck to Bob.

Attractive and charming, Bob always had been the best looking of all of us. He was tall and athletic, a happy-go-lucky type. I looked up to my big brother Don, but for my carefree role model, I had Bob. I think all of us wondered what his life would be like if he survived. It was clear that he would never be the same.

When it seemed that there was a slim chance Bob might pull through, my father, who had to return to his job, left my mother in Washington to stay with Bob through his long recovery. But as it turned out, Bob could not be saved. He lived for seven days and no more. On the seventh day, he died. I am not so sure [but that] the number failed him.[6]

Bob's body was returned home to California, and he was buried at Oakdale, a community on the Stanislaus River not far from Grandma Sitton's place. Bob's death left the entire family reeling. Wilma was in shock. Weeks later, she couldn't recall who had told her that her brother had died. "All I know is, I just stood there and screamed," she said. "I screamed as loud as I could, hoping that my screams would drown out those awful words I did not want to hear. I was fifteen years old, and the loss of Bob was the closest I had ever been to death up to that point."[7]

Wilma's parents were devastated. The loss of any family member is painful; the loss of a child is the worst possible experience. Parents never expect to outlive their offspring. Charley and Irene dream-walked through several weeks of their lives, lost in the oblivion of their son's premature departure. And then, unexpectedly, "something very good" happened to the family. "My mother, who was forty years old, became pregnant the same month my brother Bob died," Wilma recalled. "Everyone was quite surprised. Nine months later, my brother William was born. No one can take someone else's place, but after losing Bob as we had, all of us were happy when Bill arrived."[8]

Meanwhile, Louie Cole remained hospitalized in Washington for several more months before he had healed enough to allow his return to California. He lived near Riverbank, where Wilma had first met him while living with her grandmother. She stayed in touch with the boy after he returned home to recover, but the baggage between them proved too much to overcome, and they never thought of themselves as girlfriend and boyfriend again.

"Every so often we wrote to each other, and then finally that stopped," she said.

Many years later, long after I had come home to Oklahoma and had become involved in tribal politics, Louie came to visit me. He had been married several times, and he still collected disability because of the injuries he had received in that fire so many years before. I was not totally comfortable seeing Louie again. There was something brooding about him, and he wanted only to focus on the past, especially the bad times. About a year after his visit, I received a letter from Louie's mother informing me that he had been shot and killed by one of his former wives during a quarrel.[9]

Although Louie had been Wilma's first boyfriend, he wasn't her last. While shy around members of the opposite sex, she nonetheless managed to meet several interested young men at the Indian Center. One of them went by the name of Ray Billy.

Wilma was sixteen when the two began dating. He was a Pomo, from the California tribe, and a bit older than she. He also had his own apartment. Charley liked him, and that counted for a lot in Wilma's eyes.

Occasionally, Ray got the use of a car, and he would come to our house at Hunter's Point and ask my dad if he could take me for a ride. Other times, my dad let us go for rides in our family car. Everyone liked Ray. He was a gentleman—most of the time.

He was also crafty, and I had to watch my step. One night we were down on the beach. I was getting cold, so he suggested that we go to his place to get a jacket and warm up. It was a classic trick, and I almost fell for it! When we got to his apartment, he said he was tired and we ought to rest on his bed for a while. I came to my senses. I put my foot down and would not cooperate. He thought I was stupid for reacting as I did. A short time later, he dropped me for a girl who had just been crowned Miss Indian San Francisco, or some such title. Ray and I did not see each other again. I was hurt by his treatment, but I pulled through. I learned that most first crushes—even second or third crushes—can be survived.[10]

Friends and family helped Wilma heal her broken heart. Music helped. Wilma and her girlfriends got together often to listen to rock and roll and to swing to the latest soul music. "Hit the Road, Jack" and Fats Domino's "Blueberry Hill" were among their favorite tunes of the day. They listened to them on two soul stations, DIA and KSAN, and fantasized about the time they would be out of school and free to live as adults.

Not much of an academic achiever, Wilma garnered grades that shot all over the place from A to F, depending on the subject and her innate level of interest. Science and math were predictably her downfall, but she had "an affinity for" English and literature. Her teachers didn't help much; none of them left enough of an impact for her even to recall their names.

Predictably, Wilma Pearl was no big girl on campus. Just the opposite. Never a joiner, she struggled to participate in Junior Achievement for a short time before dropping out. Mostly, she got her after-school strokes from the Indian Center, which always ranked high in her memories. She loved the Ping-Pong games and the dances, the organized picnics and the staged plays.

And then something else began to take root. Slowly but surely, a wind was blowing in the air. It was the early 1960s, and changes were coming. Palpable changes one could actually feel. Wilma Pearl could practically *smell* them. Among the most obvious was the realization that all those recently funded US government programs designed to improve the lot of

America's Native people had done nothing to help. Just the opposite. She realized at last that the government had developed a program of coerced resettlement to open up Indian lands to the benefit of white real estate developers and greedy politicians.

Gradually, Wilma grew angrier. The more she went to the Center, the more she spoke with others who felt the same as she did. Before long, this painfully shy, resentful, reclusive young girl began to identify with her heritage as a young Cherokee *woman*. She started to feel the strength of the pull of the bonds that had existed between herself and other Cherokee people for centuries—their mutual history, experiences, and traditions.

Along that road, she began to see her father not so much as she had when she was a child or a teen but more as he really *was*—a mere mortal, a cog in the machinery of Social Progress. She found within herself a young woman with questions that needed to be answered—questions that Charley Mankiller had somehow managed to avoid confronting himself. Or, perhaps, it was she—the once diminutive and frightened Wilma Pearl—who had avoided confronting her *father* about those things that now ricocheted around her brain, those myriad concepts and curious notions that she had only recently begun to explore.

She realized at last that her father may not have fit the mold of the perfect Cherokee Indian, but he was a good man and a devoted parent who had worked hard to instill in his children pride in their heritage. He shared with them what the white man's world had taught him, particularly his love for books and learning. But, she wondered, had that been enough?

Her father, she realized, was only one man. While children have an innate need to look upon their parents as the best, the strongest, the smartest, and the most ambitious anywhere, eventually reality sets in. Undoubtedly, young Wilma had no reason to believe that Charley Mankiller hadn't given everything for his family's welfare that he was capable of offering or that he hadn't fought long and hard to improve the plight of the Mankiller clan. Just as surely, she recognized that he had not always succeeded and, in some cases, hadn't even come close.

Could there be more to Indian pride than what a father teaches a young girl? Could there be other sources of knowledge, of inspiration, of faith and hope? Wilma Pearl believed in her heart—for the very first time in her life—that there were.

As she confessed years later in a speech given at Sweet Briar College, her formative experiences in living in a poor black neighborhood had taught her many valuable lessons in life—some of which would remain with her until her final days.

"What I learned from my experience in living in a community of almost all African-American people," she said, "is that poor people have a much, much greater capacity for solving their own problems than most people give them credit for."[11]

One thing the Center had *not* provided for Wilma was an appetite for formal education. While she had never been particularly fond of her junior high school days, she was even less enthused with her high school experiences. Her feelings toward school ranged from benign acceptance to abject hate. She disliked most of her classmates and eschewed everything she was forced to learn of the white man's world.

When Wilma finally managed to escape from school via her commencement ceremony in June 1963, she breathed a sigh of relief. At last, she felt, she was liberated, free of the artificially imposed white man's world of formal education. She was finished, she vowed, with classrooms forever. Higher education? Vocational training? College? They were out of the question. Wilma never in her wildest dreams planned to take another class. *Ever.* The thought never entered her head.

Instead, in 1963, the seventeen-year-old pretty girl with the roiling soul and the dark, flashing eyes reminiscent of actress Natalie Wood set out to live the life of an independent woman. She was becoming Americanized, acculturated, *comfortable* with herself in her new surroundings. She took a menial job as a clerk with a small local company and enjoyed looking forward to receiving a regular paycheck. She had high hopes, dreams, and ambitions for the future, just like everybody else. But after several months of the same day-in, day-out experiences and no chance for advancement, she began rethinking her philosophy of life. Fortunately, she had the intelligence and instinct to see that without a college education, her chances for advancement, for grabbing a bigger piece of the American Pie, were gradually slipping out of reach.

So, against every instinctual bone in her body, Wilma Pearl Mankiller decided to give higher education a chance. She enrolled in Skyline Junior College in San Bruno before transferring to San Francisco State College. There, she found an educational dialogue different from any she had ever known before. SFSC was unique as an educational facility. It was a vanguard for political activism, a springboard for political thought. Its instructors challenged every student's viewpoints about *everything*. The teachers forced their charges to think for themselves. While there, Wilma met a group of Native American activists who would play a significant role in her future development.

Shortly after entering SFSC, Wilma Pearl—by then already stunningly attractive with dark hair, fiery eyes, and pure, clear skin—met a young man named Hector Hugo Olaya de Bardi. De Bardi, four years her senior, was a handsome college student from Ecuador who came from an upwardly mobile, middle-class family, and his prospects for life in America were bright. Before long, the two entered into a whirlwind courtship resulting in marriage. They soon had two daughters together, Felicia in 1964 and Gina two years later, and Wilma Pearl settled into the role of wife and mother, the perfect New Age California *hausfrau*, complete with hippie-centric psychedelic pantsuits, fringe-trimmed baby strollers, and annual vacations to exotic European ports of call.

From the outside, everything seemed to be picture perfect. Life for the young girl who had come from rural Oklahoma was good at last. Wilma Pearl Mankiller had finally found her piece of the pie. She still missed the allure of simpler days in her home outside Mankiller Flats. She longed for life in the country and for Oklahoma. But she realized that to escape from the poverty she had known all her life, she had to change her own destiny. And she had somehow managed to do just that. She had been a working woman, a college student, and a symbol of what life in America actually meant. Now she was married, a fulfilled wife and the proud mother of two, and still moving up the ladder to social success. Things couldn't have been any better.

Or at least, so it seemed from the *outside*.

On the *inside*, though, things weren't quite so idyllic.

By the mid-sixties, the San Francisco that Mankiller had known throughout most of her school years had begun its free fall from grace. The generation gap widened between parents who became adults around the time of the Second World War and their baby-boomer children. The chasm between rich and poor led to a growing awareness of class distinction and social segregation. The disagreement between liberals and conservatives on the proper role of government to redress poverty and other social issues exploded. The war between the sexes pitted a traditionally patriarchal society against a newly emerging feminist mystique. Middle-of-the-road America—a group that by then included Wilma Mankiller and Hugo de Bardi—found itself moving increasingly toward conservatism and its ties to the Republican Party. But not all Americans, she was quickly finding out, were middle-of-the-road socialites. *Or* Republicans.

The fallout from Vietnam War–era radicalism was unpredictably real: Meteoric social and political upheavals split wide before Wilma's very eyes. Social mores evaporated. Conventional principles vanished like cumulus clouds in the sunlit skies. America teemed with anti-government movements and burst with war protests. The country seethed with anger. Society degenerated into "us" and "them," which often translated into the "establishment" versus the "revolutionaries"—the "people" versus the "pigs."

Everywhere she looked, Wilma witnessed a new struggle, a fresh contentiousness for the status quo, and a growing call to arms. She saw conflict on every corner. She was not part of the problem because she was not one of the players. She was not part of the solution either, for the same reason. She was not out marching or protesting. She was not out picketing or condemning. She was who she was. Wilma Pearl Mankiller, daughter of Charley and Irene Mankiller, the progeny of the Cherokee Nation, giver to the world and taker of nothing, wife of Hugo, mother of two daughters, a formerly miserable student, an unhappy teen, an uprooted Native American, an unfulfilled human being.

And then, as she went about her business, trying to hold her own self-image together while making some sort of sense of the world exploding around her, a remarkable thing happened. A wonderful, awesome, awful, beautiful, horrible, incredible, indelible, singular, signatory, memorable, seminal, predictive, preclusive, and entirely off-the-wall thing happened.

In 1969, on November 20, five years after congressional passage of the Civil Rights Act restored to America's reservations the tribal laws that had been gradually stripped away, a ragtag group of eighty-nine Native American men, women, and children assembled on the beach and piled onto three small, weather-beaten scows. Spurred on by *San Francisco Chronicle* reporter Tim Findley, they chugged out into the harbor on their way to Alcatraz Island. The group, spearheaded by full-blooded Mohawk Indian Richard Oakes, stepped ashore on that forlorn plot of barren ground that housed a recently abandoned federal prison. And they declared the property to be theirs. Or, more precisely, they took ownership of the island in the name of all Native Americans everywhere. Their goal: to call a nation's attention to the continuing mistreatment of American Indians by the US government.

The group's raucous cheers that evening awakened Alcatraz's sole caretaker, Glenn Dodson, who—himself one-eighth Cherokee—proffered to the invaders the deserted three-story residence that had once been the quarters of the prison's warden.

To much of white America's amusement, the "invasion" was, at first, little more than another in a long line of publicity stunts by yet another "oppressed minority"—another example of a "mouse that roared." It had been tried before—the takeover of Alcatraz by a group of half-crazed Indians—and it had been a miserable failure. It happened first five years earlier, in 1964, when a band of five Indian-activist students landed on Alcatraz and declared it to be Native American soil. The group had dipped into the sixty-dollar slush fund of the San Francisco State College Native American department, purchased twenty-four dollars' worth of glass beads and red cloth to offer to government officials in exchange for the land, and begun preparations for negotiating the purchase of the island during their occupation. After all, they reasoned, a group of white men had made a similar offer when purchasing a much more significant, more substantive island they had named Manhattan some three centuries earlier. How much could land values have changed in the intervening years?

The group based its legal precedent upon the guarantees provided to them in the Fort Laramie Treaty of 1868. It contained a provision allowing any adult male Native American whose tribe was party to a treaty to file for a homestead on abandoned or unused federal property. Well, the occupiers reasoned, *We're adult male Native Americans, we were party to a treaty, and we're on abandoned or unused federal property.* The five students felt their offer was valid. But in 1964, they had few sympathizers. So, only eighteen hours after the hastily planned takeover had begun, Coast Guard cutters were dispatched to the island docks to escort the Native people off the land, much to the disappointment of a handful of Americans who empathetically had wished them the best.

It had been an admirable publicity-generating effort whose results were destined to fail. This new one, this latest Indian invasion five years later, was even *less* suited to success. It was but a pale imitation of the first takeover, and it was a joke pure and simple. To white Americans everywhere, it was one more example of how when you give some people too much of a good thing, they take it.

But to Native American people across America, the event quickly unfurled into something much more meaningful than a crass publicity stunt.

"When Alcatraz occurred, I became aware of what needed to be done to let the rest of the world know that Indians had rights, too," Wilma wrote afterward. "Alcatraz articulated my own feelings about being an Indian."[12]

Talking with friends, Wilma admitted she was stoked. "Blown away" is how she later described her reaction. She was mesmerized by what was unfolding before her very eyes. She was stunned that her husband—who had stood beside her, brooded with her, pitied her people's plight, and supported her—for some reason didn't *get* it. He didn't understand what the Indians were hoping to accomplish, and he didn't know why his wife was so supportive of their cause.

But Wilma Pearl got it.

When she turned on the family TV that morning, she witnessed what had played out overnight, and she felt invigorated. She was emboldened. She sighed with relief. She was no longer a square peg in a round hole. Nor was she a black sheep in a flock of white karakul. She was for the first time in her adult life alive and animated. She felt fulfilled. And she was actually proud—*shout-it-from-the-highest-rooftops proud!*—of being a woman. She was proud of being a Native American woman. She was proud of being Cherokee!

That very morning as she sat down after dressing the kids and seeing her husband off to work with a belly bulging full of American capitalism, she turned on the TV to catch the latest word of the occupation. She could barely breathe for anticipation.

As she listened to the words broadcast over the airwaves, she saw the filmed images, heard the invaders talk about Indian rights and America and the government and Washington, DC, and she recalled all the broken promises. She swelled with pride and began to think that perhaps, in the end, after all was said and done, maybe she *did* matter somewhat. A little bit. Oh, hell, maybe not so little. Maybe *a lot*!

She began to think about how she could contribute. And then she paused.

Wait a minute, she reasoned. She was Wilma Pearl Mankiller, wife to Hugo Olaya de Bardi, mother of two, inoculant of the ages, nobody who *mattered*.

Yet, at the same time, she had suddenly seen what being Wilma Pearl Mankiller *really* meant to herself and her family . . . had seen it and realized how much more she and her people could contribute—not a few innocent and obtuse members of a Pentecostal church in downstate Georgia or a couple of wags sharing stories of infertility in the local beauty salon or anyone else doing anything else anywhere. She was *someone*, damn it, a member of a large group of *someones*, and they all had a vast, wide, rambling, committed legacy of freedom and democracy, of principle and integrity to uphold. She was a Cherokee, and she belonged to the same community of Cherokee men and women—and Ojibwa and Sioux and Navajo and Kiowa and dozens of other tribes from all across North America, from all across these United States of Whiteness—who

57

all believed in something. Who all mattered. Who all stood for those very same things for which she stood.

Mankiller grabbed the telephone and quickly began to dial. Friends, relatives, neighbors. Had they heard? What did they think? How did they feel about what was happening? What did they believe might happen next?

She called the Indian Center and asked for their input.

She called her aunt and uncle in Riverbank. They couldn't believe it had happened. How could it *be*? Alcatraz Island was ... the United States *Government*! Surely the occupation was illegal. It wouldn't last. It *couldn't*.

But as the days unfolded, so did the occupants' determination. It was clear that this takeover was better planned, executed, and supported than the first. At times, as many as a thousand people converged upon the island—Indian activists, Native American schoolchildren and teachers, media, civil rights supporters—all to show their support for the "stunt" that had shaken America and grown to near epic proportions.

People poured in from tiny Alaskan Native villages, from the mighty Iroquois Nation, from the Pacific Northwest, from the Great Plains states, from the surrounding coastal communities. They brought with them gifts of support and encouragement—dried fruits and salmon, freshly picked berries, canned goods, pillows and other bedding, home-made soaps, bison jerky, flowers, and more. Others brought words of encouragement from the outside world, thoughts of wisdom, prayers of hope, and pledges of support.

Celebrities came as well. Vine Deloria Jr., the Sioux who wrote the book *Custer Died for Your Sins*, was a visitor, along with Anthony Quinn, Jane Fonda, Jonathan Winters, Ed Ames, Candice Bergen, and Merv Griffin. Bergen even brought along a sleeping bag and spent the night on the cold concrete floor.

In autumn 1969, the Native Americans who occupied the abandoned remains of the federal penitentiary that once housed America's most notorious criminals before closing in 1963 were an unlikely mix. They included Indian college activists, families with children fresh off reservations, and urban dwellers disenchanted with what they called the US government's economic, social, and political neglect.

They wanted more than an apology from the US government. Since well before Modoc and Hopi leaders were held at Alcatraz in the late 1800s, US policy toward Indians had worsened, despite repeated pleas from Native American leaders to honor treaties and tribal sovereignty. Among the worst of the broken promises was the Treaty of Fort Laramie.

In September 1851, thousands of American Indians descended on Fort Laramie at the US government's invitation for a meeting. It was there that the government hammered out written agreements with the Crow, Mandan, Hidatsa, Arikara, Sioux, and other tribes. The government promised in writing that tribes would always be entitled to their land and their sovereign rights—"in perpetuity." But less than twenty years later, Congress was already undoing its own hallowed words in the treaty, despite Supreme Court Justice John Marshall's trilogy of opinions warning that tribes were domestic sovereign nations and should be treated with all due rights. Congress instead simply wrote new laws that invalidated those treaties—new laws that made it easier for non-Indian settlers to follow in the steps of Lewis and Clark and expand westward in their grand quest for more land. Little did it matter that this was land that had been occupied for centuries by many generations of Native people.

Less than seventy years later, in the 1950s, the government went back to its old tricks, peddling its new and improved policy of "termination" that literally sought to wipe out all rights and legal claims of Indian tribes. The federal Termination Era also sought to relocate thousands of Native people to the cities to be acculturated with the non-Indian world. Against that historical backdrop, the occupation of Alcatraz was about human rights, the occupiers said. It was an effort to restore the dignity of the more than 550 American Indian nations in the United States. Historians and other experts say the occupation—though chaotic and laced with tragedy—lent proof to the poor conditions suffered by two million American Indians and Alaska Natives alive at the time.

"Alcatraz was a big enough symbol that for the first time this century Indians were taken seriously," said Vine Deloria Jr., a University of Colorado–Boulder law professor, philosopher, author, and historian.[13] For him and nearly two million others, Alcatraz changed everything.

As each day unfolded, new boatloads of people risked running afoul of the Coast Guard blockade just to visit and bring their donations and offerings of food, clothing, and support. Church members and women's organization representatives came, along with the members of labor unions, the Girl and Boy Scouts of America, and the Black Panthers. In December, people brought Christmas toys for the Native boys and girls.

One person who wanted to join the protestors but couldn't was Wilma Mankiller. She had discussed her feelings with her husband, shared with him the yearnings of support she felt within, the burning desire to become "part of." And he had responded: She was a mother and a housewife with two children to care for at home. She had no place on the island with rebels and criminals and lawbreakers and publicity seekers. She had no business running off to support a cause that was doomed to fail. Her first and *only* responsibility was to her family at home.

Wilma, aching inside, yearning to offer her support and solidarity, decided instead to take her husband's advice and stay home. But she never agreed to forget.

Soon, she began organizing a behind-the-scenes drive to raise funds for the Alcatraz campaign, and she helped to solicit legal aid and counsel for the occupiers. She also spread the word about the purpose of the takeover—to bring national attention, *international* attention if possible, to the plight of the indigenous people of the United States. She rallied her own siblings to support the cause and was ecstatic when, after the occupation had begun, four of them joined the original band in protest.

Wilma's brother Richard, six years her junior, was the first of the Mankiller clan to join the Alcatraz coup, eventually serving on the group's council, a panel of Native American men and women responsible for maintaining order on the island. Wilma's sister Vanessa and baby brother James were the next to arrive, followed by Linda.

Barely twenty years old and already the mother of three small children, Linda had separated from her husband and was staying (with her children) with Wilma and Hugo. Once Linda had made up her mind to join the occupation, Wilma agreed to throw her full support behind her. After all, she reasoned, it was her little sis who had donated her hard-earned cash to help Wilma buy that first one-way ticket to her grandmother's ranch in Riverbank when she was so desperate to escape the city several years earlier. It was Wilma's turn to return the favor.

The next day, Wilma met her younger sister on the dock, and they climbed aboard a boat provided by mythic rock group Creedence Clearwater Revival and headed for the island. Of the four Mankiller children who joined in the occupation, Linda stayed the longest, remaining there until June 1971.

After returning home that evening, Wilma realized that her entire life had changed. *She* had changed. She had wanted to stay on the island with her own people, her own family, standing there against all odds, shoulder to shoulder, heart to heart. She felt as though, perhaps, she had sold out too quickly, too readily, in returning home to the comfort and security of her middle-class family. Maybe she had given in to the allure and the promises of white America too easily. Perhaps, she speculated, she had been too hard on her father for having done the very same thing. People need to act responsibly, but their needs, goals, and even responsibilities change from day to day—sometimes from moment to moment. She had succumbed to the Great American Dream that promised 2.24 children in every household and a chicken in every pot. Maybe it was *she* who was betraying the cause by not answering the call to duty, every bit as much as the government had disappointed its Native flock—the Cherokee and other tribes. Every bit as much as her father had failed *her*.

But whatever was, she understood, could be no more. Whatever had been could never be again. All the "maybes" in the world couldn't hold a candle to a single "is." Yesterday, she was a Native American woman trying desperately to fit into a non-Native society. Tomorrow, she knew beyond a doubt, she would find her way back to her roots, back to her people, back to their hopes and dreams and aspirations and experiences.

She would become "totally engulfed by the Native American movement," as she later described it.[14] The occupation of Alcatraz Island would ultimately impact her life for good forever. The fact that Alcatraz had once been a prison was ironic: The occupation of "The Rock" had finally set her free. Free to be her own person. Free to be a Native American. Free to be true to herself without sacrificing her home and her family.

She realized that her husband wanted her to be a wife and the mother of their children, and she wished that as well. But there was nothing inside of her, no one *outside* of her, stopping her from doing it all. She could be a successful wife and mother *and* a Native American woman and advocate. She could do it all. She would have to work harder, put in more hours, work smarter, and that was all right. She would do it for the cause. She would do it because she felt it was the right thing to do. And everyone—herself included—would be happy.

But over the next few months, Wilma found herself spending more time at the home of the new American Indian Center (the old one had burned down), as well as at the Intertribal Friendship House in nearby Oakland. The Indian Center played a role as a command post for the fund-raising activities and legal defense fund for the Alcatraz invaders. More importantly, it quickly evolved into the communications hub between the mainland and the island.

Each passing day, Wilma Mankiller did her part. Every passing hour led her to feel stronger about herself and her new identity—an identity she had once had as a child and lost somewhere along the way to becoming an adult. It was as if she had been asleep for years and suddenly found herself awakened to the demands and the rigors of reality. She had been kissed by the prince.

Others, too, felt that way. They blamed the legacy of European contact with America's indigenous peoples for that. Fifteenth-century Spanish explorers had brought with them the concept of Manifest Destiny, a philosophy once employed by the Roman Catholic Church to justify its crusades against the Muslim world in Europe. The concept granted the divine right to pillage and plunder, to desecrate cultures that did not embrace the authority of the Church or the Crown. Later, the Founding Fathers of America incorporated portions of the Church's philosophy into its own ways of viewing land rights and conquest. In its forced marches of Cherokees, Choctaws, and others from the South to Oklahoma—imprisoning Navajos at Bosque Redondo and rounding up Geronimo—the government's actions became palatable, if not legally justifiable. In less than two generations, a population of Native people that had once numbered more than two million had dwindled to one-tenth of that number.

"We're all just remnants today, torn and scattered all over the place," Native activist LaNada Boyer said.[15] That's why Alcatraz was so important. That's why it remained important that day. The occupation was the seed of an effort to rebuild Indian cultures and political alliances among tribes.

Boyer was only one of many who felt that way. The charismatic and eloquent Richard Oakes, a Mohawk from New York, quickly became the occupiers' spokesman. "We hold The Rock," Oakes proclaimed one day during one of many press conferences to come. His words became a motto for the occupation. Other occupiers included Luwana Quitiquit, a Pomo/Modoc from northern California; Millie Ketcheshawno (Mvskoke); Ed Castillo (Luiseño/Cahuilla); Shirley Guevara (Mono); John Whitefox (Choctaw); and thousands of others who wanted more than just Alcatraz—they wanted their right to life. They made many demands. Among them was LaNada Boyer's proposal for a grant totaling $299,424 to turn Alcatraz into a cultural park and Indian social and education center. The federal government turned the offer down as too unrealistic. So the occupation continued.[16]

As Wilma would say years later when looking back at the takeover, "Much of the credit for that awakening has to go to the young men and women who first went to Alcatraz and helped so many of us return to the correct way of thinking."[17]

More than 5,600 American Indians joined the occupation, some for all eighteen months that it survived and others, like Wilma, for only a day or less. The Native Americans, like many people of color during that turbulent era, were fed up with the status quo. The annual household income of an American Indian family was $1,500, or one-fourth the national average. Their life expectancy was forty-four when other Americans could expect to reach sixty-five.

That was no longer acceptable. It was, after all, the sixties, and all hell was breaking loose: Cesar Chavez ignited Chicano farmworkers, sparking a Hispanic civil rights movement that led to better wages and an end to stereotypes. Malcolm X, Louis Farrakhan, Martin Luther King Jr., and the Black Panthers led civil rights movements among blacks. Asian Americans in San Francisco took to the streets, protesting discrimination in schools. Young white America protested the war in Vietnam and promoted a new culture of freewheeling love and peaceful dissent.

So, too, the time had come for many American Indians to speak out. It wouldn't be the first time in history, but it *would* be the first time in a century. Not since the halcyon days of Crazy Horse, Geronimo, Seath'tl, and Manuelito had American Indians so managed to capture Washington's ear. They did so without violence. And, as it turned out, without success.

"If you wanted to make it in America as an Indian," said Santee Sioux spokesperson and occupier John Trudell, "you had to become a hollow person and let them remold you. . . . Alcatraz put me back into my community and helped me remember who I am. It was a rekindling of the spirit."[18]

The occupation was designed to change white attitudes toward Indians. Its goal was both noble and simple: "We were going to be a positive example for Indian people and show a positive face to the world," said Adam Fortunate Eagle, a San Francisco businessman who had helped organize the Alcatraz occupation and led supply rallies for those living on the island for more than a year.[19] Representing dozens of Indian nations around North America, the occupiers called themselves Indians of All Tribes.

Earl Caldwell, who was covering the black civil rights movement as a reporter for the *New York Times*, feared things would get worse before they would get better. Caldwell was one of only two reporters on the scene of the 1968 assassination of Martin Luther King. He had also covered the meteoric rise to prominence of the Black Panthers, who sought many of the same things as King but turned to violence and revenge rather than peace and negotiation.

"I got the call from New York to stop covering the Black Panthers and go to Alcatraz," Caldwell recalled. Dread, he says, swept over him. "I didn't know what to expect, except perhaps the worst."[20]

But the occupation of Alcatraz turned out to be quite different. Despite its chaos and factionalism, the predominantly peaceful event resulted in significant benefits for American Indians. Years later, Brad Patterson, a top aide to President Richard Nixon, cited nine major policy and law shifts stemming from Alcatraz. These included the passage of the Indian Self-Determination and Education Assistance Act, revision of the Johnson-O'Malley Act to better educate Indians, the Indian Financing Act, the Indian Health Care Improvement Act, and the creation of an Assistant Interior Secretary post for Indian Affairs. Mount Adams was returned to the Yakama Nation in Washington State, and forty-eight thousand acres of the Sacred Blue Lake lands were returned to the Taos Pueblo in New Mexico. During the occupation, Nixon quietly signed papers rescinding termination, that insurance policy the US government had taken out to guarantee the eventual death and destruction of Native Americans' lifestyles and cultures.

The events that led to the occupation began as far back as when the government abandoned Alcatraz in 1963, making an open question of what would become of the island. After the relatively inconsequential five-day takeover by the Sioux in 1964, US policies of relocation and termination added to urban Indian unrest. Under the Eisenhower administration, the government launched an effort called "relocation" to encourage American Indians to move away from tribal lands and into the cities, where the Bureau of Indian Affairs promised resettlement aid and job training. Relocatees such as the Mankillers were given one-way bus tickets and dreams to match, but many found inadequate housing and went unemployed for months. They were stranded in the cities, far from their native homes, with no means to return to the support systems and comfort provided by relatives and friends. At the same time, the government's termination policy sought to end the federal recognition of tribes, effectively nullifying treaties made more than a century earlier with numerous tribal nations.

Five years after the Sioux occupation of Alcatraz, all of that remained on the minds of Bay Area Indians—relocatees and subjects of termination policy. In October 1969, after the San Francisco Indian Center, that anchor for displaced relocatees, had burned down, Bay Area Indians needed a new home. Attention was focused once again on Alcatraz as Indian land.

Living on the Paiute-Shoshone Reservation in central Nevada's sur-real mix of high desert and irrigated "lush farmland," Adam Fortunate Eagle took pride in the fact that the FBI had labeled him an "enemy of the state." He confessed as much in an interview granted to Ben Winton on May 1, 2010, adding that government files had listed him as a principal organizer of the occupation. Fortunate Eagle called the label an "honor."[21]

"Indian lands were being drained. Indians were marked for destruc-tion so that the government could take over the lands and the coal, oil, uranium, timber and water on them," Fortunate Eagle said. He pointed to his wife's own reservation, where the government took twenty-six thousand acres of Paiute-Shoshone land without reparation to transform the sage-ridden desert into irrigated farmland. Two decades later, the six-thousand-member tribe won a $43 million settlement in court.[22]

The US Bureau of Indian Affairs estimates that from 1952 to 1967, two hundred thousand American Indians were lured to cities such as Denver, Chicago, New York, Los Angeles, and San Francisco with the promise of a better life. The Indian Removal Act of 1830, in contrast, forced a total of eighty-nine thousand people off their ancestral lands.

Fortunate Eagle escaped government relocation, moving from his Red Lake, Minnesota, Chippewa village to be near his mother in the Bay Area. He expected to be drafted into the army during the Korean War, but he never was. Instead, he remained in San Francisco to launch his own business. In doing so, he became part of the Bay Area's solid middle class. He made a success of himself, and he did it without any help from the BIA.

Although Fortunate Eagle wore a suit and tie and drove a Cadillac, he never forgot his roots. He helped create the United Bay Area Council of American Indian Affairs, Inc., which had set up the San Francisco Indian Center. Social gatherings were frequent and drew together a hodgepodge of displaced Navajos, Tlingits, Plains, and other indigenous people in a place where they could support one another.

The center offered some solace, but by the late sixties, many urban Indians were fed up with what they considered the BIA's fake promises.

Although Alcatraz was not to remain a sovereign Indian nation, the incredible publicity generated by the occupation served the Native American community well by drawing into sharp focus the injustices that America's indigenous people had suffered at the hands of white America for more than a century. Alcatraz nurtured among Native Americans everywhere a newly found sense that, for the first time since the arrival of the Europeans to conquer the lands of the New World, anything was possible, including (perhaps for the first time in history) liberty and justice for *all*.

California's John Trudell was among them. A college dropout in 1969, Trudell was a singer, songwriter, actor, and activist who "felt the downward pull of political, emotional, and cultural stagnation in the Native American community."[23]

When he heard about the occupation, Trudell, age twenty-three, packed a sleeping bag and headed to San Francisco. He became the voice of Radio Free Alcatraz, a pirated station that broadcast from the island with the help of several local stations. When he hit the airwaves, the response was overwhelming. Boxes of food and money poured in from everywhere to support the occupation. They came from the rock groups the Grateful Dead and Creedence Clearwater Revival (who staged a concert on a boat off Alcatraz and then donated the boat), plus celebrities Jane Fonda and Marlon Brando, along with city politicians and everyday folks.

Trudell and his wife, Lou, had the only baby born on the island during the occupation. They greeted the newborn boy as the symbolic rebirth of an earlier Indian movement. They named him Wovoka, after the nineteenth-century Paiute who introduced the Ghost Dance and the prophecy that North America would be returned to Indians.

In 1969, Millie Ketcheshawno also was among the disenchanted. A graduate of the Haskell Boarding School in Kansas, she had arrived in San Francisco a decade earlier. Recently trained in office procedures that included typing, shorthand, and Dictaphone use, she was one of fourteen former classmates who had left the reservation for the first time to move to California. "There were always seven or eight of us that traveled the city together for protection and support," she said, "like a mother hen and a bunch of chicks."[24]

After being employed as an office worker, Ketcheshawno realized her heart and soul were really in social work. She met Fortunate Eagle in the early 1960s and began working with him and several others to set up Native social service programs.

On October 10, 1969, when the Indian Center burned down, social work had been evolving into Indian activism. Protests at college campuses were becoming more frequent. By coincidence, the San Francisco City Council at the time had been considering several proposals for Alcatraz. Among them was one drafted by Fortunate Eagle, Ketcheshawno, and others to turn Alcatraz into an American Indian center. After the fire, the proposal became urgent. But the controversy over Texas millionaire Lamar Hunt's desire to turn Alcatraz into a commercial venue overshadowed the Native plan.

With no options left, "we all decided November 9 would be the day we would all go out and just stay until they gave us the island," Ketcheshawno recalled.[25] Around the same time, Richard Oakes and several other college students had been thinking about taking over the island. Oakes and Fortunate Eagle, who knew of each other, met for the first time at the home of *San Francisco Chronicle* reporter Tim Findley at a Halloween party. Findley, a former VISTA worker, had a reputation for throwing parties that mixed together people who otherwise would never have mingled, such as journalists and politicos, middle-class businessmen, and student activists.

Oakes and Fortunate Eagle decided to launch a takeover of Alcatraz on November 9, 1969. Nearly a hundred Bay Area Indians showed up at Pier 39, prepared for action. But the assault was delayed when the boats to transport them failed to arrive.

While the group waited, Oakes and others took turns reading a rambling proclamation claiming Indian ownership of Alcatraz Island by right of "discovery" and offering to buy it for twenty-four dollars in glass beads and red cloth. Meanwhile, Fortunate Eagle, in full traditional regalia, including feathers and buckskin, commandeered a Canadian sailboat, the *Monte Cristo*. Its skipper, Ronald Craig, agreed to take seventy-five of the Indians on a symbolic cruise around the island. Halfway through the cruise, an impatient Oakes peeled off his shirt and shouted, "Let's get it on!" He jumped in, followed by several others. Craig veered off to dissuade more jumpers. The tide pulled the swimmers away from the island toward the open sea, where the Coast Guard had to rescue them. Joe Bill, an Alaska Native familiar with the sea, waited until the boat reached the opposite side of the island. He then dove overboard, letting the tide pull him ashore. The Coast Guard plucked him off the rocky beach.

That same night, fourteen of the activists, still reveling in the day's excitement, persuaded local fishermen to take them back to the island, where they spent the night. Fortunate Eagle and a handful of others had returned to the mainland earlier. The caretaker returned the next day to find the fourteen Indians romping with his fierce-looking but surprisingly gregarious guard dog. The Coast Guard delivered them to stern-faced US Marshals on the mainland.

No one, surprisingly, was prosecuted. "The fact was, everybody was going out of their way for them," said Findley, who not only reported on the occupation but also helped it along by rounding up boats for the successful invasion later that month. "Everyone wanted to see them succeed."[26]

After the fiascos of November 9, the college students distanced themselves from Fortunate Eagle as they planned another invasion, the "real deal," on November 20, 1969, a date when Fortunate Eagle was scheduled to be away. Boyer claimed that the students had been distrustful of him because of his age and middle-class status in the "White man's world."[27] So, at 2:00 a.m., nearly eighty American Indians from more than twenty tribes pulled up to the island's eastern shore in three boats that Findley had secured through his friend Peter Bowman of the No Name Bar. The bar was a local hangout for journalists and other so-called intellectuals, and Bowman agreed to take the Indians to the island after he got off work after midnight. Findley rode over with them to cover the landing. When the group stepped ashore, their cheers awakened Alcatraz's only caretaker, Glenn Dodson, who claimed to be one-eighth Cherokee. Dodson offered them the deserted three-story warden's residence.

Unfazed, Fortunate Eagle continued his work from the mainland to drum up food, money, and political support for the island's occupants.

"Look at it from my perspective," he said years later. "I had a lot more to lose (than college students did) back then. I had a family, a house, a business. And, yet, I stuck with it."[28] Alcatraz had become a powerful political symbol of the need for Indian self-determination, and Fortunate Eagle and the others were determined in their own distinct ways to keep the symbol alive.

As romantic as the takeover appeared from the outside, it was anything but on the inside. Nearing anarchy, several different factions tried creating their own versions of Indian utopia. Others saw the occupation as an escape from life and held constant parties fueled by drugs and alcohol smuggled past the volunteer security force.

And then real tragedy struck. On January 3, 1970, the Oakeses' twelve-year-old daughter, Yvonne, slipped while playing inside the warden's house and fell down a three-story stairwell to her death. Oakes soon left Alcatraz amid criticism that the island's own system of government had failed. A council of island residents, including Boyer and Oakes, made many of the decisions. But power struggles were common, according to many of the veterans. Free speech and dissent were actively encouraged. Lawfulness was not.

By the final two weeks of the occupation, the Indians of Alcatraz had gotten some of the concessions they had demanded—but not many. The island remained in government hands. A leading faction turned down an offer to take control of nearby Fort Mason in exchange for leaving Alcatraz. Following that refusal, frustrated White House officials were determined to get the Indians off the island at any cost short of bloodshed, which, pundits agreed, would prove too costly to the Republicans in power.

Finally, an end to the political takeover came about when fires broke out. On June 1, 1971, four historical buildings on the island went up in flames. Because the buildings were far apart from each other, occupiers concluded that government agents had set the fires to discredit the occupation, while government officials claimed they had been started by drunken, drug-crazed revelers.

Officials increased calls to remove the occupiers. Alcatraz, one said, had become an "island ghetto."[29] Most of the occupiers began funneling off the island on their own accord, anxious to return to jobs and schools. Only fourteen remained on June 11, 1971, when US Marshals in three-piece suits arrived to reclaim the land.

But the nearly eighteen-month siege of Alcatraz had not gone for naught. The island takeover awakened something in all Americans everywhere—and particularly in one woman named Wilma Mankiller. As she grew more involved with Indian rights issues, she recognized a desire, an actual *need*, to continue with her schooling, to expand her educational horizons, and to learn more about the universe as well as her own internal thought mechanisms. She decided to continue her college education to learn more about how to go about making a difference in the world.

Her doing so did not sit well with her husband.

"Once I began to become more independent, more active with school and in the community," she wrote years later, "it became increasingly difficult to keep my marriage together. Before that, Hugo had viewed me as someone he had rescued from a very bad life."[30]

Afterward, he had trouble understanding exactly *who* she was.

She and Hugo divorced in 1974.

In the years following the "occupation," Mankiller became more active in developing the cultural resources of the Native American community. She helped build a school and an Indian Adult Education Center. She directed the Native American Youth Center in East Oakland, coordinating field trips to tribal functions. She hosted Native American music concerts and gave Native kids a place to do their homework or just to connect with one another. The youth center also enabled her to pull together Native American adults from around Oakland as volunteers, thus strengthening their tribal ties.

She accomplished it all by flying under the radar. Wilma learned virtually everything she needed to know "on the job," once joking that her enthusiasm seemed to make up for her lack of skills. But it went deeper than that.

Wilma Pearl Mankiller emerged to prominence out of the ashes of Alcatraz, snatching victory from the jaws of inevitable defeat. In the end, as Alcatraz was reclaimed by the US government and the last of the steadily dwindling band of confederates was led off the island in peace, she realized they had failed to accomplish one goal: to regain ownership of what had once been Native American soil. They had succeeded beyond anyone's wildest dreams to achieve the other: to make America aware. In time, their brazen actions would lead to so much more, propelling a small, shy, insecure Indian girl to national prominence and a revered seat of leadership and authority within the ranks of her own tribal people.

It was written on the wind. It was whispered by the gods. And before long, it would be etched in stone. But not until more happened . . . so very much more.

According to Mankiller, "Every day that passed seemed to give me more self-respect and sense of pride. Much of the credit for that awakening has to go to the young men and women who first went to Alcatraz and helped so many of us return to the correct way of thinking. One of the most influential had been Richard Oakes."[31]

Oakes was a student at San Francisco State. Formerly an ironworker in New York, he quit that job and moved to California, where he supported himself by driving a truck. He also worked at an Indian bar named Warren's in the Mission District while he attended college. A critical cog in the formation of the Native American Studies program at San Francisco State, he soon emerged as one of the most influential voices of activism and social justice at the American Indian Center.

Although they hadn't previously met, Wilma became acquainted with Oakes during the occupation. She considered him one of the most articulate leaders of the Indian cause. Still only in his late twenties, he spoke passionately about treaty rights and the need for America to honor its legal commitments to its Native people. He talked about various tribal histories and diverse cultures, enumerating the many contributions Native Americans had made throughout history. Mankiller considered his words radical in the 1970s, less so as time passed. As Oakes wrote in *Rampart* magazine in 1972:

> *Alcatraz was symbolic to a lot of people, and it meant something real to a lot of people. There are many old prophecies that speak of the younger people rising up and finding a way for the People to live. The Hopi, the spiritual leaders of the Indian people, have a prophecy that*

is at least 1,200 years old. It says that the People would be pushed off their land from the East to the West, and when they reached the Westernmost tip of America, they would begin to take back the land that was stolen from them.

There was one old man who came on the island [of Alcatraz]. He must have been eighty or ninety years old. When he stepped up on the dock, he was overjoyed. He stood there for a minute and then said, "At last, I am free."

Alcatraz was a place where thousands of people had been imprisoned, some of them Indians. We sensed the spirits of the prisoners. At times it was spooky, but mostly the spirit of mercy was in the air. The spirits were free. They mingled with the spirits of the Indians that came on the island and hoped for a better future.[32]

Oakes and his wife, Annie, a Pomo woman, had five young children and took care of several others. In January 1970, three months into their island occupancy, the aftermath of their daughter's death struck home. According to Mankiller, Annie had a premonition that something terrible was going to happen to her family.[33]

The girl's death had cast a sickening pall across the island. Richard expressed his belief that, even in death, his daughter still lived within the circle of life. Yet, as time wore on, the grief grew. Oakes and his wife had no alternative but to pack up their belongings and leave with their other children.

Not to be denied what by now he viewed to be his mantra, Oakes helped the Pit River Indians in their struggle with a powerful utility company over land rights later that year. In doing so, he encountered teargas, billy clubs, and jail, only to end up in a bar brawl back in San Francisco, where two men beat him to a pulp with pool cues. Oakes somehow survived, but he never again returned to his earlier level of enthusiasm. He moved north with his wife to Pomo Country near Santa Rosa, where, in September 1972, a caretaker of a YMCA camp claimed that the Indian man had threatened him with a knife. The white man shot and killed Oakes. He was thirty years old.

Wilma thought a lot about Richard and Annie after his death, more so as Annie gradually withdrew from organizational work, turning in toward herself and severing her relationship with the community until, finally, Wilma lost contact with her. But whenever Wilma thought about the true spirit of a Native woman, she recalled her friend and cohort in life through those tumultuous days—and recalled, too, the agony and the pain caused by the young daughter's fall to her death on Alcatraz Island. And, of course, she often thought about Richard Oakes, the visionary whose turbulence in advance of his age helped an entire race of people find harmony. As Oakes had recalled in 1972:

We did a lot of singing in those days. I remember the fires at nighttime, the cold of the night, the singing around the campfire of the songs that aren't shared by the white people . . . the songs of friendship, the songs of understanding. We did a lot of singing. We sang into the early hours of the morning. It was beautiful to behold and beautiful to listen to.[34]

Another of the eloquent Native leaders who rose from the ashes of Alcatraz Island was John Trudell, a wiry young Lakota man whom Wilma once described as "one of the best thinkers I have ever met. Immensely creative and irreverent . . ."[35]

Trudell and his wife, Lou, had come from Los Angeles to Alcatraz with their two daughters to join the Indians of All Tribes. Although Wilma thought them an oddly incompatible couple—John the hyperactive and serious one and Lou the level-headed grinder—she was nonetheless impressed by their devotion to the Indian cause and politics. Before long, Lou came to be looked upon as the all-encompassing Earth Mother of Alcatraz. While living there, Lou gave birth to Wovoka.

Throughout the occupation, John was the announcer for Radio Free Alcatraz, which radical Berkeley radio station KPFA broadcast for thirty minutes each evening. Never at a loss for dreams, Trudell elaborated on the concept of an Indian complex on Alcatraz to include an educational center for Native American studies, a historical archives and museum, and a spiritual center. Grace Thorpe, a Sac and Fox and the daughter of all-time Olympic hero Jim Thorpe of Oklahoma, appeared as a guest on his program, as did many other Indian activists.

Wilma and Lou grew to become close friends, and Mankiller's affection and respect for John were obvious. Even after the federal government rejected all Native American claims to Alcatraz, proffering that the island become, instead, a park, Trudell refused to acquiesce. In an April 9, 1970, article in the *New York Times*, he wrote, "We will no longer be museum pieces, tourist attractions and politicians' playthings. There will be no park on this island, because it changes the whole meaning of what we are here for."

Some of the other Native women who befriended Wilma and continued to have a profound effect upon her even after the occupation ended included Gustine Moppin, the Klamath woman whom Wilma had known since she was a young girl, the person who had convinced her to continue her education. In later years, Wilma called her "a true inspiration. Gustine was the personification of the Cherokee concept of 'having a good mind.' Unfailingly cheerful even in the worst of circumstances, she devoted every waking moment to helping others."[36]

In turn, Gustine believed that Wilma had the potential to do something special with her life, offering encouragement and support through her toughest years as her marriage to Hugo steadily eroded. Pleased that she and Gustine had reunited for the Alcatraz experience, the women got together often over the years that followed to talk about the plight their people faced. Among the worst was a dreaded disease called diabetes, which took an enormous toll on Native people. Gustine lost an arm to diabetes and then had to undergo dialysis when her kidneys failed. She was eventually confined to a wheelchair. When Wilma last saw her in the winter of 1990, Gustine had wasted away to nothing but still worked tirelessly to help people in any way she could. She counseled other amputees on independent living and served on the boards of several Indian agencies. But, not long after Wilma's last visit, Gustine passed into the other world, and the Bay Area Native American community lost its most devoted matriarch.

Another California immigrant during those frantic years with whom Wilma stayed in touch was Bill Wahpepah, a Kickapoo and Sac and Fox.

She worked closely with him on several projects, including an alternative school, youth services, and an Indian adult education center. He brought to his home some of the most dedicated leaders of the American Indian Movement (AIM). Among them were Dennis Banks, Carter Camp, and Vernon and Clyde Bellecourt. Wilma found Clyde Bellecourt, one of AIM's founders, especially likable. He came to the Bay Area with an entourage of Native children. Wilma admired how much he cared about the children and worked hard to help them through life.

Leonard Crow Dog, another dynamic player in the Native American movement, also came to Wahpepah's place. Wilma found within him a certain spiritual presence that reminded her of the Cherokee elders she knew while growing up in Oklahoma. On one occasion, Leonard led an "impressive Lakota ceremony" at the adult education building in Oakland. He and his wife, Mary, traveled everywhere with their young son in a large truck, carrying a hallowed buffalo skull with them wherever they went.[37]

Wilma recounted in her memoir:

> *Bill Wahpepah was always there for us. He opened his home to everyone, especially the Indian children. Most of them were second-generation relocatees who would have been out on the streets without Bill's guidance. I saw Bill weep in utter frustration over a young man who continued to sniff paint. I knew those tears were real. They came from a man who had survived alcoholism and heroin addiction to emerge in the 1970s as one of our finest spokespersons for native rights. He traveled all over the world, telling anyone who would listen about the problems of Native Americans, while he searched for answers and solutions.*[38]

Bill, like Richard Oakes, died much too young. He was in his late forties and at the height of his activism when he walked into spirit country following a sudden illness. Like so many others who had been relocated, he had always spoken of someday returning to live among his people in Oklahoma. That was not to be. He died on September 20, 1972.

The same was true for Wilma's father, Charley. Only in death did he return to the place where he had been born. His passing tore through Wilma's spirit the way lightning carves a hole in the sky.

It came during the Alcatraz occupation. By that time, my parents had long since left San Francisco and Hunter's Point. The spice company my father worked for had relocated, so my folks had moved farther south, down the coast to a small town not too far from Salinas and Monterey, places that John Steinbeck had immortalized in his books. Life had finally leveled out for my father and mother. It was the best period of their life together. At last, they had a decent place to live. Most of their kids were grown and making their ways in the world, and several of us were deeply involved in the Native American rights movement.[39]

Just when it appeared that all was well, misfortune struck once more. Wilma's father developed high blood pressure along with severe kidney problems. The diagnosis was not encouraging—end-stage polycystic kidney disease. At that time, the options for treatment were few. Kidney transplants, common today, were experimental and not available to persons older than fifty-five. That meant her father had just barely missed qualifying. Dialysis, although commonly available, was not nearly as effective as it is today.

As the family began adapting to Charley's illness, Wilma suddenly developed health problems of her own. Once again, she started showing signs of urinary tract infections and the discomfort associated with kidney problems, just as she had when she was pregnant with her first daughter. After extensive testing to find out why she experienced recurring infections, she was diagnosed with polycystic kidney disease, which she had inherited from her father.

The physicians told her that the genetic condition is characterized by the appearance of numerous cysts on the kidneys. The cysts continue to grow, overtaking the normal, healthy tissue until the kidneys fail. They said that in mild cases, total kidney loss is not inevitable. In fact, some people live out their lives without even knowing they have the disease because it produces no apparent symptoms.

But further tests revealed that, just as with her father, Wilma had a severe form of the malady. In both their cases, the disease was progressive and pronounced incurable. Wilma's was not nearly as advanced as her father's was, but all prognoses were that she could expect to experience kidney failure by the time she reached her early to mid-thirties in the 1980s.

Strangely enough, Wilma reacted to the diagnosis with some sense of relief. At least she finally had an explanation for the repeated infections, which sometimes required days of hospitalization. It wasn't the explanation she had hoped for, but, still, it provided some sense of certainty.

Such was not the case with Wilma's father, whose health steadily declined. She had grown closer to him over the years, even as the miles grew farther. Suddenly, none of that seemed to have made a difference. She recalled:

> *It was so difficult to watch my father slowly leave us. He hated being sick, he hated having to give up his job, and he hated taking medicine. My mother practically had to force him to see the doctor for regular visits. We all went to see him as often as we could. He understood our involvement in Alcatraz—that we were fighting for native rights. A conservative Cherokee full-blood, Dad was pleased that his children were taking a stand. I have a strong memory of a Thanksgiving visit with my dad. He was bedfast, and while the rest of the family was busy out in the kitchen getting all the little ones fed, I brought him a plate of food. We ate together, just the two of us, a rare treat in a family as large as ours. He smiled at me and told me he was proud to have a daughter who had become a revolutionary. As it turned out, that was to be his final Thanksgiving dinner.*[40]

The end was especially difficult for the entire family. Wilma's parents had no health insurance, so the children brought him to San Francisco General Hospital, where he could be placed on dialysis. His physical reaction to the procedure was not as the doctors had expected, and he was forced to undergo cardiac surgery to remove fluid that had gathered in the pericardial sac surrounding his heart. Afterward, Wilma went to his room and walked over to his bed. A long scar and dressing crossed his chest. Her father looked up and said, "Look what they have done to me now."[41]

After undergoing that surgery, Charley quickly slid downhill. With the Alcatraz occupation still playing out, Wilma sent the boat to the island to retrieve her brothers and sisters. Although the doctors did everything possible to save their father, it wasn't enough. With his wife and children gathered around him, Charley Mankiller died in February 1971. He was fifty-six. Wilma recalled what happened next:

We never even considered leaving him in California. We brought Charley Mankiller back home to his everlasting hills of Oklahoma. My brother Don and my mother made the arrangements. Some of us flew back to Oklahoma, others drove across country to get there. Even though the lives of my brothers and sisters had taken different paths, my father's death brought us together. We took him to Echota Cemetery, just a few miles from where I now live. Waiting for him were the graves and spirits of his parents, grandparents, cousins, aunts, and old friends, all of them long departed to the other world. It was a cold February day. We formed a line of cars and pickups and followed the hearse from the funeral home in Stilwell out to the graveyard.

Even in my grief, the countryside looked so familiar to me. I was back home again. Rocky Mountain is sparsely populated, but as our procession of vehicles wound slowly down the road to the cemetery, people came outside and stood in their yards to watch us pass. You could almost hear them saying, "There goes Charley Mankiller. They are bringing Charley Mankiller home."[42]

Most of the people who spoke or sang at the funeral service did so in the Cherokee language. Some people literally walked out of the woods to attend the service. Others came from as far away as Kansas and North Carolina. He was buried beside his parents and a child whom Wilma's mother had miscarried between the birth of Linda and Wilma. "There was something very natural about laying him to rest in that ground near people he loved," Wilma said later. "It was so peaceful, and I knew the trees would protect him."[43]

Still, as they left to return to California, the entire family was numb. The anchor that had always kept the Mankiller clan together was gone. In many ways, none of those left behind would ever be the same.

For Wilma's mother, it was a difficult adjustment. Part of her spirit went with her husband when he departed. They had fought for his life together. Now that he was gone, she looked as if she had waged her last great battle. From then on, according to Wilma, life for her would never be the same. She had been married to him since she was a fifteen-year-old girl, and for more than thirty years, they had gone through hell and back, always emerging victorious. They had raised a family, buried children, and gone through the trials of relocation. Besides loving him, Wilma's mother truly respected and liked him. He'd been her best friend. Watching someone she cared so much about suffer through such indignity, Wilma explained, wasn't easy. But her mother made the necessary adjustments and, like the rest of the family, persevered. Just as Charley Mankiller would have wanted—and expected.

So, Wilma returned to Alcatraz and her Native American issues for a few months until the occupation ended, after which she returned to community work. By then, she had come to realize she could no longer be content solely as a housewife and a mother.

Hugo, unhappy with his wife's involvement in the Alcatraz takeover and any of the other Bay Area projects with which she became associated, was especially irritated whenever she held meetings at their home. He also opposed the idea of his wife's traveling anywhere without him, even if only a short distance. When Hugo informed her that she couldn't have a car, she didn't say a word but, instead, went straight to the bank, withdrew some money, and bought an entry-level Mazda. "It took a little bit of doing," she later recalled, "but I figured out how to operate the stick shift on those terrific San Francisco hills."[44]

Buying that little red car without her husband's approval was Wilma's first act of rebellion against a lifestyle she had come to believe was too narrow and confining for her. She longed to break free to experience all the changes going on around her—the politics, literature, art, music, and the role of women in society. Once she had her own car, she felt free to travel to many of the tribal events held throughout California and even up into Oregon and Washington.

And there were a lot of them. All around her, change was exploding. Before long, the young Cherokee woman took on the task of director of the Native American Youth Center in East Oakland. She not only discovered the building destined to house the organization at Fruitvale and East Fourteenth Streets but also drafted some volunteers to slap a fresh coat of paint on the place, pulled together some school curricula and a cultural program, and opened the doors. Her previous experience at the San Francisco Indian Center served her well. Some of the young people who made their way to this new youth center were dropouts. Others came at the end of the school day. All were there to live, learn, and survive.

In effect, Wilma proved successful despite herself. "I had no idea what I was doing when I became involved at the youth center, but I learned quickly—on the job," she wrote in her memoir.

My enthusiasm seemed to make up for any lack of skills. There were field trips to plan and coordinate, and visits to various tribal functions all over northern California. At the center, while the kids did their homework after school, they listened to the music of Paul Ortega, Jim Pepper, or some of the other talented native singers and musicians who came there. All the while, we tried to instill pride in our Native American heritage and history, and to encourage our young people to use that pride as a source of strength to survive the tough streets of East Oakland.

We also worked on basic educational needs. I worked very hard with a young Klamath girl to get her to return to school. I scraped up a little bit of money to pay her, and she helped me with the center's office work. She was just fine with running errands, but when it came to jotting down telephone messages or filing, she became terrified. Finally, she broke down and admitted that she had absolutely no reading skills at all. I immediately got her into a literacy program.[45]

81

At the center, Wilma, too, learned invaluable lessons about self-help. When she had no clue as to where to go to raise funds for a renovation project, she turned to a bar a block from the center. The sister of her friend Gustine owned Chicken's Place, and many of East Oakland's Native people hung out there. Targeting it as a likely starting place, Wilma went in and announced that she was seeking volunteers. To her shock, several people jumped up, ready to dig in to help.

From that point on, whenever the center needed funds for a field trip or warm bodies to do some manual labor, she went to Chicken's Place. The bar never let her down. Wilma, recalling those days fondly, said, "A little of that absolute faith in our ability to get things done by helping one another sustained me later when I returned to Oklahoma. But it was in Oakland where I formed a belief that poor people, particularly poor American Indian people, have a lot more potential and many more answers to problems than they are ever given a chance to realize."[46]

Beyond the youth center, she also became a volunteer worker for the Pit River people in what she described as their fierce legal battle with the powerful Pacific Gas and Electric Company over the rights to millions of acres of the tribe's northern California land. That was the tribe that her former friend, Richard Oakes, had tried to help. Wilma got inspired to act after seeing a report on the six o'clock news about the tribe's efforts to reclaim ancestral lands. They were rural people trying to get back what was rightfully theirs. Something about them reminded Wilma of the Cherokees. When she heard their lawyer speaking out, she rushed to call him and volunteer her services, launching a nearly five-year association with that tribe until the mid-1970s, when she finally left Hugo and California behind.

During her time working for the Pit River people, she managed to absorb much of the history and culture of the Native tribes in California. While most of her time was spent organizing a legal defense fund at the tribe's legal offices in San Francisco, she and her daughters occasionally visited the traditional leaders out on their land. They stayed in a small cabin not far from the home of Raymond and Marie Lego. Wilma recalled:

Raymond was a traditional tribal leader, and the Lego home became the center of activity for those of us taking part in the land fight. Often in the evening, we sat on the front porch, and Raymond and Marie told us about their long struggle to get back the land. Sometimes Raymond would bring out an old cardboard box filled with tribal letters and documents, which he treated as though they were sacred objects. We were privileged to be able to see those things and to spend that time with such people. I felt at home there. The Legos grew a garden. They hunted, and lived a simple life. The demeanor and lifestyle of the Pit River people put me in mind of my own people back in eastern Oklahoma.[47]

From the time she spent with the Pit River tribe, Wilma evolved a world of information that would come in handy later in life. She learned about treaty rights and international law. When she and her daughters drove to Mendocino on the northern shore of a half-moon-shaped bay, they stopped to visit with some of the Pomo people she had met at Alcatraz, and she gathered seaweed with them along the shore. Collecting seaweed was one of their seasonal rituals, she said, "and we placed what we found in special baskets that were family heirlooms. The seaweed was quickly fried in very hot grease and wrapped in thick bread. It was delicious."[48]

After spending time there, Wilma traveled to Kashia, a Pomo *rancheria* in the mountains near Santa Rosa. Only about five acres in size, it was where some of the activists sought refuge after the 1973 AIM takeover at the hamlet of Wounded Knee on the Pine Ridge Reservation in South Dakota. Wounded Knee was the site of the 1890 massacre where, according to legend, the Lakota Nation's sacred hoop was broken and where many dreams died along with hundreds of slaughtered Native Americans. Some of the soldiers who participated in the killings received medals from the United States. Russell Means, John Trudell, and other committed activists went to Wounded Knee in 1973 to demand reforms. Their seventy-two-day standoff with the FBI resulted in a shoot-out and deaths on both sides, but it focused more attention on the injustices in Indian life.

Wilma's brother Richard demonstrated at Wounded Knee. After Alcatraz, he had worked at a television station in San Francisco before leaving for South Dakota because he felt an obligation to join the protest. Their mother was very worried about his welfare, but he was never shot or otherwise hurt.

"Like many other young native men of that time," Wilma later wrote, "Richard heard the call to help the people at Pine Ridge, and he went. Whether the occupation of Wounded Knee helped or hurt Pine Ridge continues to be the subject of debate among the people most affected—those who live on Pine Ridge Reservation." She continued:

There was still much talk of the bloodshed at Wounded Knee when my girls and I camped at Kashia. We stayed with the parents of my friend Maxine Steele. Her brother Charles had gone to Wounded Knee. We cooked our meals outside, and we talked. We felt it was a magical place. It still is today. There are several Indian doctors there, mostly women. We attended dances in the traditional Pomo round house. Under the stars, we listened to stories of history, medicine, and ceremonies.

All of it was a remarkable experience. All of those trips and visits. All of the music and dancing. All of the hard, hard work. All of the time spent in the fight for Alcatraz, at the youth center, with the Pit River people gave me precious knowledge. All of the people I encountered—the militants, the wise elders, the keepers of the medicine, the storytellers—were my teachers, my best teachers. I knew my education would never be complete. In a way, it was only beginning. I felt like a newborn whose eyes have just opened to the first light.[49]

More and more, Wilma found those eyes turning away from the sea and the setting sun and gazing east to where the sun begins its daily journey. That was where, she suddenly realized, she had to go next. Not to heal and regenerate for a few weeks after a marital squabble, not to lay a loved one to rest and then leave again. This time, she knew, she had to go back to stay for good. Back to the land of her birth, back to the soil and trees her grandfather had touched. Back to the animals and birds whose calls a young Native girl had memorized before the family packed up their things and headed out of town on a westbound train so very long ago.

She had to go back, she realized, to complete the circle. Everything suddenly seemed to be so simple, so clear. So *easy*.

Wilma Pearl Mankiller was going home.

The Long Way Back

The year: 1984. Two downhill ski instructors and a third skier, a ski writer working for *Ski Magazine*, load their gear into a rental car and head down I-25 southeast from Denver toward Taos, New Mexico. Their destination: Taos Ski Valley, where they have reservations for a week, which include complimentary dinners, lodging in Taos owner Ernie Blake's personal guest condo, and a week's worth of lift tickets.

Ski reports tout a 180-inch base, 12 inches of fresh powder, and a massive storm moving in from the Pacific Northwest. The three could not be happier.

As the car tools along the highway, the skiers pass an old Chevy pickup truck with a blown-out tire pulled off onto the shoulder. Two Native American men are at the rear. One is leaning against the fender, and the other is seated on the open tailgate. They are wearing lightweight white T-shirts and tattered jeans, despite a temperature in the low fifties.

As the skiers pass them by, the driver of the car hits the brakes and pulls off the road.

"What's up?" the writer, who had been dozing in the backseat, asks.

The driver—an aging, distinguished-looking man with silver hair and a four-o'clock shadow—tells him that they're going back to see if they can help.

The car backs up to within a few feet of the truck and stops. The three skiers get out and, after brief introductions, inspect the tire. It is worse than it looked from the road: a total blowout, the thread-worn rubber shredded on the inside.

The skiers volunteer to help change the tire, and one of the Indians, short, muscular, and drinking from a Schlitz beer can, waves his hands. "We don't have no jack."

He finishes his beer and holds one out to silver-hair, who politely declines.

"We've got a jack," silver-hair tells the man, to which the Indian replies, "Don't matter. We don't have no spare either."

The ski writer walks up and asks the Indians if they want them to stop at the next exit to call for help.

"Thanks," the first Indian says. "But we don't have nowhere to go," and he offers the writer a beer. The writer notices a dozen or more empty cans lying in the bed of the truck and likewise waves him off. "We were on our way to Santa Fe to join our tribe. Part of a *gov-er-ment* plan for resettlement." He says the word as if it is poison. "That's when the tire blew, which is okay. The engine was running hot anyways. And we're out of gas."

"Well, what are you going to do?" silver-hair asks him.

The Indian on the tailgate slides his weight forward and jumps down from the truck. He goes around to the passenger side, opens the door, and pulls out a couple of sleeping bags from behind the seat. Handing one to his companion and hoisting the other over his shoulder, he points his thumb south.

"A.T.," he says, laughing.

Silver-hair looks at him. "A.T.?" he asks. "What's that?"

The second Indian grins. "Alternative transportation," he says, and the two turn toward the desert and begin walking.

The skiers look from one to the other, and silver-hair chuckles. "You ever see anything like that? They're going to walk across the desert all the way to Santa Fe. That must be a hundred miles or more."

The other skier turns to the writer. "They'll never make it. They'll freeze to death."

And as the writer turns toward the desert to catch sight of the Indians once more, he notices something peculiar.

They're gone.

THREE

Trail of Tragedy

"It is wise to learn from the past while keeping an eye peeled on tomorrow," Wilma once wrote. "But often it is best not to know everything that the future holds. All the while I volunteered with the Pit River tribe, took my courses at San Francisco State, and feasted on the harvest of seaweed near Kashia, I had no inkling of what lay ahead."[1]

That's not to say that some of the life events facing Wilma weren't predictable. She knew that divorcing Hugo was inevitable. But beyond that, she didn't realize just how much pain lay right around the corner. If the gods could have spoken, they would have told her of the death and dying tempered with an equal amount of happiness and fulfillment just beyond her reach. "Still," she said, "since I am no soothsayer or medicine person, I could not be sure just what to expect. But sometimes I caught glimpses of harbingers."[2]

She couldn't have realized amid the tumultuous seventies that, inside of a decade, she would not only return to Oklahoma to work for her tribe but also become principal chief of the Cherokee Nation. She learned later that others had that knowledge. Years before being honored as the first woman to serve as chief, a Cherokee spiritual leader saw it all in visions as clear as the mountain waters of spring. According to that sacred leader:

I am a spiritual person, born with a gift inherited from my fore-fathers. . . . One of our prophets is a woman, the First Woman . . . a woman came out from the place where the holy spirit had gone into. She was an ideal woman, an ideal Cherokee woman, and she was nice and she smiled. And I thought, I'm not dealing with gods now. This is a human, I can talk to her.

At that moment, as she smiled at me, I knew that she was the Red Lady of the Eternal Flame. That she was in the third form of our deities, our ancient deities. . . . Then we moved from that scene to a higher ground where I observed a large arbor all made of natural material. And under that arbor were all people that had passed us. They didn't have a care in the world. . . . And then she smiled. I was again talking to a spiritual representative. And at that point, I woke up from that vision, or dream. . . . I knew right then and there, five years ahead of time, that she, Wilma Mankiller, was going to be chief. With experience of this nature, we could only say that she is a special gift. She is somebody special.[3]

This spiritual leader later told that to Wilma when they first met, startling her because he had recognized her not by sight or by name but from the vision.

Around that time, in 1977, Wilma returned to Oklahoma for good. Her last years in California were hectic and, according to her, disturbing. Throughout the unraveling of her marriage, she struggled with the handsome man she had married when she was barely out of high school, with whom she bore two children. He was the same man, she imagined, who had liberated her from the silent hell of Hunter's Point before going on to smother her. The two had by then grown so far apart, she could no longer simply turn on the radio, hum along with the music, and mentally fly away.

For a while, she found refuge at the home of Lou Trudell. Lou and her three children lived in a housing complex on East Fourteenth Street in Oakland. Their house was close to an alternative school run by the Black Panther Party, only a few blocks from the site of the Indian Adult Education Program, a popular gathering spot for Indian activists.

But Lou and her husband, John, were not the ideal married couple. Eventually, their differences caught up with them, and they divorced. He eventually married a Paiute woman named Tina Manning, and they all got along surprisingly well as an extended family. In time, whenever John and Tina and their children visited the Bay Area, they stayed in Oakland with John's ex-wife and her family.

As Wilma departed California for Oklahoma for good, one of the last stops she made was at Lou's place, and John and Tina were there with her. They made some sandwiches for Wilma and her daughters to eat on the trip. Wilma hadn't been back in Oklahoma very long when she received word that Tina Manning Trudell, who was pregnant with John's child, along with three of their children—Ricarda, age six; Sunshine, three; and Eli, one—had been killed in a mysterious fire on the Paiute people's Duck Valley Reservation in Nevada. Tina's mother, Leah Manning, was also killed in the blaze. Tina's father, Arthur Manning, a former tribal chairman, was severely burned. John was attending a demonstration in Washington, DC, at the time. Until the day he died, John contended that the fire was arson, and many others agreed. He strongly suspected FBI involvement.

Wilma found the pain that John experienced impossible to understand. After a time, he used his immense talents and energy to create music and poetry. One of the many ballads he wrote and recorded was "Tina Smiled." He also collaborated with Robert Redford in the making of the documentary film *Incident at Oglala*, as well as played a leading role in *Thunderheart* behind Val Kilmer and Sam Shepard. That film was loosely based on the life of Leonard Peltier, a Native American activist serving a life sentence for allegedly murdering two FBI agents in 1975. Many Native people believe Peltier is a political prisoner who should be released or, at the very minimum, receive a new trial. Wilma was among them. For a long time, she kept a poster that read "Free Peltier."

In later years, John Trudell traveled to Oklahoma to visit his old friend at the Cherokee Nation Tribal Headquarters. Wilma recalled the joy mixed with shock when she saw him, saying,

It was good to be able to spend time with him again. He still lives life on his own terms. He was barefoot, had a sort of half Mohawk haircut, and wore a long silver earring dangling from one of his ears. When we sat down for coffee, I told him that he had to be one of my most bizarre friends. John laughed at that comment. "You have the nerve to sit there and tell me that I'm bizarre?" he asked. "Here you are in this complex running a great big bureaucratic organization. What about you? I think you're the one who is bizarre." On days when the political headaches of my job as chief become almost surreal, I recall John's words and I smile. I also remember the old times in Oakland with John and his two wives, our time together at Lou's place. John's friendship continues to be very important to me.

Everyone who showed up in those days in Oakland found Lou warm, witty, and very generous. Her house was a place of comfort. I especially liked her kitchen. Lou and I gathered there with some other women at least once a week to share our thoughts. It was a most eclectic circle of women.[4]

The friends included Wilma's old Klamath compadre, Gustine Moppin, always optimistic even if her latest lover had just run off or she was without a penny for her rent. Gustine would just smile and say somebody else better was in store for her, or she would somehow come up with enough rent money before an eviction notice arrived. As if by magic, Gustine was always right.

Another of the group was Susie Steel Regimbal, Wilma's self-assured Pomo friend with a biting wit. Susie came from a tribe whose spiritual leaders were women, including writers. Because many authors write from either a patriarchal or white feminist perspective, the value of Native women, according to author Devon Abbott Mihesuah, is vastly underrated despite overwhelming oppression at the hands of whites. Mihesuah wrote:

Natives have persevered but men have not been the only catalysts for survival, adaptation, and development. Women have been just as crucial to the economic, social, religious, and political survival of tribes. "Activism and Expression as Empowerment" is an overview of how some Native women have empowered themselves and have striven to empower their tribes. Women such as Wilma Mankiller, Ada Deer, and Winona LaDuke not only devote time and energy to what white researchers consider "female issues"—health care, education and social work—but they also contend with economic development, environ-

mental protection, treaty rights, and tribal sovereignty. Almost all prominent female Native leaders have stated that they gain confidence and strength to persevere from the knowledge that their female ances- tors also were striving for many of the same goals. Strong women participate in their tribal ceremonies and serve as political leaders and as social and environmental activists. We read their forceful words in poetry and novels and watch documentaries and movies they write and produce.[5]

From her friend Susie, Wilma learned of these tribal concepts of traditional female leadership and the belief that their indigenous value systems far exceed those of Western society.

Yet another participant in their regular women's circle was Linda Aaronaydo, a Creek and Filipina and the youngest of the group of five. A preschool teacher, she had the demeanor and looks of the stereotypical country schoolmarm and the heart of an anarchist. She regaled the group with stories of her experiences on the social-protest front, including the 1968 Poor People's March to Washington, DC.

The women talked about many different subjects, from their children and the emerging women's movement to the role of Native American women, indigenous rights, the environment, and politics. They also gos- siped about men, of course, each sharing things they would never have admitted to a man. "We spoke of our innermost angers, fears, and vul- nerabilities," Wilma recalled. "We spoke of dreams—our secret dreams. These were shared only when we were all together in Lou's kitchen."[6]

Occasionally, Wilma added, the group went on picnics, to activist meetings, or to a "rather raunchy bar" in East Oakland. Sometimes, they would attend powwows together. Mostly, though, they simply met at Lou's house "to talk and sing and dream. None of us was quite sure where we were headed, but we all knew there was no turning back. The outward foundations of our lives had already crumbled, and we had to move on."[7]

And move on they did, making the journey from the safety and secu- rity of Lou's kitchen to places none of them had ever been before.

Gustine, who inspired so many others, stayed active in Indian affairs in the Bay Area until 1990, when she "walked into spirit country." Susie entered into a partnership with a Seminole Indian named Kenneth Tiger, who shared her love of books, art, music, health food, and the Pomo culture. She became the first female tribal chairperson of her Pomo band just before she died of stomach cancer in late 1992. Linda ended up becoming a physician and established a practice in Santa Rosa, where she raised her children and devoted more time to learning about her Creek history and heritage. Lou went on to become a nurse practitioner in rural New Mexico, living near her ancestral home, with a clear view of the mountains and "an even clearer view of her future."[8]

Wilma wrote in 1993:

The three of us from that group who remain—Lou, Linda, and I— see one another only occasionally. I visited with Lou at a Farm Aid concert in 1992 in Texas, and we fell into easy conversation, as we always do. We also talk on the telephone and correspond. No matter how much time passes or what happens, that special bond between us is still there. I have heard people speak of a bond that develops between survivors, people who have come through some sort of threatening experience together. I suppose that is what our bond is like. We are survivors of a battle to gain control of our own lives and create our own paths instead of following someone else's. And because our lives are still evolving, it will be interesting to see where and when we will complete the journey that began so long ago in that sanctuary, Lou's kitchen.[9]

Following those last few months in California, Wilma reclaimed her maiden name, which had always been a part of her Cherokee heritage, becoming Wilma Pearl Mankiller once again. Although her ex-husband helped Wilma and the girls out financially from time to time, making a go of things mostly fell on Wilma's shoulders. But her flight from the coast was held up suddenly when, while she and her daughters lived in Oakland, Hugo picked up Gina, who was barely ten, to take to a circus at the Cow Palace in San Francisco. Wilma tells the story of what happened next:

Late that evening, I received a phone call from Hugo informing me that he had decided to keep Gina with him and go on a trip. I told him not to do that, and he responded that he would bring Gina home on one condition—that I tell him I loved him.

I flatly refused. So Hugo kept Gina and did not return her to me for almost one whole year. It was a horrible time, an unbelievably horrible time. Hugo called periodically to tell me that Gina was OK, and then he would always ask about our getting back together. I was frantic and very worried about Gina, but I could not give in and go back to the kind of life I had had with Hugo.

During the time Hugo had Gina with him, using her as some sort of bargaining chip, they went to Chicago to see his snobbish relatives, whom we had visited on our honeymoon in 1963. Then he took her to live in Berkeley for a while, and from there, they traveled abroad and ended up at his family's home in Ecuador. Gina was sent to school, learned Spanish, and was given all sorts of presents and fancy dresses. Although she was generally spoiled by her father and his family and, I am sure, loved all the attention, she was not really a happy little girl. She missed being with her sister and me. Eventually, Gina began to lose her pretty hair, and she developed an ulcer.

Finally, Hugo and Gina returned to the United States, and they came to San Francisco for a visit. When he brought her by the first time, I saw that she was different. She acted very formal at first, but by the end of the day, she was back to her old self. I took a chance and let Hugo return for her, because he promised to bring her back again the following week. I held my breath and waited, and sure enough, the next week, there was Gina.[10]

When Wilma asked her daughter how she felt about staying with her mother and sister, she hesitated before replying. She had a birthday coming up, and her father had planned a big party for her in Ecuador with lots of gifts. Knowing all that, the youngster still managed to say that she felt good about not going back with her father. She wanted to stay with her mom. Wilma picked up the phone, called Hugo, and told him the news.

Once reunited with her daughter, Wilma was still concerned that Hugo might eventually show up; she wasn't sure what he was capable of doing. So, she quickly arranged for a trip to Oklahoma. There, Wilma had to reconnect with her past while introducing her daughters to a world they had never known. She wrote about the experience:

On the first Saturday of every month from April to October, the members of the Four Mothers Society and friends would gather. The men tested their skill with bow and arrow by shooting at bales of hay. Families watched while comfortably seated on blankets and quilts on the ground. Later there would be a stickball game, then the evening meal. In summer when vegetables and fruit were in season, the dinners were sumptuous. Meals usually included sliced tomatoes and cucumbers, corn harvested that day, green beans, okra, freshly dug potatoes, and onions. Dessert was fresh blueberries, huckleberries, or peaches, cobblers made from those fruits. Later, when the time was right, the evening ceremonial dances began. They sometimes lasted until sunup.

Aunt Maude Wolfe, my father's cousin, told us about an empty cabin near one of the ceremonial dance grounds. That was where we stayed for most of the visit. There was electricity, but no running water. It was quite a dramatic change for the girls. In some ways, it must have been as strange for them as when I went to San Francisco as a child. The girls had had some experience getting along with few amenities when we had gone to Pit River or visited some of the other rural tribes in California, but they were not prepared for such living on a daily basis. After a few weeks, we returned to California. But my mind was made up—we would move back to Oklahoma permanently the following summer.[11]

When they finally arrived at her mother's place that summer, Wilma realized she had twenty dollars to her name, no car, no job, and few, if any, prospects. But the family was happy. At last, she and her girls were home to stay.

Wilma's mother had already moved back to Adair County a short time ahead of the clan. She had rented a house not very far from Mankiller Flats, and everyone crowded in with her until they could find their own place and Wilma landed a job. Later, after things finally settled down, Wilma built a house of their own before doing the same for her mother and youngest brother, Bill, just up the road. Their old house, which they had abandoned in the 1950s, was gone. So were the smokehouse and most traces of the old gardens. But the cold-water spring where her grandfather and father had drunk and where she had collected water when she was a little girl was still there. So were the trees and the hills, the birds, and the rest of the animals.

"Gradually, most of my brothers and sisters also came home to live in Oklahoma," Wilma recalled.

Frieda lived in Tulsa, never having moved away from Oklahoma. Vanessa had returned before I did. Richard, my brother who had gone to Wounded Knee, and Frances and Linda all followed. One by one, with their families in tow, all of them drifted back—all of them but Don and John, two of my older brothers. They stayed. Don has a ranch to run near Yosemite, and grandchildren to fuss over. Johnny remains in San Francisco, kind of an unofficial caretaker of the Mankiller legacy we left behind in California.[12]

When they first moved back, Wilma spent a lot of time looking for work. It was tough, but she was determined to remain positive. When she wasn't interviewing, she played her guitar and sewed to keep her mind occupied. She made ribbon shirts and clothes for her brothers and sisters and school clothes for Mitchell, her sister Linda's youngest son. Most of all, she refused to get discouraged.

Then, finally, during that first autumn after their return in October 1977, she found a job working for the Cherokee Nation of Oklahoma. Based on all of her experience with various tribes and Native American issues in California, it seemed logical for her to do something on behalf of her own people. Finding a job wasn't easy at first until, finally, she got fed up with hearing how "overqualified" she was or simply just didn't fit in. She got tired of being turned away, so she walked right into the office and said, "I want to work! Whatever you have, please let me try it. I need to go to work!"[13]

The direct approach paid off, and she was hired as an economic stimulus coordinator. Her starting salary of $11,000 a year was a princely sum for a low-level management job. Besides that, the cost of living was so much lower in Oklahoma than in the Bay Area that she felt as if she'd suddenly struck gold. One of the first things she did was go out and buy a used station wagon.

Wilma's primary duty in her new job was to get as many Native people as possible trained at the university level in environmental sciences and health and then help them integrate back into their communities. It seemed like a rewarding enough job, but as she dove into the work, she had mixed feelings. She had been involved with the nitty-gritty issues of Indian activism for so long, she suddenly felt overwhelmed by the bureaucracy that engulfed her. It was difficult to find *anyone* who believed in grassroots democracy.

In time, though, she found the task of working with a male-oriented tribal power base rewarding, particularly since her efforts were designed to bring about a rebirth of Cherokee government. At last, there was something the US bureaucracy hadn't stripped away. The Cherokee Nation, the country's second-largest indigenous tribe behind the Navajo, was once again electing its own chief, and it had a brand-new constitution.

Former principal chief William W. Keeler was the one who had started the reforms rolling with a constitutional revision in the early 1970s by appointing a committee to draft a new governing document. Keeler had been appointed in 1949 to head the Cherokees, and in 1971 he became the first chief elected by *all* of the Cherokee people since 1903. After serving a four-year term, Keeler withdrew from active participation in politics and retired to take care of his ranch and his other business interests.

Keeler was succeeded by Ross O. Swimmer in August 1975. An attorney and the president of First National Bank of Tahlequah, Swimmer was elected principal chief by a narrow margin out of a field of ten candidates. A staunch Republican and graduate of the University of

Oklahoma, the High Church Episcopalian had begun his service to the Cherokee Nation in 1972 as tribal attorney.

After taking office as chief, Swimmer immediately saw to it that the new constitution drafted during Keeler's term was modified and finally passed. He moved quickly to adopt a new constitution because the election for principal chief had been so close and contentious, he feared someone might vote against the measure. He hoped that the new governing document would have a unifying effect on the people, showing them that he didn't intend to usurp the government but rather to lead as an executive with the power of the tribe divided among three separate entities.

Under the terms of the newly adopted document, a principal chief and deputy were to be elected every four years. A fifteen-member tribal council would act as the legislative branch, and a three-member judicial appeals tribunal would serve as the judiciary. The constitution promised "speedy and certain remedy" to all Cherokees who suffered wrong and injury. It also established a checks-and-balances system within tribal government, allowing for all registered Cherokees to vote in tribal elections. After federal approval of the constitution by the US Department of the Interior, the Cherokee Nation ratified it in June 1976.

But the new document, which was supposed to unite the Cherokees, failed. Some Natives thought the requirement of one-quarter blood should have been enough to qualify them as Cherokee, while others felt that those who lived outside the Cherokee Nation should be barred from voting in tribal elections. Some people objected to the inclusion of the Delawares and Shawnees as Cherokee tribal members, while others lamented the exclusion of Cherokee freedmen and intermarried whites.

Wilma met Chief Swimmer not long after she began working for the tribe. The meeting was curt, since she was occupied with her job. But, as she finished her assignments, she began looking around for something else to do. After all the time she had spent trying to raise money for various Native American causes and projects in Oakland and San Francisco, she had learned to write a strong grant proposal. She was never at a loss for work—or, it seemed, words.

The five years spent with the Pit River people alone were invaluable when it came time for her to speak up for her own tribe's needs. At

Pit River, she had learned a great deal about treaty rights and the government-to-government relationship between Indian nations and the United States. When folks at the Cherokee Nation discovered that she possessed some ability, she was kept busy churning out proposals.

As her workload grew, so too did her reputation as a knowledgeable and dedicated employee. By 1979, she had been named program development specialist for the Nation, a job she went on to hold for two years. When a couple of the grant proposals received funding and she began earning substantial revenue for the tribe, Chief Swimmer and the council sat up and took notice.

Also, in 1979, Wilma returned to her college work to complete the last few remaining course credits for her bachelor of science degree in social work. She took the Graduate Record Examination and chose to attend the University of Arkansas at Fayetteville for her graduate work in community planning. Located in northwestern Arkansas not very far from the Oklahoma state line, Fayetteville is a picturesque city with rolling hills and shady residential streets. Although the university campus was a little more than an hour's drive each way, she enjoyed the commute. It gave her a chance to think and make plans—and even dream about the future. She had secured a graduate assistantship to help defer some of her expenses, and she never did have to take a formal leave of absence from her post with the Cherokee Nation. That gave her peace of mind, because she had the understanding that she could come back to her full-time position as a program specialist whenever she desired.

Meanwhile, Wilma's daughters were busy with their own schoolwork and making new friends. Finally, everything appeared to be falling in place. Work was coming along well; college was progressing nicely. Everything had turned out for the best since the family returned to Wilma's hometown. Wilma enjoyed renewing old acquaintances with various folks and family members while making new friends, including many non-Native persons. In fact, two of her very closest compatriots were a white couple, Mike and Sherry Morris. With their little girl Meagan, they had moved to eastern Oklahoma a couple of years before Wilma. In 1979, Mike accepted a position with the Cherokee Nation as director of education. Wilma reflected upon their relationship:

Sherry and I were about the same age, but other than that simple fact, there were very few similarities between us—at least on the surface. For example, Sherry came from the Deep South, a totally different background, lifestyle, and culture than mine. A strikingly beautiful woman, she had been concerned with her physical looks as a girl and young woman. But even though she was a former beauty queen and had been a first runner-up for Miss Mississippi, we hit it right off when we met. Sherry became one of my best friends.

Sherry was just beginning to come into her own as a person. She had finally stopped being so concerned with her physical self, and was starting to turn inside as well as looking beyond at the world around her. Over time, rural health-care issues and early child development became her primary interests. She also was so great with Meagan, her exceptional three-year-old daughter. It was good to see how Sherry nurtured her child. As someone who had experienced my own evolution into a more independent woman, I felt privileged to be able to watch Sherry grow and find her own path.[14]

And then something strange happened. It occurred on November 8, 1979, a Thursday. A sign, an omen that calamity was approaching, had shown up at the Mankiller household the night before.

That evening, Wilma's second cousin Byrd Wolfe and his wife, Paggy, came to visit. Byrd was active at the Flint ceremonial grounds in their community, and Paggy was a shell shaker at their dances. As the old friends sat and talked of the world of Cherokee medicine—a unique world that few outsiders realize still exists to this day—Wilma became aware of two realities the Cherokee Nation people maintained. The first was that the two worlds, Native and non-Native, are very different, with the Indian world functioning within the non-Native world surrounding it, while the second dictated that Native Americans have to retain their ancient Cherokee belief systems, values, customs, and rituals regardless of the surroundings in which they find themselves.

An essential part of that system in some communities is the belief in the power of medicine people. That evening with the Wolfe family, they discussed those practitioners. Wilma recalled the outcome:

We sat around the fire burning in my stove, and we talked about how medicine people usually practice two kinds of old medicine. One type requires the use of herbs, roots, and other gifts of creation for curing, for something as simple as a headache or as complex as a blood ailment. The other type draws on ancient tribal rituals and customs, which sometimes include songs, incantations, and other thoughts or acts. Many of the prescriptions and rituals are preserved in medicine books written in Cherokee and passed down from medicine person to medicine person.

That November evening, our conversation turned to the use of medicine to settle disputes or cause harm. As time passed, the gist of our talk centered on how, even in contemporary Cherokee society, some of our people still use medicine to "settle scores."[15]

As the three of them sat around the fire talking, they became aware of a presence outside the Mankiller house. They heard sounds coming from the darkness, and peering out the windows into the night, saw movement up in the trees. Closer inspection revealed some owls—and more of them, still. Some had taken flight, while others rested in the trees. "We heard their voices," Wilma said.[16]

Many Native Americans, including the Cherokees of the Mankiller family, are taught to beware of owls. They're told that a *dedonsek*, or "one who makes bad medicine," could change into an owl and travel through the night skies to visit Cherokee homes. That usually brought bad luck. Wilma had heard stories that if owls came close to the house, it often meant bad news was coming. Just the hooting of an owl could make some people wary. In eastern Oklahoma, there are still Cherokee tales of *Estekene*, the Owl, who can change shape to appear in almost any form. Other Native people also consider the owl to be an omnipotent figure of death. They throw rocks and sticks at owls that gather near their homes to chase them away.

That November evening, Wilma's house was suddenly surrounded by owls. They were everywhere. Despite what she had been taught as a child, she believed that owls were harmless unless you bothered them. But the owls thought otherwise. That night was anything but quiet as the birds roosted near the house, creating all sorts of raucous noises. As the activity increased, Wilma became uneasy. By the time her cousin and his wife had departed, leaving Wilma alone with her two daughters, the owls' screeching had grown louder. The Cherokee woman couldn't help recalling an ancient legend recited by Margaret Craven, writing in *I Heard the Owl Call My Name*:

> *The Indian knows his village and feels for his village as no white man for his country, his town, or even his own bit of land. His village is not the strip of land four miles long and three miles wide that is his as long as the sun rises and the moon sets. The myths are the village, and the winds and rains. The rain is the village, and . . . the talking bird, the owl, who calls the name of the man who is going to die.*[17]

The next morning, Wilma arose and prepared for a trip to Tahlequah to speak to the personnel director at the Cherokee Nation about working on a study to provide her with a little extra cash. At the time, she was living on $300 a month from her graduate assistantship, a few grants, and food given to her by her Cheyenne friend, Jerri Warledo. She needed the extra money for necessities.

Just as she headed out the door, something on the television caught her eye, and she froze. Years later, she couldn't recall what she had seen precisely. Perhaps the hostage crisis in Iran had just erupted, or something else of international importance had exploded over the air. Later, she thought about how her stopping to watch television threw off her routine and upended her normal timing.

She finally left the house and pulled out onto the road several minutes late. She drove the station wagon up the backcountry roads to Highway 100 as usual. Everything seemed fine as she approached a small hill. On the opposite side, hidden from view, a car headed for Stilwell pulled out to pass two slow-moving vehicles. Wilma never saw the car until it crested the hill. By then, it was too late. Wilma yanked the steering wheel violently to one side, but in a split second, she saw her life pass before her eyes and heard the jarring sound of metal on metal as she felt the impact of the collision.

She remembered virtually nothing afterward except for several figures running around, trying to decide how to extract her from the wreckage. The front of the vehicle was pushed in so far that the rear edge of the hood cut into her neck. Her face was literally crushed. Her right leg was mangled, and her left leg and both ankles were broken. So were many of her ribs. Blood gushed from the cuts and abrasions. Death was near. She felt it. Wilma reflected upon the head-on collision:

Two ambulances tore down the two-lane asphalt highway to the scene of the crash. Of course, I had no way of knowing it at the time, but there was only one person from the other vehicle involved in the accident. Only much later would I find out that the other victim was also a woman. Her car was much smaller than my station wagon, and sustained even more damage. She lived only a short time. Unbelievably, she was someone I knew. She was my friend—my very good friend. The woman who died was Sherry Morris.[18]

The odds of two friends crashing into one another on a rural road were virtually nil. Wilma had just seen Sherry earlier that week to make plans to go together to Arkansas to hunt for antiques. She was anxious to find an oak table. Her husband, Mike, was away at an educational conference. Fortunately, their daughter, Meagan, was not with Sherry on that fateful ride when the two cars met.

One of the ambulances carried Sherry to the hospital in Tahlequah, but her neck was broken, and they pronounced her dead on arrival. The other ambulance rushed Wilma to Stilwell, where she was stabilized. From there, they transported her to a larger hospital in Fort Smith. She recalls fading in and out of consciousness. As the ambulance sped down the highway, she believed she was actually trying to die; her spirit was struggling to leave her body. Strangely, she felt no urge to fight it. She described the sensation:

It was such a wonderful feeling! That is the best way to describe what I felt. I was dying, yet it was all so beautiful and spiritual. I experienced a tremendous sense of peacefulness and warmth. It was probably the most profound experience I have ever had. All these years later, I can still recall how it felt, but it is difficult to explain. It was overwhelming and powerful. It was a feeling that was better than anything that had ever happened to me. It was better than falling in love.

I had this feeling all the while the ambulance raced me to the hospital. There was a woman there in the ambulance. I later learned she straddled me and tried to stop me from dying. She fought to keep me alive. But there was this tremendous pull toward what seemed to be an overpowering love. The woman was pulling me back toward life.

I recall that while I was in that condition, Felicia and Gina came into my mind. Then I made an unconscious choice to return to life. I did not see any tunnels or white lights There was none of that. It was more as if I came to fully understand that death is beautiful and spiritual. It is part of life, and when I finally came out of it, I vowed to hang onto that experience. I wished to retain that feeling, and I did so. As a result, I have lost any fear of death. I began to think of death as walking into spirit country rather than as a frightening event. Even though more brushes with death were ahead, the idea of dying no longer frightened me.[19]

That first day, right after the accident, Wilma was in surgery for six hours. She was then moved to intensive care. Some of the people who were at the scene told her later that her body was so badly mangled, they couldn't tell if she was a man or a woman. Wilma didn't regain full consciousness until two days later. When she realized she had been in an accident, she asked if anyone else was injured. Her friends and family assured her that everything was okay. She didn't find out the truth for three weeks.

Friends and relatives came to visit, including Mike Morris, but he didn't bring Sherry, which she thought was odd. Finally, she asked about her friend, and he replied that she was busy, but that didn't make much sense. She and Mike were close friends, and she wondered if something was wrong. Then, finally, Mike asked the family and the doctors if he could visit with Wilma alone. That's when she learned that the other woman in the accident had been Sherry.

Wilma, stunned, began to cry so hard that she hemorrhaged from her wounds, and medics had to be called in once more to stop the bleeding. Her sister, who was waiting in the hall outside, said that a few minutes after Mike had gone into the room, she heard Wilma scream. Later that day, when her sister stopped by to visit, Wilma asked if she went to the funeral. She said she had, and Wilma returned to her silent mourning.

A local Tahlequah newspaper account of the accident didn't help Wilma's depression. Under the headline, "Park Hill Driver Dies in Wreck," the article went on to detail the event:

One woman was killed and another critically injured in a three-car accident on SH 100 about 16 miles south of Tahlequah in Cherokee County Thursday.

A motorist identified by the Highway Patrol as Sherry Ethridge Morris, 32, Park Hill, was pronounced dead in a Tahlequah hospital from multiple injuries.

Listed in critical condition at Sparks Regional Medical Center in Fort Smith, Ark., was Wilma Mankiller, 33, Stilwell.

Investigators said the cars driven by the two collided head-on at the crest of a hill about 10 a.m. and that one of the vehicles then careened into another car on the highway.

The driver of that car, Alexia K. Brown, Park Hill, was not reported injured. Investigators said Mrs. Morris was trapped in the wreckage of her car for 55 minutes.[20]

Having to deal with the shock of Sherry's death, combined with her own physical and emotional pain, made the suffering unbearable. She carried with her a certain amount of survivor's guilt that frequently accompanies such circumstances for what seemed an eternity. Relating to Mike was awkward, but he had little emotional support on which to lean, so she tried to be there for him and his daughter despite his growing depression.

In the meantime, Wilma had to overcome her own remorse and keep moving forward, despite her lingering pain and injuries. Her first hospital stay lasted for more than eight weeks. During that time, she underwent numerous surgeries to put her face and shattered bones back together. Before it was all over, she had endured seventeen operations, mostly on her right leg. At one point, the doctors told her she would never walk again, and they even considered amputation. It was a frightening thought that Wilma recalled with difficulty:

> *The pain was unbelievable, and I had to wear full casts on both legs. I was confined to a wheelchair for some time, and would be somewhat incapacitated for almost a year. I could not even go to the bathroom or brush my teeth without assistance. To this day, I am not sure how I managed to regain mobility.*
>
> *But throughout the entire ordeal, I never allowed myself to become depressed—not once. I had faced death, and I had survived. I would not permit myself to sink into a negative state. Recovering at my home, I had the time to examine my life in a new way—to reevaluate and refocus. The entire family was a big help to me during those troubled times. My sister Linda came to my house every day for about six months. I will always be indebted to her. Mother also helped to care for my daughters, and our friends pitched in to see that our basic needs were fulfilled. I was so proud of my girls. They rolled with the punches. They did not allow the chaos in our lives to best them.*[21]

During the long healing process, Wilma turned inward to embrace her Cherokee heritage, adopting what the elders call "a Cherokee approach" to life. They say it is *being of good mind*. That means one has to think positively, to take what is handed out and turn it into a better path. At the beginning of some Cherokee traditional prayers and healing ceremonies, everyone is asked to remove all negative thoughts, to have a pure mind and heart for the prayer and the ceremony ahead. Wilma tried to do that in the process of healing and ultimately attributed her recovery to her efforts.

But the accident changed her life. She had experienced death, felt its presence, touched it, and then let it go. It was a very spiritual thing, she admitted later, a rare natural gift. From that point on, she thought of herself as the woman who lived *before* and the woman who lived *after*.

Throughout the recuperation process, Wilma made steady if slow progress. She read and made plans and worked hard at improving her physical self. She was determined not to have to wear leg braces. Her goal was to get out and walk a quarter of a mile to the mailbox and back each day. At first, she couldn't make it out of the yard without stumbling and falling. That both frustrated and angered her, but it also steeled her will to keep trying until she succeeded. Week after week, she was able to walk a little farther at a time.

But her trials were far from over. In time, she would experience even more physical woes before she could ever be weaned off the crutches from the accident. She recalled them clearly:

It was in early 1980, and I began to experience muscle problems. At first, it was relatively minor. For instance, I had a little trouble peeling a grapefruit and holding a pencil. Then it became worse. I dropped my hairbrush constantly and lost my grip. Before long, I could not even hold my toothbrush. Then I started to experience severe double vision. My sister Linda took me to several physicians, including an optometrist and neurologist. They did not help. They could not confirm any specific disease or ailment.

My strength was leaving me. I was growing weaker and weaker. Before too long, I lost control of my fingers, my hands, my arms. Then I could no longer stand up, even on my crutches. I would rise and then crumble and fall. I could speak only for short periods of time because my throat muscles would give out. My breathing became labored, and I could not hold my head up. I lost the ability to chew except for very short periods of time. Soon, I had lost forty pounds. I was afraid to drink water because it would come out of my nose. Some days I could not keep my eyes open for very long, so I would just lie down and keep my eyes closed. That became my existence.[22]

For someone who had absorbed life internally, loved to read, and was always on the go, the inability to see things around her or to move around freely was nearly intolerable. During that time, Linda took her sister to Oklahoma City to visit Mary Barksdale, an activist lawyer and good friend. Wilma lay on the backseat of the car all the way there to conserve her energy. When they drove up to Mary's house, Linda helped Wilma out of the car with her crutches. As she began to walk toward the front door, her muscles suddenly gave out, and she fell face-forward onto the sidewalk. She broke her nose once more as blood gushed all over. She began to choke.

Suddenly, the thought struck her that her destiny was to continue to erode until death overtook her. It was a struggle she was clearly losing. Several nights later, as Wilma lay on the sofa, her brothers and sisters came to visit. Her breath grew increasingly strained. "I felt my old friend death approach me," she recalled. "Somehow, I knew what to do. I found that if I relaxed and closed my eyes, everything would get better, and that is what I did that night. I lay there absolutely still, and the moment passed."

Nearly ten months after the automobile accident and seven months after her muscle problems began, Wilma was watching the Jerry Lewis muscular dystrophy telethon when a woman appeared and described her muscle problems and how she had come to be dependent on a respirator. As she spoke, Wilma realized the woman's symptoms were identical to her own. "My God!" she said. "That is what I have!"[23]

The woman had a disease called myasthenia gravis, a form of muscular dystrophy that can lead to permanent paralysis. Finally, Wilma knew what was wrong with her.

The following week, Linda drove her to Tulsa, where they met with the staff at the local Muscular Dystrophy Association. They conducted tests that verified Wilma's worst fears. She had systemic myasthenia gravis. She wrote about what happened next:

> I went to my sister's car and wept quietly. I was spent. I needed to collect my thoughts before proceeding. I thought about how I had somehow managed to get through the trauma of the automobile accident and Sherry's death, and then had faced the continuing problems with my legs and regaining use of my limbs. Now this had happened to me. I was stricken with a disease that most people had never even heard of. I was very discouraged, but I knew I could not give in. I

went home and prepared to battle this latest assault on my physical self and spirit. I could feel the anger running through my body. I was determined to win. I drew on the strength of my ancestors and of present-day Cherokee medicine people, and on my own internal resolve to remove all negative factors from my life so I could focus on healing.[24]

In November 1980, Wilma checked into a Tulsa hospital to undergo more tests and procedures. She had quit smoking and worked hard to prepare her body and mind for what lay ahead. The physicians presented her with various options, including chest surgery to remove her thymus gland. They told her she would also need to endure further treatment involving high doses of steroids. Although that approach seemed drastic, it made sense. She didn't want simply to cope with the disease. She wanted to *beat* it. She wanted to rid herself of it once and for all. She opted for surgery.

The operation was a success, and Wilma felt a sudden surge of strength when she awoke on a respirator. Within less than a week, she was on her feet, washing her hair, and caring for herself. She was determined to get on with living and with work. The surgery and the intensive drug program "truly worked miracles," she said. "Although the drugs had side effects, such as causing a significant weight gain, the worst of my symptoms were completely gone within four to six weeks after the operation. I continued to experience moderate muscle dysfunction, but even that was under control in less than two years after the surgery. The drug therapy continued until late in 1985, yet I was able to return to my post with the Cherokee Nation in January of 1981."[25]

Little could she have realized back then, but within only a very few years, she would become deputy chief and then principal chief of the entire Cherokee Nation. Her vision of spiritual leadership would come true. But none of that would have happened, she believed, if it hadn't been for the ordeals she'd been forced to endure. After that, she realized she could survive anything. She had stared down adversity and turned it into a positive experience—a better path for her to follow. She had found the way to be strong of body and clear of mind.

The Cherokee and the Women

In the times before the Cherokees learned the ways of others, they paid extraordinary respect to women. When a man married, he took up residence with the clan of his wife.

The women of each of the seven clans elected their own leaders. These leaders convened as the Women's Council and sometimes raised their voices in judgment to override the authority of the chiefs when the women believed the welfare of the tribe demanded such an action. It was a common custom among the ancient Cherokees that any important questions relating to war and peace were left to a vote of the women.

There were brave Cherokee women who followed their husbands and brothers into battle. These female warriors were called War Women or Pretty Women, and they were considered dignitaries of the tribe, many of them being as powerful in council as in battle.

The Cherokees also had a custom of assigning to a certain woman the task of declaring whether pardon or punishment should be inflicted on offenders. This woman also was called the Pretty Woman, but she was sometimes known as Most Honored Woman or Beloved Woman.

It was the belief of the Cherokees that the Great Spirit sent messages through their Beloved Woman. So great was her power that she could commute the sentence of a person condemned to death by the council.

The last of the Beloved Women, the Ghigau, known by her later name of Nancy Ward, earned her title, the highest honor that a Cherokee woman could achieve, by rallying the Cherokees in a pitched battle against the Creeks in 1755. As a War Woman of the Wolf Clan, she accompanied her first husband, Kingfisher, into battle. In the field, she prepared food for him and chewed his bullets to cause fatal damage when they struck their marks. When Kingfisher was killed in the heat of the fray, she raised his weapon and fought so valiantly that the Cherokees rose behind her leadership and defeated the Creeks.

In recognition of her courage in war, Nancy was given her prestigious title. She spent the remainder of her life as a devoted advocate of peace between the Cherokees and all others.

Four

The Long Way Home

IN 1981, WILMA RETURNED TO HER OLD JOB, WRITING GRANT PROPOS-
als for the Cherokee Nation. But things had changed. She was angry, but
it was a healthy anger. It was a rage produced by the battle she'd just come
through with Western medicine and the overall dehumanization of its
patients. That had been her experience during the long road to recovery,
and it was not at all pleasant.

To help channel her anger and maintain a positive outlook, she
decided to write a short story that addressed the issue of cultural clashes.
It was the story of the aging Ahniwake, a kind of Cherokee "every-
woman" who found herself at the mercy of the American system of medicine after a lifetime of turning to traditional Cherokee doctors to treat
her ailments. Another character in her story was a young woman named
Pearl, the older woman's granddaughter, who was trying to guide Ahniwake through unfamiliar surroundings and the ways of white people.

Wilma called the story "Keeping Pace with the Rest of the World."
It didn't appear in print until 1985, when *Southern Exposure*, a publication
of the Institute for Southern Studies, picked it up and published it. That
issue was called "We Are Here Forever: Indians of the South." The story
was the first she'd ever published, and it helped to quench within her the
trauma she'd endured. It was pure fiction, but it was filled with the stalk
of truth.

"[The doctor] did not know how to heal an illness, only how to cut it
out," she wrote, following up with Ahniwake telling her granddaughter:

"He did not know my clan, my family, my history. How could he possibly know how to heal me?"[1]

During her long, grueling months of rehabilitation, Wilma had little else to do to pass the time than read and write. She also studied some tribal issues and realized that she had been given a chance to think about what she wanted to do with the rest of her life. When she realized how fragile life is, she set about tackling projects she would have never otherwise even considered. "Fortunately," she wrote, "Chief Ross Swimmer was willing to allow me to go back to my position with the tribe. I was still in my recovery phase when I hobbled into his bank in Tahlequah and asked him if I could return to my job. He did not hesitate for a second, and for that I am grateful."[2] But, as she fell back into the natural rhythm of work, she realized something within her had changed.

When I returned to my duties with the Cherokee Nation, I did so with a fury. I was not particularly anxious to move up the ladder of hierarchy in my tribe. My work was my main priority. I was determined to work closely with self-help projects and program development. I wanted to see to it that our people, especially those living in rural areas, had the chance to express their own special needs. I was determined to do this by using the "good mind" approach.

In 1981, I helped to found and subsequently was named the first director of the Cherokee Nation Community Development Department. I did not necessarily seek the job. In fact, I first headed a national search to locate a director before I finally decided to accept the position myself. Immediately, we set out to identify new ways to implement renewal projects in rural Cherokee communities. This department grew from important development work carried out in the tiny Adair County community named Bell. As this project evolved, we needed a new department so we would be eligible to receive grants.

I had assumed that Swimmer and his consultants had located some funding for the project. Not so. We immediately put together several federal and foundation grants. We also recruited many volunteers to allow local citizens to construct a sixteen-mile water line and to revitalize several of their homes.[3]

The rural community of Bell was a poor, blue-collar area with some 350 people, 95 percent of whom were Cherokee. Most of them spoke their Native tongue. If she was looking for an ideal starting place for her pet project, Wilma thought she'd found it in Bell. Not everyone agreed. As Gloria Steinem wrote of the project:

Bell, a town in a rough and rural part of eastern Oklahoma with about 300 mostly Cherokee families, had no school that went above the eighth grade, little indoor plumbing, a lot of conflict, and widespread hopelessness. Because residents were dependent on government handouts and treated as invisible to the outside world, they had come to feel powerless over their fates; adults with all the vulnerabilities of childhood and none of the rewards. The few who managed to escape were often ashamed to admit they had ever lived in Bell.

When Wilma Mankiller, a Cherokee community renewal leader, said she wanted to start a project there, she received two warnings from people who knew Bell: first, "these people" would never work, much less volunteer, to help themselves; and second, she shouldn't stay in town after nightfall.

Nonetheless, she posted notices in Cherokee and English asking people to come to a town meeting to discuss "what you would like Bell to look like in ten years." No one came. She called another meeting. A handful of residents came, but only to complain. She called a third, and convinced now that she really wanted to listen, about a dozen people showed up.

"I've always trusted disenfranchised people to come up with their own ideas," Wilma said later. Therefore, she didn't dictate or even suggest. She just asked a question: "What single thing would change this community the most?"

The answer was not a project for school dropouts or any other program to help young people who still had a hope of escaping Bell, which was what Wilma had expected. Instead, they chose something that was more democratic and crucial to everyone, regardless of age or intention to leave: a water supply that was connected to every house, plus indoor plumbing. This would cut school dropout rates, too, as they explained to Wilma. Their kids had to bathe in polluted streams or in water carried from a single spigot outside the school-house, and when they failed to bathe as often as their less poor classmates in Stillwell, a neighboring town with the nearest high school, they were ridiculed.[4]

As effortlessly as Wilma had started the project with an opportunity for local residents to exercise their power of choice, she continued it with an agreement. She would get the materials, tools, supplies, federal support, engineering reports, and other necessary items only if the residents of Bell built the water system with their own two hands. After enduring generations of promises fallen by the wayside, the residents were skeptical about obtaining real outside help. They also realized, after years of failing to act on their own, they were incapable of succeeding without it. Still, there was something in this woman's demeanor with which they felt comfortable, so they gave themselves the name Bell Water and Housing Project, and they set about work.

Each family was assigned one mile of ditch to dig and lay pipe. Those residents who could read and write English also worked on helping Wilma with her fund-raising plans. Those who spoke Cherokee did everything else, from marking the path of the ditches to carrying sand, gravel, and rocks to be used for backfill. Everyone understood one thing: Each job was critical to the project's success, and no one was more so than another. Even though the women had been "just part of the woodwork," as Wilma put it, convinced that they were too weak to carry pipe or perform other construction tasks, they soon learned manual labor was no harder than carting water or doing their other household chores. Wilma finally knew she'd succeeded in instilling the residents with pride when the families began holding relay races to see which could lay pipe the fastest!

According to a letter sent to the families in Bell, only 5 of 103 families had failed to do any work at all on the project, which included 350 "man" hours of construction work per family. A letter written on behalf of the project later commented: "Some people [of Bell] did not think they really had to work." Nevertheless, it continued, the vast majority dug in and did the work, improving their community, and "had a lot to be proud of."[5]

To Wilma, the Bell project represented the perfect example of community self-help at its best. The locals were able to build on their Cherokee *Gadugi*, or tradition of sharing physical tasks and working collectively. That instinctively restored much of the confidence that had been lacking among the residents for decades.

The Bell project served as a model for Wilma and the Cherokee Nation in a number of other communities, too. After establishing a partnership between the residents of Bell and the Cherokee Nation, Wilma worked to bring members of the community together so they could identify and solve their other mutual problems. From the beginning, the Bell residents realized they were responsible for the success or failure of the project. They knew they were expected not only to develop long-range plans but also to implement their community renewal. The national association was geared to act as project facilitator and funding broker only.

The program ended up costing a million dollars in hard cash, all funded by grants. It was money well spent. Instead of surrendering to defeat, the people of Bell pitched in to change their entire outlook on life. They accomplished all of the once-impossible goals that had been set out for them. A new rural water system brought the town's first running water in pipes installed by the community. More than twenty homes were rehabilitated, and the dilapidated community center was rebuilt. Steinem took note of the remarkable progress being made in the rural Oklahoma town and wrote about it in her book *Revolution from Within*:

> *Though failure had been the unanimous prediction of Bell's neighbors, people from surrounding communities came to see what was happening. So did several foundation executives who viewed this renewal project as an example of Third World development; certainly few places in the world were poorer than Bell. When a local CBS television crew—attracted by Bell's reliable scenes of poverty—came to film powerlessness, they played an inadvertent role in changing the situation by letting residents see themselves on the evening news and begin to feel less isolated. Soon, even the non-Indian residents of Bell*

were saying positive things about this water project in the newspapers, and the Indian community began to feel visible for the first time. Most important, they had become visible through something they were doing for themselves.

The next fourteen months encompassed a novel's worth of personal change and problem-solving, but by the end, the water system was complete. The CBS crew returned to document success, and the seven-minute story that resulted appeared on "CBS Sunday Morning" with Charles Kuralt. Now known as "the town film," it is often replayed with pride.[6]

Since the community of Bell lay a scant ten miles from Mankiller Flats, Wilma recognized the similarities between the two places from the start. That was one of the reasons the project's success was essential to her. Bell represented achievement where everyone else had anticipated failure. For Wilma, the Bell project also validated a lot of the things that she intrinsically believed about her people—most notably that they retained a great sense of interdependence along with a willingness to pitch in and the pride required to help one another. She also knew that they could solve their own problems if they were helped along the way to do so.

Although the unanimous prediction of Bell's residents was ultimately failure, things quickly turned around. Perceptions changed. Realities set in. Bell's neighbors, people from surrounding communities, came to see what was happening. So did several foundation executives who viewed the renewal project as an example of Third World development.

The Bell project meetings swelled from a dozen skeptical residents to most of the town's inhabitants, by then brimming with optimism. They served as a model for Wilma and the Cherokee Nation in a number of other communities. According to author Sarah Eppler Janda:

Mankiller's experience with the people in Bell deepened her desire to help Cherokees in other poor communities, such as Kenwood. This, in part, inspired her involvement in Cherokee politics. Bell, which many described as the Harlem of eastern Oklahoma, was one of the poorest communities in the state. This project brought considerable attention to Mankiller and opened the door to her political involvement. Swimmer, the principal chief of the Cherokee Nation, brought in people to train Mankiller in community development. He also created the new department of community development and asked Mankiller to serve as the first director, which she did until she resigned to run for deputy chief in 1983.[7]

So confident were the people of Bell that the group decided upon its next project: improving housing. Again, Wilma got federal funds through the resources of the Cherokee Housing Authority as the locals once more served as their own labor force. "Even if families didn't like each other," Wilma explained, "they were learning to work together. They were beginning to bond as a community."[8] Because federal funds had been earmarked for Indians only, the five or six non-Indian families in Bell weren't eligible for housing assistance. But, after considered discussion, the Cherokee community decided to hold fund-raisers so those families could benefit, too, even though some had behaved badly toward them in the past. As always, self-esteem had created an open door toward generosity. "It began to restore the Indian principle of reciprocity," as Steinem wrote, "wrongly characterized as 'Indian giving' by whites but really a balance of giving and receiving."[9]

So, as that first meeting in 1979 had produced grumbling and sentiments of "nothing will change," in the end the sessions took on a different slant. Suddenly the attitude was, "Look what we've done; what else could we take on?" As Steinem explained:

Since renovating Bell's housing, members of the steering committee have overseen a senior citizen education project, an annual "fund-raising powwow," a speakers' bureau that carries Bell's lessons to other rural communities, and a bilingual education program to help preserve the Cherokee language and culture. The school dropout rate has fallen, and other nearby communities like Burnt Cabin and Cherry Tree have begun water and housing projects, too. Those who were once ashamed of living in Bell have become proud.

But for Wilma, watching individual people flower was the greatest reward. Sue and Thomas Muskrat, a Head Start worker and farmhand respectively, had been too unconfident and skeptical to speak up at all in the early meetings. They became members of the school board and the speakers' bureau. With beadwork, drawings, and elkhorn carvings they had always made but realized had value only after outsiders commented on their beauty, they opened a craft store. Because their one son had grown up before this change in their lives, they decided to share their good fortune by adopting a child, an abused, part-Cherokee little boy from Dallas.[10]

Wilma experienced an unanticipated change in her life as a result of the Bell community project as well. During construction activities, she came to know a man who proved to be a critical part of her life. His name was Charlie Lee Soap, a full-blooded, bilingual Cherokee who was, according to Wilma, "probably the most well-adjusted male I have ever met."[11]

She was introduced to Charlie Soap in 1977 shortly after the Mankiller family moved back to Oklahoma. He was working with the Cherokee Housing Authority, and she had consulted with him about a housing matter. Charlie had a reputation as someone who could get things done in the housing office. He was quiet and unassuming but upbeat and efficient.

Wilma had heard from some of the women who worked at the housing authority office that Charlie was not only tall and handsome but also talented. An accomplished ceremonial dancer, he learned in college to do many different war dances while dressed in full regalia, complete with colorful eagle-feather bustle and Angora leggings. His dancing at pow-wows was renowned throughout the region. He was that rare breed who could walk into a school filled with children and captivate his audience in moments. The children sat spellbound as they watched him dance, his long, black hair flying in time to his spritely steps. Later, they crowded around him to ask questions as they ran their hands across the feathers.

"Charlie is indeed like a Pied Piper," Wilma commented later after getting to know him, "particularly with children and young people. They love him and his stories, and he enjoys working with them to help them build self-esteem and to encourage them to remain in school."[12]

During the Bell project, Charlie was assigned to work with Wilma as a co-organizer. After their long, drawn-out meetings in Bell, he often drove the Cherokee woman home to Mankiller Flats, where they sat outside in his pickup truck, chatting about everything from work to their personal dreams and aspirations. She learned a lot about him, realizing quickly that he was more than merely a skilled dancer.

Charlie, slightly older than Wilma, was born March 25, 1945, at Stilwell. His mother's name was Florence Fourkiller Soap, and his father was Walter Soap, a farmer who also worked for the railroad. After his father died, Charlie's mother remarried, taking the name of Florence Hummingbird. Charlie's parents traced their family lines back to their people's original homelands in the Southeast. Like Wilma's family, the Soap clan included eleven children. He had one sister and nine brothers, including two half-brothers.

Learning as a boy how to work hard and pull his own weight, Charlie and his siblings cut railroad ties, cleared land for crops, picked strawberries and beans, hauled hay, and did about anything else they could to earn money for the family. The Soap clan lived just outside Bell before moving to the nearby community of Starr. They lived as traditional Cherokees, and at one time, Charlie's father was very active in the Keetoowah Society, the surviving core of the Cherokee religious movement led by Redbird Smith in the nineteenth century. Its aim was to preserve the culture and teachings of the Keetoowah in Oklahoma after the removal of the tribes from the American Southeast. One of the earliest records of the Keetoowah movement is dated August 15, 1888. In traditional Keetoowah fashion, the Soap family spoke primarily Cherokee.

For much of his young life, Charlie attended country schools. He became an accomplished athlete, excelling at basketball in college and during his service in the US Navy. Married twice, he had two sons from his first marriage, Chris and Cobey; another son had died during heart surgery as an infant. Charlie's youngest boy, Winterhawk, was from his second marriage. By the time Wilma met him, Charlie reluctantly admitted his second marriage was in trouble.

At the time, Wilma and her daughters were living near Rocky Mountain on her ancestral land. The girls busied themselves with school-work and friends, while their mother saw to her tribal duties and, of course, her recovering health. It had been several years since her marriage to Hugo had ended, and she wasn't especially interested in more than a casual relationship with a man. Besides, Charlie was strapped with his own problems, so the two didn't pay much attention to one another socially until the Bell project had concluded. After building a solid work-ing relationship, their friendship continued to grow, proving to provide the strongest foundation for them until, one day, the two realized they were in love.

From the start, Charlie and Wilma recognized that their personal values were the same. They complemented one another in different ways. Wilma instilled in Charlie some of her self-confidence, and he helped her understand how to get things done within a bureaucratic system. He taught her about traditional Cherokee medicine through many of the old stories that had been passed down from one generation to the next, and she taught him how to persevere in whatever he chose to do.

Of course, they had their differences, too, particularly in the areas of religion and spirituality. Charlie had been raised in the Church and had taught Sunday school at one time. While Wilma had some exposure to Christianity, she had never read the Bible and didn't attend regular ser-vices. Despite these differences, both were highly spiritual people.

Charlie's marriage ended in 1983, but he and Wilma didn't marry for three more years, until October 1986, after their relationship had time to develop and he had time to mend. Both remained cautious about jumping ahead too quickly. Wilma recalled the day everything changed years later:

Charlie stopped by my house for a cup of coffee. We had been sitting there in the kitchen talking when he kissed me. It was so unexpected. We embraced and kissed again. Both of us were wondering what was going on. For about a week or so after that, we shied away from each other, but that did not last. We missed being with each other too much.

From the onset, our relationship was as solid as a rock. It all stemmed from a deep respect. It is the strongest love I have ever known. We genuinely like each other. We never seem to get bored, and I think we continue to bring out each other's strengths. That is so important. It has been said that when someone asks Charlie or me to name our personal heroes, we start our lists by naming each other. It's true.[13]

Charlie quickly became the one constant in Wilma's life. She never saw him intimidated or threatened by strong women or even by other men. Years into their marriage, she recalled, "He still is one of the most unusual persons I have ever met. He is bright, never pretentious, and he genuinely enjoys helping people. He is free from all traces of racism and sexism. He likes children and is respectful of old people. Charlie Soap is a comfortable man. He is comfortable to be with, and he is comfortable with himself. He is guileless. He is my best friend."[14] Charlie wrote of himself in 1992: "I know who I am, what I am, and what I can do or cannot do. I am a Cherokee and I am proud of it. There is no one who can take that away from me."[15]

Wilma reflected upon the first few years they were together in the early 1980s as among the most pivotal of her life. Everything about Charlie and the Bell experience was positive. Her daughters were doing well in their schoolwork, learning more each day about their Cherokee heritage. Many members of Wilma's family were living within easy reach, and she found her work satisfying. She was, as she recalled later, "beginning to feel complete."[16]

After enduring two back-to-back assaults on her body, the comfort she suddenly felt with life was rewarding—the best medicine she could have had. Serving as the primary organizer and enabler at the Bell community marked the first time she had been given any position of real responsibility within the tribe. Chief Swimmer listened to her requests for more duties and responded, and Wilma quickly learned to use all available federal grants to finance her people's dreams and aspirations.

Finally, in 1983, history in the making unfolded when Ross Swimmer asked Wilma to run as his deputy chief in the coming election. He had been deserted by most of his closest political supporters only a year earlier, after being diagnosed with lymphatic cancer. The reason his backers decided to oppose him for chief was that they thought he was too ill to remain in office. They wrote him off for dead. So, the following year, when the time came for Swimmer to announce his bid for reelection for another four-year term, he remembered his right-hand "man." He trusted Wilma and was pleased with both the quality of her work and her dedication to her people.

By the time Swimmer announced his candidacy, he had begun to recover his health. The chemotherapy treatments had been effective. His prognosis was good, but he had also chosen to seek internal Cherokee healing from William Smith, a traditional medicine person, and from the Seven Medicine Men at the ceremonial grounds. He stepped inside the circle and asked for their help. Wilma wrote later that Chief Swimmer made the point that he did not seek the traditional Cherokee healing as a symbolic gesture, but because he believed in its power.[17] He later wrote:

I know just from my own knowledge that most, or many, contemporary medicines are derived from the natural medicines that the Indians developed years ago and . . . the folks there certainly have a handle on those medicinal roots and herbs and things. They might well have a lot of the answers to common illnesses. A lot of those roots and herbs have been synthesized into drugs today, and combined with some other chemicals that make them more potent, still serve the same purpose.

In my ancestry, one of the Swimmers was a medicine man and listed all the herbs and the roots and the mushrooms and everything else that were used medicinally and many of them are extracted today and used in everyday medicine. So, I was fairly confident that [Cherokee traditional medicine] certainly wasn't going to hurt me and if anything it might hold some secret to helping.[18]

Swimmer was taking a massive leap of faith in bypassing his male friends to select Wilma as his running mate. But he was convinced she was an effective leader and manager. Wilma laughed afterward, "He must have forgotten that I am also a liberal Democrat."[19]

Although Wilma was flattered by Swimmer's selection of her, she thought the entire notion was ridiculous. The tribe was so large that running for office was similar to running for the US Congress. It would entail all the hoopla surrounding a typical political campaign—print and broadcast advertising, campaign billboards, rallies, interviews, and more. Wilma viewed her chances of getting elected as one step beyond impossible. Even with her years of tribal experience, she couldn't picture herself in high tribal office. She told Chief Swimmer she was honored that he had chosen her but that she was forced to turn him down.

But almost immediately after she had given him her answer, she began thinking about what was transpiring around her. She went out among some of the rural communities in eastern Oklahoma, where they were facilitating development projects. In one small town, she came across three people living in an abandoned bus without any roof. Most of the clothes they owned were hanging on a line. They had few other possessions. It burned a hole in Wilma's heart.

Worse, she realized that this was not an isolated situation. Many Cherokees were forced to put up with inadequate housing, rising medical costs, and "educational deficits." She realized she was being allowed an opportunity to create change for Cherokee families such as those living in the old bus; if she didn't act, she would have no right to criticize those who did.

The visit to that small community had a major impact on me. I drove straight to Ross Swimmer's home. I told him I had reconsidered, and I would run for election as deputy chief in the 1983 election. I quit my job with the Cherokee Nation so there would be no conflict of interest, and I filed for office.

From the start, I figured most people would be bothered about my ideas on grass-roots democracy and the fact that I had a fairly extensive activist background. I adhered to a different political philosophy than many people living in the area. But I was wrong. No one challenged me on those issues, not once. Instead, I was challenged mostly because of one fact—I am female. The election became an issue of gender. It was one of the first times I had ever really encountered overt sexism. I recalled that my first real experience with sexism had occurred in California. I had once slugged a boss during a Christmas party in San Francisco when he came up behind me and tried to kiss me. He did not fire me, but I do believe he got the message that I did not want to be mauled. The memory of that time came back to me during the 1983 campaign.

I heard all sorts of things—some people claimed that my running for office was an affront to God. Others said having a female run our tribe would make the Cherokees the laughingstock of the tribal world. I heard it all. Every time I was given yet another silly reason why I should not help run our government, I was certain that I had made the correct decision.[20]

Still, the unreasonable reactions to Wilma's candidacy devastated her. It was a "very low time" in her life, but she was determined not to falter. She decided the best way to silence her critics was to ignore them. "I remembered a saying I had once read on the back of a tea box," she wrote in her memoirs. "It said something like this—if you argue with a fool, someone passing by will not be able to tell who is the fool and who is not. I did not wish to be taken for a fool."[21]

So, she began building her campaign on a positive foundation to counter the irascibility she faced wherever she turned. Regardless, the campaign was far from easy. In fact, she recalled, "To say that the campaign was heated would be the understatement of all times. Most of the negative acts did not originate with my opponents for office, but with those who did not want a woman in office. I even had foes *within* the Swimmer-Mankiller team. Toward the end of the campaign, some of them openly supported one of my opponents."[22]

Occasionally, the actions of those who were out to stop her election grew violent. She began receiving hate mail, including several death threats. After one memorable night's rally, she returned to her car to discover all four tires had been slashed. On other occasions, she received threatening messages over the telephone. Once, she answered the phone to hear the unmistakable sound of a rifle bolt being slammed closed.

She also had a daunting experience while riding in a parade. As she waved and smiled at the crowd along the route, she noticed a young man toward the back with his hand cocked and his finger pointed at her as if it were a pistol. He drew his hand back as he fired an imaginary round. She did not even blink, choosing instead to look away.

Despite her concern, the scare tactics didn't work. One reason was that the people in Bell and throughout other rural Cherokee communities where she had worked fully supported her. Unfortunately, that couldn't be said for the voters elsewhere. She wrote:

> *My two opponents for office were J. B. Dreadfulwater, a popular gospel singer and former member of the tribal council, and Agnes Cowan, the first woman to serve on the tribal council. She was older than I was, and already established in our tribal government. They were worthy opponents who liked to criticize me for having no experience in tribal politics. In truth, I had a great deal of applicable experience, but I did have much to learn about political campaigning.*[23]

One of the things she learned quickly was that you could never count on anything. After sending out invitations and preparing for a first campaign event, she was shocked to find that five people showed up to hear the candidate speak. And three of them were relatives! Still, Wilma smiled through it all, realizing things could only get better.

And they did. Putting to use all of her experience as a community organizer for the Indian Center in San Francisco, Wilma began stumping, going from door to door with her campaign. She attended every event and rally. She kept encountering opposition as a female candidate, but she refused to make that a campaign issue.

Finally, election day came, and when the ballots had been counted, Ross Swimmer was reelected to his third term. Wilma beat out Dreadfulwater in that first election but had to face Cowan in a July runoff. In a grueling political battle, she defeated Cowan and emerged as the tribe's new deputy chief. It was a moment she would recall forever. The first woman deputy chief in Cherokee history. She took office on August 14, 1983. The local press gave scant notice, saying:

> *Inaugural ceremonies for principal chief Ross Swimmer and 16 other Cherokee Nation officials will be held this afternoon at Northeastern Oklahoma State University.*
>
> *Also taking oaths of office at the public ceremony will be Deputy Chief Wilma Mankiller and 15 tribal council members.*[24]

Others weren't quite so blasé about the results. As one of Wilma's supporters put it, at long last a daughter of the people had been chosen for high tribal office. It was a historic moment because it had been over one hundred years since a woman had held a leadership role in the Cherokee Nation. "Most people felt the tribe would fall apart," she said in an interview for the Corporation for Public Broadcasting.[25]

Swimmer admitted that his decision to tap Wilma for the role of deputy chief was not one "with which everyone agreed. I had some very dedicated campaign people that said they couldn't work for Wilma because she was a woman."[26]

In a speech given in Denver the following year, Wilma put those antiquated notions to rest, saying, "Women can help turn the world right-side up. We bring a more collaborative approach to government. And if we do not participate, then decisions will be made without us."[27]

Winning the election had been difficult, but not nearly as difficult as serving her first two years in office. As in most of politics, she had inherited many people on Ross Swimmer's staff and wouldn't have her own people aboard for some time. Although Swimmer had chosen her as deputy and had stuck with her throughout the campaign, there were significant differences between the two. For starters, he was a Republican banker with a very conservative viewpoint, and Wilma was a Democratic social worker and community planner who had organized and advocated for Indian civil and treaty rights.

She had also been elected along with a fifteen-member tribal council that, for the most part, didn't support her. Many had openly worked against her election. Suddenly, they found themselves confronted by a young, radical idealist—not to mention a *woman* veteran of Alcatraz— who was not only the new kid on the block but also president of the council on which they sat. Wilma was shocked at just how petty and political some of them behaved, even after the election.

Serving as president of a council that, at least in the beginning, failed to support her was an "interesting experience." Several members were openly hostile, but what surprised her most was the lack of support she received from the three women on the council. She recalled later:

Of course, they had also opposed my election, but I had naively assumed that once I was in office, we would all work together. But the situation did not get any better. In the subsequent election, two of the women supported my opponent, and the third did not seek reelection. I suppose that throughout those first few months, I felt a real lack of personal power. I had all the responsibility with none of the authority. Mostly, I just coped.[28]

In time, she learned to adjust, as did many of the council members. Still, it took awhile to figure out individual styles and the different ways of doing business.

Wilma's first two years spent helping to govern an Indian nation spread over fourteen counties in northeastern Oklahoma kept her busy. Despite their inherent differences, she and Swimmer shared an absolute commitment to rebuilding and revitalizing their rural communities. As deputy chief, Wilma helped supervise the daily operations of the tribe, which was composed of more than forty tribally operated programs ranging from Head Start classes, daycare, and elderly assistance to health clinics, water projects, and new-home construction.

Then in September 1985, just shy of two years into her term, more change emerged. Chief Swimmer had been tapped to go to Washington to head the BIA after being nominated by President Ronald Reagan to serve as Assistant Secretary of the Interior for Indian Affairs. To assume the top Indian Affairs post in the federal government, with fourteen thousand employees and a $1 billion annual budget, was an offer that Swimmer, then forty-one, couldn't possibly refuse.

But who, everyone wondered, would replace him locally? Article Six of the Cherokee Nation Constitution, ratified in 1976, provided the answer. The replacement of a principal chief who left office before the expiration of his term would fall to the deputy principal chief. The Cherokee Nation Tribal Council would then elect from within its ranks a new deputy principal chief. Members of the council would then recommend a name to fill the vacancy, after which the nominee would be confirmed by the full tribal council.

When Wilma first learned about Swimmer's upcoming departure, she was concerned that she would go through the same ordeal as before, when she ran for deputy chief. She immediately began girding, both spiritually and emotionally, for the onslaught. But remarkably, the transition was not that difficult. Her move to chief ran smoothly, probably, she assumed, because "many people who were opposed to me thought they could live with the tribal laws and wait for two years until the next election, when they could clobber me at the polls. My problem seemed clear. I had to serve the balance of Ross Swimmer's term—from 1985 to 1987—without any real mandate from the people."[29]

When news of Swimmer's appointment leaked out, the press had a field day. "Woman to take over as chief of Cherokees," an article in the *Salina Journal* screamed. It elaborated:

> *A woman is in line to take over, for the first time, as chief of the Cherokee Nation.*
>
> *Deputy Principal Chief Wilma Mankiller will automatically become principal chief and fill out the remaining two years of Chief Ross Swimmer's four-year term as soon as he receives Senate approval to head the Bureau of Indian Affairs.*
>
> *Swimmer was named to the post by President Reagan on Sept. 26, and confirmation is expected by year's end.*
>
> *The slowness of the Senate progress on Swimmer's nomination gives tribe members time to adjust to the idea of a woman becoming principal chief, said Mankiller, who was elected deputy principal chief in 1983.*

"By-and-large, Cherokees have stated they are ready for female leadership. It's no longer a major issue," she said.

"We have the same problems the state has," she said, explaining that Oklahoma has relied too heavily on oil and agriculture. Now, she said, the state and the Cherokee Nation must find other assets to develop.

One of 11 children, Mankiller spent her childhood in rural Oklahoma where her family grew strawberries and chopped wood to scratch out a living.

As head of the nation's second largest, and one of its most progressive, Indian tribes, she says she'll champion the cause of the poor.

"My goal for the next two years is to spend an awful lot of time developing the economy of this area," Mankiller said, referring to the 14-county area of northeastern Oklahoma where the majority of the Cherokee Nation's 62,000 registered members reside.

"For our tribe, I don't see bingo as a viable economic base," she said, referring to the recent development of high-stake bingo games by other tribes.

"I'm looking for a more stable base."

The Cherokee Nation, which has assets of $23 million and an annual payroll of $9 million, has hired a director of its Business Development Department.

The tribe employs more than 550 people, owns a 160-acre industrial tract in Stilwell, and a business complex in Tahlequah, operates a cattle and poultry ranch and a woodcutting operation, and is planning to build a $100 million hydroelectric plant on the Arkansas River.[30]

Swimmer's nomination was ultimately confirmed by the US Senate, and on December 5, 1985, Wilma was sworn in as principal chief of the Cherokee Nation in a private ceremony. As such, according to activist/feminist Gloria Steinem, it was an "office that carries more responsibility than those of state governor and senator combined."[31] Formal ceremonies were held on December 14 at the tribal headquarters. Memories of her public inauguration would remain with Wilma as long as she lived. For her, it was not the happiest of occasions. Swimmer had had little time to prepare her for all the complex issues she would face. His staff members and many other people felt that the Cherokee Nation would crash and burn with a woman at the helm. Wilma, always wary, knew full well what pitfalls lay ahead.

Still, the ceremony was critical if for no other reason than its symbolism. Wilma selected a business-like dark suit and white blouse for the occasion. Snow littered the ground that day, but the sky was clear, blue, and cloudless. So many people came to her with hugs and smiles and good wishes that she thought for a moment she was a celebrity. People cried tears of happiness. And when Wilma slipped into the chair behind the chief's desk for an official photo, she beamed with pride.

The council chamber was packed for the occasion, filled with photographers, reporters, and guests. Wilma stepped forward and placed her hand on a Bible. She raised her other hand to take the oath of office, a no-nonsense pledge of allegiance:

> *I, Wilma P. Mankiller, do solemnly swear, or affirm, that I will faithfully execute the duties of Principal Chief of the Cherokee Nation and will, to the best of my abilities, preserve, protect, and defend the Constitutions of the Cherokee Nation and the United States of America. I swear, or affirm, further that I will do everything within my power to promote the culture, heritage, and tradition of the Cherokee Nation.*[32]

The room erupted in applause as the new chief stepped up to the podium. As the crowd stilled, the only sound was the clacking of the cameras as Wilma began to speak. She thanked everyone in attendance, along with all of her friends, family, and supporters. She spoke of the honor of assuming the position of chief. After complimenting Ross Swimmer for his leadership, she talked about the numerous tasks before her.

> *I think there's a bit of nervousness in the Cherokee Nation. I think any time there's a change, people wonder what's going to happen, is there going to be some kind of major change. And my political adver-*

saries like to spread around rumors that there's going to be a purge
of employees. That's just not the case. I like what's going on at the
Cherokee Nation. There will be very little that will change. The only
thing that will change is that there will be more of an emphasis on the
development of the economy.[33]

By the time she took the oath of office in 1985, Wilma's eldest daughter, Felicia, had married, and she had delivered her first grandchild, Aaron Swake. Wilma was both the first woman to serve as chief of a principal tribe and a forty-year-old grandmother. She told reporters that the only people who were really worried about her serving as chief were members of her family. All of them knew how much time she tended to devote to her work. Her daughters were concerned about her health. But her little grandson thought it was great that his grandma was the chief.

One thing that Wilma knew was that she'd never become "one of the boys" nor a "good ol' girl." She knew both how to be political and how to get the job done, but she drew the line at sacrificing her principles. Rural development remained a high priority, an important goal required to break the circle of poverty in which so many of the area's families found themselves. Wilma had seen just how tenacious the Cherokee people were, having survived everything from major political and social upheavals to land grabs and outright war. Through it all, they managed to sustain and grow the Cherokee government.

Toward that goal, the new chief made sure the Cherokee government was staffed with professionals—educators, physicians, attorneys, business leaders. All worked diligently to help erase the stereotypes created by decades of media and by Western films depicting the drunken Indian on a horse, chasing wagon trains across the prairie. She recalled in her memoirs:

I suppose some people still think that all native people live in tepees
and wear tribal garb every day. They do not realize that many of us
wear business suits and drive station wagons. The beauty of society
today is that young Cherokee men and women can pursue any profes-
sional fields they want and remain true to traditional values. It all

comes back to our heritage and our roots. It is so vital that we retain that sense of culture, history, and tribal identity.

We also are returning the balance to the role of women in our tribe. Prior to my becoming chief, young Cherokee girls never thought they might be able to grow up and become chief themselves. That has definitely changed. From the start of my administration, the impact on the younger women of the Cherokee Nation was noticeable. I feel certain that more women will assume leadership roles in tribal communities.[34]

The effect of negative stereotypes upon Native people was profound. Wilma Mankiller, a victim of stereotypes herself, agreed that "there are so many stereotypes about us that we begin to believe that crap ourselves. When people know there's discrimination, and they can feel it, they've got to internalize some of that eventually. They've got to. So we've got to learn!"[35]

On the other hand, positive stereotyping might have accounted for some non-Native and mixed-heritage people's decisions to identify themselves as Native Americans. Individuals with little knowledge of Natives might become enamored with images of Indians as physically attractive, valiant warriors and mystical environmentalists who are "one with nature." Positive imagery of Native Americans in the 1960s and 1970s probably accounted in part for the dramatic increase in the number of Natives in the 1980 census.[36]

Positive stereotyping also accounted for the number of people who claimed to be part Native—and still do today—regardless of how much they know about their ancestors. Actors Val Kilmer, Chuck Norris, Kim Basinger, Cher, and Connie Sellecca claim to be part Cherokee or Choctaw.[37] Illustrating the vacuous knowledge of many people regarding their "Indian ancestors," disco queen Gloria Gaynor writes in her autobiography, *I Will Survive,* about her relatives: "The only thing I do know is that my great-grandmother on my mother's side was a full-blooded Blackfoot Indian, with hair down to the bend of her knee."[38]

Meanwhile, in 1992, never having reason to doubt her own heritage, Wilma met a Native man who told her that he was an Oneida and that one of the prophecies he had heard was that the time was right for women to take on a more critical role in society. He described it as "the time of the butterfly."

When I read recently of Judge Ruth Bader Ginsburg's nomination to the Supreme Court, Hillary Rodham Clinton's work on health-care reform, the appointment of Ada Deer as assistant secretary of the interior in charge of the BIA, and the election of a female Canadian prime minister, I smiled and thought about the prophecy of the anonymous Oneida man who had driven all day to pass along his message to me.[39]

Wilma's former political foe, J. B. Dreadfulwater, writing in the *New York Times* on December 15, 1985, said of her, "I had negative thoughts [about women leading the tribe] before. But I have had the opportunity to work with her [Mankiller]. I have been impressed with her leadership."

In 1987, after fulfilling the remainder of Ross Swimmer's term as chief, Wilma reached a decision to run on her own for a four-year term. It was not an easy decision. She knew the campaign would be difficult. She talked to her family and to friends and neighbors. She spent hours on end discussing the issues with Charlie Soap, her husband of one year. Charlie had contracted with private foundations to continue development work with low-income Native community projects. Wilma recalled:

His counsel to me was excellent. He encouraged me to run. So did many other people.

But there were others who were opposed to my continuing as chief. Even some of my friends and advisers told me they believed the Cherokee people would accept me only as deputy, not as an elected principal chief. Some of those people came to our home at Mankiller Flats. I would look out the window and see them coming down the dirt road to tell me that I should give up any idea of running for chief. Finally, I told Charlie that if one more family came down that road and told me not to run, I was going to run for sure. That is just what happened.[40]

Wilma Pearl Mankiller announced her candidacy in early 1987, calling for a "positive, forward-thinking campaign." She chose John A. Ketcher, a member of the tribal council since 1983, as her running mate for the June 20 election. In 1985, John had been elected by the council to succeed Wilma as deputy chief. An eleven-sixteenths bilingual Cherokee, John was born in southern Mayes County in 1922. A veteran of World War II and a graduate of Northeastern State University in Tahlequah, Ketcher agreed with Wilma that unity and economic development were the top priorities for the Cherokee Nation. Wilma considered him a great asset to his people.

Running for principal chief against Wilma that year were three people: Dave Whitekiller, a postal assistant from the small community of Cookson and a former councilman; William McKee, deputy administrator at W. W. Hastings Indian Hospital in Tahlequah; and Perry Wheeler, a former deputy chief and funeral home director from Sallisaw in Sequoyah County.

From the very start, the most accurate description of the unfolding campaign came from a council member who said there was an "undercurrent of viciousness." Still, Wilma ignored the things going on around her and campaigned as she always had—by going out to the communities and talking about the issues to as many Cherokee people as possible. Her opponents, meanwhile, tried blaming Wilma for failing "to properly manage and direct the Cherokee Nation, which was obviously false," she recalled. "Revenue for 1986 was up $6 million, higher than it had ever been to that point. And I was not about to lose focus by warring with my opponents."[41]

Wilma relived the action as election day dawned:

The election eliminated all the candidates except for Perry Wheeler and me. None of us had received more than 50 percent of the votes. I had polled 45 percent to Wheeler's 29 percent. We had to face each other in a July runoff. My supporters worked very hard during those last few weeks. Charlie was one of my main champions. On my behalf, [he] visited many rural homes where English is a second language to remind the people that prior to the intrusion of white men, women had played key roles in our government. He asked our people to not turn their backs on their past or their future.

Charlie's help was especially important because I was stricken with my old nemesis, kidney problems, during the final weeks of the campaign.

Finally, just before the election, I had to be hospitalized in Tulsa, but the physicians never determined the exact location of the infection and could not bring it under control. The lengthy infection and hospitalization . . . nearly cost me not only the election but also my life, since it brought on extensive and irreversible kidney damage. From that point forward, I was repeatedly hospitalized for kidney and urinary tract infections, until I underwent surgery and had a kidney transplant in 1990.[42]

Wheeler, an unsuccessful candidate for the chief's job against Ross Swimmer in 1983, tried to make Wilma's hospitalization a significant issue. He waged a well-financed negative campaign, claiming that his opponent hadn't been truthful about her health. It reminded her of the way Swimmer had been attacked when he was battling cancer. Wheeler, whom Wilma described appropriately as an old-style politician, also made claims that his opponent had not hired enough Cherokee people for what he called the higher-paying tribal posts. Writing in the *Tulsa Tribune* in 1987, he tried to paint Wilma as a typical Californian, tying her to a different world: "When she [Mankiller] came back here [to Oklahoma], she had a different philosophy. She grew up in a time when the hippie craze was going on."[43]

The night of the runoff, Wilma and Charlie went to the Tulsa Powwow, where her daughter Gina was being honored. In a photograph taken that evening, Charlie, Gina, Felicia, and Wilma looked worn out, as if having just survived a battle, which indeed they had. Later that night, they returned to Tahlequah to check on the election results. Despite the dirty politics, once all of the ballots from thirty-four precincts plus the absentee votes were tallied, the woman who supposedly knew nothing about politics was declared the winner.

At last, the Cherokee Nation had elected its first woman as principal chief—the first woman chief of a dominant Native American tribe. Wilma Mankiller had outpolled Wheeler, while John Ketcher had retained his post as deputy chief. At long last, Wilma had the mandate she had wanted. She had been chosen as principal chief of the Cherokee Nation—this time by her own people. It was a sweet victory. At last, she felt the question of gender had been put to rest. As Gloria Steinem wrote:

> *She won reelection by an unprecedented 83 percent of the vote. The projects she has helped to start during her reign as chief range from adult literacy programs to a communally owned manufacturing plant, and she oversees a total annual budget of $54 million, more than half of which is now self-generated by the Cherokee Nation. Before community renewal programs began, 80 percent of all funds came from the federal government.*
>
> *Wilma Mankiller became the best kind of leader: one who creates independence, not dependence; who helps people go back to a collective broken place and begin to heal themselves. Though there is a long way to go before the Cherokee Nation restores in a new form the dignity and self-sufficiency it knew 500 years ago, before the terrible centuries of genocide and the banning of even the Cherokee language and religion, now there is a way of making progress that is their own.*[44]

Many Americans, both Cherokee and non-Cherokee, breathed a sigh of relief. Women had finally broken that glass ceiling, at least in Native America. No longer would they be confined to supportive roles in their tribes, and in time, the same would become true in the US government. Or would it?

Wilma pointed out that while white and sometimes even black Americans often rally around a single shared culture, there is no such rallying cry in Native America. Just because the culture in one tribe changes doesn't make it so in all tribes. There is no universal "Indian language" in Native America. All Indians have their own distinct languages and cultures. They have their own art forms and social systems, and their tribes are radically different from one another. As the new chief explained:

Many tribal groups do not have women in titled positions, but in the great majority of those groups, there is some degree of balance and harmony in the roles of men and women. Among the Lakota, there is a very well known saying that "a nation is not defeated until the hearts of the women are on the ground." I think in some ways Rigoberta Menchu, the Nobel Peace Prize winner—a Guatemalan human-rights activist—may be a good rallying force for all of us. She represents to me the very best of what native womanhood is about. I am awestruck by her life and accomplishments, as are many other native people in Central, South, and North America.

In the instance of the Cherokees, we are fortunate to have many strong women. I have attained a leadership position because I am willing to take risks, but at the same time, I am trying to teach other women, both Cherokees and others, to take risks also. I hope more women will gradually emerge in leadership positions. When I ran for deputy chief in 1983, I quit my job and spent every dollar of my personal savings and proceeds from the car-accident settlement to pay for campaign expenses. Friends describe me as someone who likes to dance along the edge of the roof. I try to encourage young women to be willing to take risks, to stand up for the things they believe in, and to step up and accept the challenge of serving in leadership roles.[45]

If she was to be remembered, she insisted, she wanted to be remembered for being fortunate enough to have become her tribe's first female chief. But she also wanted to be remembered for emphasizing the fact that Native Americans have indigenous solutions to their problems. Cherokee values, especially those of helping one another and of their interconnections with the land, can be used to address contemporary issues. As she said in a speech given at Harvard University in 1987, "True tribal tradition recognizes the importance of women. Contrary to what you've probably read in history books, not all tribes were controlled by men."[46]

During those first few years serving as chief, Wilma began to feel an immense responsibility. She realized that if she wasn't accepted at a meeting or session, all women everywhere would feel that sense of rejection.

Not only was her own credibility on the line, but also that of all women who might follow after her.

In time, those fears began to fade as she grew more comfortable in her new position. Before long, she realized she was accomplishing more for her people than she'd been able to before. She had even grown used to the snide or caustic remarks some people made following her election. As Wilma's mother said in an article appearing in *Oklahoma Today* in February 1990, "When I look at her, I just see Wilma. But sometimes I think about what she has done . . . and I can't believe it."

Although Wilma's spirits were buoyed by the milestones accomplished by the Cherokee people, she was still battling her personal demons. Among the most critical were her ongoing problems with her kidneys. She had been misdiagnosed by doctors in Tulsa, after which she sought medical advice in Denver. Although she knew she had polycystic kidney disease, she continued to hope that she wouldn't sustain total kidney failure, as had been predicted years earlier by a group of California physicians. She even went so far as to try several controversial and experimental procedures to see if she could stave off the disease. "Most of those attempts," she admitted later, "were acts of desperation," doomed to fail.[47]

On the advice of a kidney-disease researcher, Wilma traveled to the University of Oregon in spring 1989 to undergo yet another procedure. Surgeons made a fifteen-inch abdominal incision to expose both kidneys so they could remove the tops of the cysts and bathe the area with antibiotics. At the very minimum, the procedure was believed to lessen the number and severity of the damaging kidney infections and, at best, slow the progress of the disease.

It didn't work. Shortly after returning to Oklahoma, she was again hospitalized with a severe kidney infection.

By autumn 1989, Chief Wilma Mankiller realized that kidney failure was imminent. She was hospitalized again and advised that she would need to begin kidney dialysis treatment soon. Within six months, she would need to consider undergoing a kidney transplant.

Wilma devoured every bit of material she could find about the disease. For a time, she felt exhausted as she found herself having to face yet another major health battle to stay alive. As if the automobile accident, the trauma of Sherry's death, the continual surgeries, and the bout of myasthenia gravis hadn't been enough, now she was being asked to stand up and fight yet another battle.

As she lay in one more hospital bed, a woman doctor came in to speak to her about her options. "I was struck by her youth and vigor," Wilma recalled. "Earlier, she had told me about her marriage plans, and how excited she was about beginning her medical practice. As she spoke, I allowed myself the rare luxury of wondering what it would be like to have her life—a life without constant social and political struggle, without endless battles with disease."[48]

Later that afternoon, after agonizing about her future, she slept. And she dreamed. And, when she awoke, she felt suddenly refreshed, as if she had come back to a safe place. Once again, she knew she could make the next journey in her life and survive. This one, though, she knew she couldn't keep to herself. This one would need to be shared with others every step of the way, almost as if it were televised, with the American public and the entire Cherokee people looking on.

The transplant team projected that Wilma could wait six months before the surgery. They wanted to allow her diseased kidneys to fail completely before removing them. They then would place her on dialysis and add her name to the national waiting list for a donor kidney from a cadaver.

Wilma wasn't overjoyed with the strategy. She was already growing weak from the disease and seriously doubted she'd be able to survive the procedures to come. She learned a lot about the large number of people already on kidney waiting lists, and she knew the list was growing longer each day. That didn't begin to cover those in line for new hearts, livers, and other organs. Although a swell of public awareness about the donor crisis had finally hit America, the number of donors hadn't increased appreciably in years.

So, while Wilma waited, she asked her immediate family members to be tested as possible donors. Charlie asked all of his wife's brothers and sisters plus her mother and two daughters if they would be willing to donate a kidney. Six relatives signed aboard—three brothers, two sisters, and Wilma's daughter Felicia. After they were all tested, only her sister

Frances tested positive as a viable donor. Most of the others had some form of genetic kidney disease of their own, although not nearly as severe as Wilma's. Frances, although clear of the disease, had slightly elevated blood pressure and blood-sugar levels that disqualified her. After further tests, the doctors decided that unless her conditions could be cured, she would also be struck from the list of potential donors.

Dissatisfied with much of the medical advice she'd received, Wilma told her doctors she was considering getting an opinion from another transplant center. Her primary physician became defensive and told her she couldn't dictate the terms of her treatment.

All the while, Wilma shared the ongoing episodes of the soap opera with her good friend, feminist author Gloria Steinem. She told Wilma about a physician who she believed could help. After noticing some hesitation, Gloria insisted that Wilma set up a meeting with the doctor at his office in Boston. Wilma reflected upon the advice:

She was right to persist. Dr. Anthony Monaco, a skilled transplant surgeon affiliated with New England Deaconess Hospital and Harvard Medical School, saved my life.

Only fifteen minutes into our first meeting, I knew I had found the right person. He asked that further tests be conducted on Frances, and although she again appeared to be a good match for the procedure, Dr. Monaco was concerned about her blood-sugar level and blood pressure. He ordered more tests.

Meanwhile, my condition was worsening. I was becoming badly anemic, and I was coping with profound weakness. My kidneys were barely functioning when Frances took the final battery of tests. Charlie and I were at a fund-raiser in New York when we received word that Frances had failed the tests and was definitely eliminated as a donor. We had come full circle and had nowhere else to go.

But then a few days later, Charlie called my last remaining sibling, who had not been tested—my big brother Don in California. Charlie explained the situation, and Don agreed immediately to take blood tests and consider serving as a donor. The results were good—Don was free of any disease and could serve as a donor. The decision to donate one's kidney is difficult. This was especially true for Don, who hates being near hospitals and medical doctors and made it a point to stay healthy so he would not have to get even remotely close to a medical facility.[49]

Don talked to his wife and children about the situation, and they were naturally concerned for his safety. But he accompanied his little sis to Boston for a final test to make sure there was an absolute match of blood and that everything was in order. It was.

So, in spring 1990, Don agreed to go ahead with the surgery and to give Wilma one of his healthy kidneys. The operation was set for June. As he had been so many times throughout their lives, Wilma's big brother was once again a hero. Wilma wrote in her memoirs:

The surgery took three hours. My brother's kidney was removed and transplanted, and it began to work almost immediately after it was placed in my body. Don experienced incredible postoperative pain, but both of us soon mended, although I suffered much guilt from watching Don go through a painful rehabilitation. But except for a few minor problems, there have been no real complications since the operation. I was back to work in Oklahoma in August, less than two months after having received my new kidney. I am much more respectful of death than to declare myself a clear victor, however. With an illness such as this, even though I feel well most of the time, I am aware that things could go wrong again, that I could experience kidney rejection or other problems related to the transplant.[50]

Following the operation, Wilma went back to work, throwing herself into her duties as if nothing had ever stopped her. Although she accomplished several important things, she realized much still needed to be done. So, in 1991, after discussing it with her family, she decided to run for another four-year term as chief of the Cherokee Nation so that she could continue working on various health and housing issues for her people. Although she drew two experienced opponents, William K. Dew and Art Nave, she won another term by a broad margin.

"The newspapers called my victory a landslide because I received 82.7 percent of the votes," she recalled. "I really did not expect to do that well. I was only hoping to avoid another runoff. But by receiving so many votes, I felt that our people were saying the issue of gender and doubts was at last buried."[51]

Wilma's inauguration ceremony was held on August 14, 1991, when she played to another full house. Charlie held the Bible as his wife took the oath of office once again. There were a lot of speeches and warm words, and Wilma felt she had made the right decision as she stood at the podium to deliver her address. She knew many others were present there that day besides the people gathered in the auditorium. She felt their presence.

> It's a fine time for celebration because as we approach the twenty-first century, the Cherokee Nation still has a strong, viable tribal government. Not only do we have a government that has continued to exist, we have a tribal government that's growing and progressing and getting stronger. We've managed not to just barely hang on, we've managed to move forward in a very strong, very affirmative way. Given our history of adversity I think it's a testament to our tenacity, both individually and collectively as a people, that we've been able to keep the Cherokee Nation government going since time immemorial.[52]

Although the tribe had continued to make remarkable progress, Wilma felt they still had a long way to go, including developing a new educational plan and installing Cherokee language and literacy programs, developing Sequoyah High School into a magnet school, initiating a comprehensive health-care system, settling old land claims, making taxation more equitable, enacting new housing initiatives, safeguarding the environment, and growing economic development.

Throughout everything, Chief Wilma Mankiller never forgot about her family—from shy and retiring daughter Felicia to bright, outgoing Gina—and spent as much time as possible with them. Both of her daughters married men with Cherokee ancestry.

"When my girls were growing up," she recalled, "I encouraged them to read, appreciate music, maintain a sense of humor, and dance. We danced to all kinds of songs, but our favorite was Aretha Franklin's 'Respect.' After the car accident in 1979, I could no longer do that type of dancing. I am always saddened when either of my girls refers to 'the time when Mom danced with us.' I still do ceremonial dances, but I no longer do very much contemporary dancing."[53]

Charlie's thirteen-year-old son, Winterhawk, lived with them and, like his father, became a prominent Plains-style dancer. He attended Cherokee ceremonial events and studied Cherokee culture. Wilma recalled in her memoirs:

> I recall the numbers of Cherokees who, in the last two centuries, left behind our traditional ways. Those Cherokee elite, as I call them, adhered to the white ways. I also think of their counterparts, the traditionalists who remained true to our tribe's past. I remember hearing that this division created incredible stress and confusion within our Nation, and in 1811, a large comet blazed across the sky for weeks. There was talk of more war with the British and with the Creeks. I recall the old stories.
>
> It was during that time that our people reached a crossroads. It was a period of great uneasiness, and that year and the next, there were severe earthquakes that caused fear to spread among our people. An indication of this turmoil was conveyed by the Warrior's Nephew to the Moravians. He reported that some native people—led by a man beating a drum—had descended from the sky. The man had warned the Cherokees that the Mother of the Nation was unhappy. She was unhappy that we had given up planting corn. She was unhappy that we had let the whites take over our sacred towns. The Mother of the Nation wanted the Cherokees to return to the old ways.[54]

According to the oral tradition, it was during that time that a great Cherokee prophet named Charley claimed to have received a message from the Great Spirit, the Creator of Life and Breath. Charley emerged from the mountains accompanied by two wolves. He told an assembly of

Cherokees that the Great Spirit was displeased that they had given up their old ways in favor of the white man's stores, clothing, and culture. He told them that the Great Spirit was angry and wished the Cherokees to take up the old dances and feasts—to return to the time when they listened to the Great Spirit in their dreams. Charley warned that if they ignored the message he delivered, they would face death. But when death did not strike those who chose to ignore his warnings, his power shrank in the eyes of the people. Some of them, though, realized that the death Charley warned about may not have been physical death but, rather, one's spiritual demise.

"This is one of my favorite stories," Wilma wrote.

It is a lesson. When it is told well, I can visualize the prophet and his two wolves coming out of the night to warn the Cherokees about the impending loss of our traditions and culture.

Among the artworks I keep in our home are a painting and a wood sculpture. They are depictions of Charley and the wolves appearing before the council of Cherokees. Having Charley in my home reminds me every single day of the need for contemporary Cherokees to be on guard. Having Charley nearby reminds us to be sure to do everything we can to hold onto our language, our ceremonies, our culture. For we are people of today—people of the so-called modern world. But first and foremost, and forever, we are also Cherokees.[55]

The Ending of War

Gana was a Seneca war chief who called a council to make peace with the Cherokee. He sent a large party of warriors far away into the deep forest by the riverside, where they drank medicine every morning, purged themselves, and washed in the river.

Afterward, the chief said, "Now we must get the eagle feathers." So, the members of the tribe went to the top of a high hill and dug a trench there the length of a man's body and put a man into it, with boughs over the top so that he could not be seen, and above that, they put the whole body of a deer. Then the people hid and prayed to invite Shada ge'a, the great eagle that lives in the clouds, to come down.

The man under the brush heard a noise, and a common eagle came and ate a little and flew away again. Soon it came back, ate a little more, and flew off in another direction. It told the other birds, and they came, but the man scared them away because he did not want common birds to eat the meat.

After a while, he heard a great noise in the air and knew it was Shada ge'a, the bird he wanted. Shada ge'a looked around in every direction for some time before he began to eat the meat. The man raised his hand and caught hold of the bird's tail. Shada ge'a rose up and flew away, but the man had pulled out one feather. They had to trap a good many eagles in this way, and it was two years before they could get enough feathers to make a full tail and were ready to start off for the Cherokee country.

They were many days on the road, and when they got to the first Cherokee town, they found there was a stockade around it so that no enemy could enter. They waited until the gate was open, and then two Seneca dancers went forward, carrying the eagle feathers and shouting the signal yell. When the Cherokee heard the noise, they came out and saw the two men singing and dancing, and the chief said, "These men must have come upon some errand."

The leader led the Seneca tribe to the meeting house for discussion, where the Seneca chief said, "We have thought among ourselves that it is time to stop fighting. Your people and ours are always on the lookout to kill each other, and we think it is time for this to stop. Here is a belt of wampum to show that I speak the truth. If your people are willing to be friendly, take it," and he held up the belt.

The Cherokee chief stepped forward and said, "I will hold it in my hand, and tomorrow we will tell you what we decide." He then turned and said to the people, "Go home and bring food." They went and brought so much food that it made an enormous pile across the house, and all of both tribes ate together, but could not finish it.

The following day, they ate together again, and when all were done, the Cherokee chief said to the Seneca, "We have decided to be friendly and to bury our weapons, these knives and hatchets, so that no man may take them up again." The Seneca chief replied,

"We are glad you have accepted our offer." Afterward, all threw their weapons in a pile.

Then the Cherokee chief said to his people, "Now is the time for any of you that wish to adopt a relative from among the Seneca to do so." Some Cherokee women went and picked out a man and said, "You shall be our uncle," and some more took another for their brother, and so on until only Gana, the chief, was left. But the Cherokee chief said, "No one must take Gana, for a young man is here to claim him as his father." Then the young man came up to Gana and said, "Father, I am glad to see you," and he led Gana to his own mother's house, the house where Gana had spent the first night. The young man was really his son, and when Gana came to the house, he recognized the woman as his wife, who had been carried off long ago by the Cherokee.

FIVE

In Control of Change

The Cherokee people stand upon new ground. Let us hope that the clouds which overspread the land will be dispersed, and that we shall prosper as we have never before done. New avenues to usefulness and distinction will be opened to the ingenuous youth of the Country. Our rights of self-government will be more fully recognized, and our citizens be no longer dragged off upon flimsy pretexts to be imprisoned and tried before distant tribunals. No just cause exists for domestic difficulties. Let them be buried with the past and only mutual friendship and harmony be cherished.

—CHIEF JOHN ROSS[1]

BY THE TIME WILMA DECIDED HER HEALTH NO LONGER ENABLED HER to serve as head of her people's government, she realized that change had become an inevitable part of life. Not only her life but also the life of the Cherokee Nation. It was part of life's cycle, unfolding "like the passing shadow of a hawk in flight."[2] Despite the most daunting challenges change can bring, nearly all offer hope and, eventually, joy. To Wilma, change meant an opportunity for renewal.

Following in the footsteps of her ancestors and their approach to life's difficult times, she recalled the example of John Ross. Writing in her memoirs, she said:

A bright star for the Cherokee people and one of our most esteemed leaders, Ross served as Principal Chief of the Cherokees after the tribe's forced removal from our beloved ancestral homelands along the Trail of Tears to what became Oklahoma. It was a period of great discord and drastic change.

[Chief Ross's] remarks were taken from an address delivered before the Cherokee National Council in Tahlequah on October 9, 1861. Ross uttered his stirring words as bloody Civil War divided not only the United States but our own Cherokee tribe.

On August 14, 1999, when newly elected Principal Chief Chad Smith gave his inaugural address at the historic Cherokee capitol in Tahlequah, he quoted excerpts from Ross's 1861 speech.

Despite the passage of time, the sage advice Ross offered so long ago remains relevant today. Even now, as our people emerge from several years of political upheaval and internal strife which have to rank as one of the most difficult and distressing periods in our history, we find comfort in knowing that nothing is as enduring as change. This knowledge helps us restore our balance as once more we stand on the new ground of another century. I remain confident that if we all work together, the Cherokee Nation will heal its wounds and will unite.[3]

Another event that the passage of time foreshadowed was Wilma Mankiller's retirement from tribal politics. All her life, she enjoyed the ability to know when the time was ripe for change—and that included within her own life's sphere. After devoting more than a third of her life to the Cherokee government, she felt it was time to move on to new experiences and challenges and to allow someone else to guide the second-largest Indian tribe in America.

In her wisdom, she showed how she understood the role she played within her people's lives: It was important, necessary, and basic but hardly critical. "I never overestimated my importance to the Cherokee Nation," she wrote, "and the history of my people. In the totality of Cherokee history, my time at the Cherokee Nation was very brief. I remained focused on the challenges and tasks of serving as chief rather than the historical implications of the work."[4]

Perhaps her realistic attitude toward her own role within and contributions to her political leadership enabled her to recognize that the time had come for her to step down. "I had begun to sound like the people I used to protest against," she wrote, "and I had said if that ever happened, I would leave."[5]

Throughout her seventeen years of tribal service, she felt blessed for the positive experiences she'd had—her marriage to Charlie Soap, the growth of her two daughters into bright and caring young women, and her overcoming a "daunting set of health problems" that might well have decimated a lesser person.

She had met with three presidents and was honored at the White House; she lobbied Congress for everything from health clinics to the national Head Start program; she received more awards than most people could imagine; and she had the opportunity to work with and get to know the people within her own Cherokee communities of Bell, Kenwood, Cave Springs, Burnt Cabin, and White Oak. But the accomplishment she said she appreciated most was when a group of male Cherokee elders officiating at a memorial service asked her to sit with them in a spot usually reserved for respected elders. *That*, she emphasized, was a moving experience.

Naturally, Wilma's decision not to run for yet another term as chief didn't come easily. She discussed the prospect with Charlie, her daughters, and other family members and friends. After spending hours weighing all sides of the proposition, she reached a decision that was far from unanimous. But it was the right one for her.

After stepping down as the Cherokee Nation's principal chief, Wilma entertained several offers. She accepted a Montgomery Fellowship to Dartmouth College in Hanover, New Hampshire, for the winter term of 1996. The college had an impressive Native American Studies program, and Wilma looked forward to the opportunity to interact with Dartmouth's president at the time, James Freedman.

Because her stepsons, Winterhawk and Cobey, were still in high school, she and Charlie decided that he would remain home in

Oklahoma with the boys while she went off to Dartmouth for the semester. She arrived on January 1, 1996, and inherited a hectic schedule crammed with seminars, guest lectures, and meetings. She spent much of her time with Native American students exploring issues such as the pros and cons of Indian gaming, Native American spirituality, and Native American identity.

The only real problem she had with Hanover was the freezing weather. She had to buy winter shoes and a heavy coat and gloves. When she came down with the obligatory colds and flu and finally pneumonia, she assumed her health problems were due to the weather. But with her kidney transplant in 1990, she had taken immune-suppressant drugs to prevent rejection of the new organ and realized her sicknesses were related to them. She was being treated for pneumonia at Dartmouth Medical Center when she complained of severe night sweats. Finally, a young resident said, "You know, your symptoms sound like lymphoma, but that couldn't be the case because your blood is all right."[6]

In late February 1996, Wilma called her kidney-transplant surgeon, Dr. Anthony Monaco, and he brought her back to Boston for tests and a biopsy. The following week, she was back in New Hampshire, preparing to attend a reception for Hillary Rodham Clinton sponsored by the New England Circle, when Dr. Monaco called and told her that the biopsy indicated she had lymphoma. He asked her to make immediate arrangements to return to Boston for further tests.

By the time she hung up the phone, she'd gone numb. She had often wondered how she'd react if she learned she had cancer. Now she knew. She remembered sitting down, trying to absorb everything the doctor had told her. She recalled her telephone call back home:

I called Charlie, and he cried when I told him the news. He asked if he should come up, and I told him to wait for a while. I wanted a chance to deal with this situation on my own. Our conversation was interrupted by President Freedman's driver ringing the doorbell. I decided to go to the Hillary Clinton event. I was glad I did. I found a chance to speak to the First Lady and tell her that history would prove she had been correct about her national health-care plan. On the way home, I told President Freedman about my condition. Because he had been successfully treated for lymphoma, he offered me some insight.[7]

On February 25, Wilma left Dartmouth a week short of the winter term's end. A car picked her up early that morning, and she had the driver stop for coffee and the *New York Times*. But she never remembered taking a single sip or reading a single article on the two-hour drive into Boston. She later related the events:

When I was a girl and young woman living in the San Francisco area, I had experienced several earthquakes. They came on suddenly, without any warning, and turned my life completely upside down. Now I once again felt as though I had been hit by an earthquake and that my life was spinning out of control.[8]

In Boston, Wilma breathed a deep sigh as Charlie and her daughters reunited with her. She was by then ready for their help and comfort. After more biopsies, blood tests, CAT scans, and bone-marrow tests, she gathered with the family to hear the news: She had second-stage large-cell lymphoma.

Because of her suppressed immune system, the oncologists wanted to explore treatments other than traditional chemotherapy and radiation. She remained hospitalized for five grueling weeks while her physicians searched for the most effective protocol for their patient. Gloria Steinem joined her there, and together they researched several treatment alternatives. They contacted the National Cancer Society, the National Institutes of Health, and many other organizations.

They read books on nutrition and employed various relaxation techniques and visualization exercises designed to function as a mind-over-matter antagonist to the cancer. Before long, Kristina Kiehl, a Democratic Party political operative and photographer/videographer, joined Gloria and arranged for a massage therapist to visit Wilma once a week. The visualization program didn't work. She was supposed to envision the cancer cells as the enemy and then destroy them. But every time she tried, she saw these "poor little stick figures cowering in the face of their enemy, and I could go no further. I must be a dedicated pacifist if I cannot even make war against a disease that could destroy me!"[9]

Fortunately, they found other ways to combat the illness. Gloria called the Harvard Mind/Body Institute, and the staff showed Charlie and Wilma a simple meditation exercise that she used almost every day over the next few months. "Gloria sent music, books, wonderful scents, and a striking red shawl for my room," she relayed. "During those uncertain weeks a small circle of trusted friends—Kristina Kiehl, Bob Friedman, Jean Hardisty and, of course, my associates at Dartmouth—drew near and gave me comfort. Kristina completely altered my view of nutrition and forever changed my eating habits. I even learned to love tofu."

Wilma continued her story in her memoirs:

> I felt that everything about me was changing. My world narrowed significantly. I found myself spending much of my time thinking about red and white blood-cell counts and anticipating my next clinic appointment. My relationships with people changed as well. I had always been the helper, the enabler, the leader. People who knew me in those roles had a great deal of difficulty relating to me as someone in need of help. Some people I considered my friends dropped away, but many more rallied to support me.
>
> Eventually, we all decided the best option for me was traditional chemotherapy, coupled with Native American teas and herbs. In March 1996, I took my first chemotherapy treatment and was released from the hospital to my friends Bill and Suzanne Presley. I went to their home in Boston. Within several days, I became extremely ill with a fever of 104 degrees, chills, and vomiting. I was rushed back to the hospital, isolated, and given intravenous antibiotics. At last I rallied, and on the sixth day, I was allowed to return to the Presleys' home.[10]

After the initial hospitalization, Wilma's chemotherapy treatments continued, no worse nor better than any others. As expected, she experienced the predictable nausea, weakness, loss of hair, and abandonment of appetite. Then a routine CAT scan detected spots on her lungs, so doctors ordered another biopsy. It occurred so quickly, she hadn't even had time to notify her family.

The oncologist thought the lymphoma had moved to my lungs. Dr. Monaco was present during the biopsy surgery and came to see me later in the recovery room to tell me the good news—it was not a recurrence of lymphoma. He said it turned out to be a severe lung infection caused by my lowered immune system and chemotherapy. The treatments were stopped and I was given a strong antibiotic. At the time, I had just two chemotherapy treatments to go, but my transplanted kidney was still working fine. That would soon change.

When chemotherapy was resumed in late July 1996, my transplanted kidney began to fail.[11]

In September 1996, with her chemotherapy treatments completed, Wilma returned to Oklahoma. By October, she had started six weeks of radiation treatments for which she drove an hour and a half each way to a hospital at Fort Smith, Arkansas. She completed the treatments in late November. By December, it was clear that her kidney problem was worsening. When her kidney failed, she asked for peritoneal dialysis at home, which only served to bring on new challenges, including severe anemia.

By spring 1997, Wilma was receiving regular blood transfusions, but she continued to grow weaker and more fatigued. That summer, doctors ordered more scans and tests in Boston, and the oncologist became concerned about a suspicious new strand, or growth, that he discovered. In autumn, she received two stem-cell treatments in Nassau, Bahamas, that had a positive effect on her anemia and caused the strand to disappear. In spring 1998, she was declared cancer-free, but her health problems were far from over. It was time to face another kidney transplant.

To her complete amazement, five people offered to donate a kidney. All of them went through genetic testing. Two were unsuitable, but three of the volunteers were deemed compatible.

Wilma had difficulty approaching any of them to undergo major surgery for her benefit. She had found it tough enough when her eldest brother had donated a kidney in 1990. But, eventually, one of her nieces,

Virlee Williamson, the best of the donor candidates, volunteered. When Wilma asked why the thirty-two-year-old working mother was willing to go through such an ordeal, she said she had always admired Wilma, and it was difficult for her to watch her decline while knowing there was something she could do about it. Wilma wasn't surprised that Virlee had stepped forward. The young woman had always been an idealist and someone who was moved to help others.

So, Virlee and her nine-year-old daughter accompanied Charlie and Wilma to Boston. On July 22, 1998, the women underwent simultaneous operations at Deaconess Hospital. Doctors removed white blood cells from Wilma's niece and implanted them into her aunt's body, followed by the donated kidney, which began functioning normally. Once again, a family member had saved Wilma's life. An article in the *Daily Oklahoman* detailed the event.

> *Former Cherokee Nation Principal Chief Wilma Mankiller was in stable condition following a kidney transplant Wednesday.*
>
> *Her doctors at Beth Israel Deaconess Hospital said she was "doing very well."*
>
> *In April, Mankiller said she was looking forward to the operation—her second kidney transplant—after apparently beating the cancer she had battled for two years. The kidney was donated by her niece. She received a kidney from her brother in 1990.*
>
> *Mankiller served 10 years as chief of the Cherokee Nation in northeastern Oklahoma, the nation's second-largest tribe. She stepped down in 1995.*
>
> *She became seriously ill in January 1996, and cancer was discovered the following month. Doctors said she suffered from lymphoma, a tumor-related disease.*
>
> *The chemotherapy that apparently cured her cancer, however, destroyed a kidney.*[12]

During all of her physical ordeals, Wilma never lost belief in her faith, remaining spiritually active through prayers, meditation, and "the realization that although many people love and support me, this was really a solitary and often lonely journey that I had had to walk alone."[13]

She read the Bible and the writings of the Dalai Lama. Once, during her recuperation in Boston, when she felt as if she were faltering, she sat on the ground in a friend's backyard, faced east, and prayed as hard as she could for the illness to leave her body.

This prayer is supposed to be done near fresh water, but I just dipped the tip of the eagle wing in a glass of water and hoped the Creator would understand my special circumstances. Although I was thin, bald, and weak, and the traffic noises kept interrupting me, I still felt such wonderful peace. It was almost as if I were back in Oklahoma on my own beloved land.

Throughout all the treatments and operations, I managed to coedit a women's history book, raise funds for several worthy organizations, and stay engaged in local community activities, including helping Charlie build a Boys and Girls Club in Tahlequah.[14]

As a result of her tireless efforts on behalf of others, Wilma received the Presidential Medal of Freedom—the nation's highest civilian honor—from President Bill Clinton in January 1998. She recalled feeling strange at the time for being rewarded simply for doing the work she felt she was born to do. She accepted the medal on behalf of all Native American people, including women, whom she felt had done much more work than she.

As she entered the White House with her family and friends that day, she couldn't help but think back over what a long, long way it was from her carefree, loving, protected childhood in Mankiller Flats to where she was now.

Back in Oklahoma, surrounded by my loved ones and old friends on ancestral land that means so much to me, I ponder my whole life— past, present, and future. I also reflect on the Cherokee Nation. Many times, I have been given a new lease on life, just as my own people have. All of us have survived adversity and have persevered.[15]

In 1999, with another election looming, the Cherokee people went to the polls in a hotly contested tribal battle following four turbulent years of rule under Joe Byrd, who had been steeped in controversy and whose administration was marred by constant turmoil. In a May 22 election that prompted a remarkable number of nine candidates to run for the office of principal chief, Byrd received 32 percent of the vote. His runner-up, with 19 percent, was Chad Smith, a Sapulpa attorney and a great-grandson of revered Cherokee traditional leader Redbird Smith.

With backing from Ross Swimmer and Wilma, a powerful coalition swelled up behind Smith, who ended up defeating Byrd in a July 24 runoff that drew 56 percent of the vote. Wilma claimed it was the most significant Cherokee election of the century. After his extraordinary victory, Smith gave his inaugural address on August 14, 1999, concluding with a brief but critical thought:

Let us move forward to our final destination and fulfill our designed purpose. Let us, armed with our indomitable Cherokee spirit and ancestral pride, proceed on our journey, relying on the strength and wisdom of our Cherokee women and guided by our Creator.[16]

Writing of the event in her memoirs, Wilma later said:

Today—on the brink of a new millennium—the Cherokee Nation not only has a new lease on life but also has new leadership to restore financial and political stability. In a simple act of faith in their own ability to create change, Cherokee people who had seen their tribe raked by controversy for too long went to the polls and voted for leadership that promised to heal, renew, and rebuild the Cherokee Nation.

Who knows what the future will bring? I have always heard that the best way to make the Creator laugh is to plan for the future. Nevertheless, I cannot help but believe the future looks bright for the Cherokee Nation. I also know my own prognosis is good. I intend to live fully for as long as I am granted this precious gift called life.[17]

The Lost Cherokee

When the first lands were sold by the Cherokee in 1721, a part of the tribe bitterly opposed the sale, saying that if the Indians once consented to give up any of their territory, the whites would never be satisfied but would soon want a little more, and a little again, until at last there would be none left for the Indians.

Finding all they could say not enough to prevent the treaty, they determined to leave their old homes forever and go far into the West, beyond the Great River, where the white men could never follow them. They gave no heed to the entreaties of their friends but instead began preparations for the long march until the others, finding that they could not prevent their going, set to work and did their best to fit them out with packhorses loaded with bread, dried venison, and other supplies.

When all was ready, they started off on their journey under the direction of their chief. A company of chosen men was sent with them to help in crossing the Great River, and every night until they reached it, runners were sent back to the tribe, and out from the tribe to the marching band, to carry messages and keep each party posted as to how the other was getting along.

At last, they came to the Mississippi and crossed it with the help of those warriors who had been sent with them. These then returned to the tribe, while the others kept on to the west. All communication between the two groups was now at an end. No more was heard of the wanderers, and in time the story of the lost Cherokee was forgotten or recalled only as an old tale.

Still, the white man pressed upon the Cherokee as one piece of land after another was sold until, as years went on, the dispossessed people began to turn their faces toward the west as their final resting place, and small bands of hunters crossed the Mississippi to learn what might be beyond. One of these parties pushed on across the plains, and there at the foot of the sprawling mountains—the Rockies—they found a tribe speaking the old Cherokee language and living still as the Cherokee had lived before they had ever known the white man or his ways.

Six

Where Activism and Feminism Collide

Life to Wilma Mankiller was precious—but not so much as what one did with it. Living for the sake of breathing and taking up space was not her idea of living. Within her own ranks and social hierarchy, she was a mover and a shaker, a doer and a leader. She was and always would be, first and foremost, a chief.

She had been born at the right time. A decade or two earlier, and she would have been too old to have considered tackling some of the most significant inequities and injustices facing the Cherokee Nation along with indigenous people everywhere. A decade or two later, and she would have missed the cusp of the revolution.

Not that Wilma Pearl Mankiller was a revolutionary in the most conventional sense of the word. That was a job for others—to spearhead a movement, to rattle society, to upset the status quo. For a chief named Mankiller, the thrill of the battle was in ferreting out the causes of injustice, exploring them, and reaching a conclusion as to how best to defeat them. Violence and marches and protests were less her modus operandi than they were for others. Slow, deliberate, contemplative actions were more Wilma Mankiller's weapons of choice. Although less flashy than sit-ins, marches, rallies, and demonstrations, her approach to solving age-old problems relied more upon mental acuity, solid compromise, legal action, and the dedicated support of her people.

That was a lesson she most likely learned from her father. He had taken all the abuse he could swallow, watching firsthand how those around him suffered at the hands of a callous and careless ruling class and government, before playing his own role in the legal system, placing his support where he deemed it would do the most good and never backing down. He traveled through life unnoticed but not unnoticing. His goals were the same as those of the most fervent fomenters—but more effective in the long run. It was a lesson he hoped to teach by example to his children. It was a lesson that Wilma Mankiller learned well.

Do what you do best. That may well have been the motto Wilma carried with her through life. If so, she lived up to it time and again. Failure was not in her vocabulary. Awareness was. For a Mankiller from a small rural community in south-central Oklahoma, it was ordained for her destiny. For a curious and displaced young girl who might as well have found herself growing up on the moon, she emerged to become a powerful voice in the American Indian landscape—whether or not that had been her intent. Mankiller, in her adult years, admitted that she felt "uncomfortable with being cast as a role model" because people get upset if you fail to live up to the image they have of you. "I can't do my work or live my life being conscious of the fact that some people view me as a role model," she continued, or "I would begin to suffer from paralysis."[1]

Despite her discomfort with the concept—or perhaps because of it—Wilma Mankiller received numerous awards and other forms of recognition throughout her adult life, ironically enough for being an outstanding role model. One of the awards was the highest honor that could be bestowed upon a private citizen, the Presidential Medal of Freedom.

For the American Indian, political activism hit its stride in the 1960s at a time when Wilma was hitting hers. It was an era when many groups were actively organizing in the pursuit of civil rights and, for some, a more radical approach to a shift in power. Among the most prominent civil rights groups of the era were African American organizations such as the National Association for the Advancement of Colored People (NAACP), Martin Luther King's Southern Christian Leadership Conference (SCLC), the Student Non-Violent Coordinating Committee (SNCC), and the National Organization for Women (NOW). Civil rights groups most often focused on lobbying, education, and creating change via whatever legal mechanisms were available. Power groups responded to the limits of civil rights groups with more radical rhetoric and actions. Among the wide-ranging power groups were those advocating black power, brown power, red power, and radical feminism—groups such as the Black Panthers, Brown Berets, American Indian Movement (AIM), and New York Radical Feminists.

Many of the power groups borrowed strategies, tactics, theory, and rhetoric from the African American movement, among the first to grab national attention. While similarities in goals and tactics mark these groups, American Indian organizers differed from others in several key areas, drawing upon their own unique history of continued resistance and conflict over land use, ownership, and resources.

One of the most significant differences was that the Native focus was less on integration with the dominant (white) society and more on maintaining their unique cultural integrity. While African Americans had been denied their rights to integration, American Indians had faced a history of *forced* integration called "assimilation."[2] American Indians also differed in their problems from African Americans in that they were landowners with central resources whose focus was less on obtaining civil rights as it was on gaining enforcement of legally binding treaty rights already in place. The Indian movement focused more on empowering the tribe to procure and recover its previously given rights than on individuals seeking those rights, and that stood in marked contrast to the common theme among other civil rights groups.

At a time when white student groups advised against trusting anyone over the age of thirty, American Indian youth actively pursued bonds with their elders and looked to them for cultural knowledge and leadership.[3] While elders enjoyed a revered status within their tribes, they lacked tribal authority. Many tribal councils were governed by members of a middle generation who had survived boarding schools and who never understood the tribe's traditional values or the interest among youth in reconnecting to their heritage.[4]

Divisiveness in Indian goals often extended to geographical differences. Indians on reservations were frequently compared to poor southern blacks, while those residing in urban America often gravitated toward the "rhetoric of power groups."[5] According to author Donna Hightower Langston:

The National Congress of American Indians (NCAI), founded in 1944, was one of the prominent Civil Rights groups of the American Indian movement during this time period. Unlike earlier groups, NCAI membership was restricted to people with Indian ancestry, and Bureau of Indian Affairs (BIA) employees were barred from leadership positions. Ruth Bronson (Cherokee) was the first executive secretary of the NCAI and served in this position until 1956. In general, the NCAI worked on issues more pertinent to reservation Indians than urban communities. NCAI campaigns included voting rights in the Southwest where Indians were prohibited from voting in state and local elections. Among the lobbying victories of this time period were the 1965 Indian Self-Determination and Education Act, the 1968 Indian Civil Rights Act, the 1972 Indian Education Act, the 1975 Indian Education Assistance and Self-Determination Act, the 1978 Indian Child Welfare Act, and the 1978 Religious Freedom Act.[6]

Although much of the work done by the NCAI flew under the radar of many Native Americans, something that stood out was the organization's well-structured lobby against the 1953 Termination Act passed by Congress and signed by President Eisenhower to dissolve the legal status of all tribes and, in so doing, eradicate them from being. In a 1947 report by William Zimmerman, the Acting Commissioner of Indian Affairs, tribes were divided into categories of immediate versus eventual termination.[7] The process began with the termination of the Paiutes of Utah in 1954, when the government denied the tribe building permits for hospitals and schools so the tribal members could remain on their land. Worse, Congress refused to consider compensation for "acquired" land and resources unless the tribes were willing to develop an acceptable plan of termination.

The termination policy was conceived during the "red scare" of the McCarthy era, when the House Un-American Activities Committee, headed by Senator Joseph McCarthy of Wisconsin, held daily hearings to ferret out "communists," communist sympathizers, and other threats to American democracy from within the US government and the ranks of

Hollywood's studio system. Widespread fears that American values were under threat from outside as well as within exploded.[8] Indians who had not assimilated into the dominant culture were viewed as un-American. Not coincidentally, Dillon Meyer, who had directed the Japanese American relocation camps during World War II, was named Commissioner of Indian Affairs in 1960.

One part of the termination policy was the relocation program begun in 1952, offering reservation Indians one-way bus fare and the promise of assistance in finding jobs and housing in urban areas. In 1940, 87 percent of Indians lived in rural areas, but by 1980, fewer than 50 percent did so. The BIA estimated that nearly a quarter-million Indians were relocated under the program. The high point of the termination policy occurred during the period from 1952 to 1962, slowing considerably after the election of John F. Kennedy in 1960. By the late 1960s, both Johnson and Nixon had renounced termination, which was formally overturned in 1972, twenty years after it had been initiated—and many years, as it turned out, too late.

What resulted from those two decades of misguided legislative abuse was an awakening within Native American communities to the inequities of the termination policy and the damage done to tribal America. It was an awakening that Wilma Mankiller and her contemporaries could no longer ignore. "A renewed interest in tribal values was the exact opposite of what the Relocation Program was supposed to achieve," wrote Donna Hightower Langston. "Both African-American and Indian militancy had increased with migration to urban areas. The growth in urban Indian populations unwittingly set the stage for a renewed radicalism among youth."[9]

In the African American movement, with which a teenaged Wilma Mankiller readily identified, a younger group of students grew disillusioned with the limits of civil rights and turned to the Southern Christian Leadership Committee to form the offshoot Student Non-Violent Coordinating Committee. This type of split also occurred in the American Indian civil rights movement, as students founded their own organization separate from the NCAI. The National Indian Youth Council (NIYC) was founded in 1961 after an NCAI conference in Chicago during which disputes between Oklahoma and Great Plains tribes occurred, resulting in a falling out between tribal leaders who dominated NCAI and younger urban Indians.[10] While the NCAI by tradition held its conventions in large metropolitan areas, the NIYC held its meetings on reservations, instilling each session with traditional tribal songs and ceremonies.

The group employed nonviolent, often humorous, and always symbolic ridicule of white society through their publication *ABC* (*Americans Before Columbus*).[11] Most likely influenced by Third World Liberation movements, they perceived the status of reservations to be that of internal colonies under the rule of the BIA. The NIYC supported African American groups and borrowed many of their ideas and rhetoric.[12]

One of the first Indian activists to use revolutionary rhetoric, Clyde Warrior (Cherokee), was also one of the original founders of NIYC. He spent the summer of 1961 working with the SNCC on implementing various voter education projects, and was the first to label the BIA a white colonialist institution. Correspondingly, Vine Deloria Jr. (Lakota), at a national NCAI conference in 1966, was the first to use the term "red power," which was broadcast initially in 1967. In the broadcast, Warrior promised that the NIYC would lead an uprising that "would make Kenya's Mau Mau look like a Sunday school picnic."[13] One of the first actions the student activists joined was the Fish-in movement in Washington State in 1964. A movement of open resistance had begun that would support new tribal achievements nationwide.

In 1968, two new youth-led power groups emerged, one on the West Coast and one in the Midwest. Lehman Brightman (Lakota), director of the Native American Studies program at the University of California, Berkeley, formed the United Native Americans, whose members played a role in the occupation of Alcatraz. Although they viewed themselves as a national organization, most of their support was in the Bay Area. They were best known for publishing the first intertribal militant newspaper, *Warpath*, in 1968, calling for an insurrection against the BIA.

A second group of young community activists, this one centered in urban Minneapolis, grew to become the American Indian Movement. Modeled after the early prototype of the mostly peaceful Black Panther

Party, they spoke out and demonstrated against urban police harassment and quickly found themselves on the FBI's most-watched list. At the time of the group's founding, the Twin Cities' Indians made up "a third of the state's indigenous population, more than any [other] single reservation in the state."[14]

The first red power action that grabbed the national and international spotlight was the 1969 occupation of Alcatraz Island. Other occupations followed, including one at Fort Lawton, Washington, in 1970; the Washington, DC, occupation of the Bureau of Indian Affairs in 1972, and the Wounded Knee, South Dakota, takeover in 1973. These post-Alcatraz intertribal groups aimed their protests at various national sites and symbolic monuments.

The occupation of Alcatraz galvanized Indian pride and consciousness and heralded a new era in American Indian activism. The landmark occupation began in November 1969 and ended nineteen months later, in June 1971. (An earlier, mostly symbolic four-hour takeover of Alcatraz occurred in March 1964, organized by Bela Cottier [Lakota], which attracted little more than curious regional media attention.) The latter Alcatraz incursion group, led by representatives from the United Bay Area Council of American Indian Affairs, drove claim stakes into the ground (a broom handle was used for one), symbolizing the discovery sticks Lewis and Clark had used in the opening of western America to white settlement. The protestors offered the government forty-seven cents an acre for a total of $9.40 for the island. The occupying party of forty included twenty-six-year-old Russell Means (Oglala Lakota) and his father. Bela Cottier also pressed a claim to the island through the courts under the Fort Laramie Treaty, granting Native Americans the right to claim abandoned federal property, but was unsuccessful. The action launched a topic of conversation among urban Bay Area Indians that lasted for years.

Several prominent leaders, including Wilma Mankiller and Russell Means, had grown up in California; their families, along with others from tribes throughout the United States, had moved there as part of the federal government's relocation program. In 1958, four out of the eight original relocation centers were located in California—one each in San

Francisco, Oakland, San Jose, and Los Angeles. California was a natural, then, to become a hotbed for Indian activism.

Before long, there were as many Lakota Sioux in California as there were on reservations in the entire state of South Dakota. The Indian population in California was 82 percent urban, in contrast to states such as Arizona, New Mexico, Alaska, and North Carolina, where urban Native communities made up less than 30 percent. Urban residents at the time had more education and lower rates of unemployment: 11 percent in urban areas compared to 40 percent and greater in rural reservation settings. Being an urban Indian provided an important identity, and the Indian population had become a younger group overall. An unintended consequence of this concentration of young Indians in urban areas was an increase in American Indian militancy. Urban militancy was matched by a resurgence of nationalism on reservations.[15]

The 1969 occupation of Alcatraz, with all its accompanying media coverage, was led by students from California campuses and supported by community members of the San Francisco Indian Center. Indian centers in urban areas were an unanticipated result of the government's relocation program. In urban settings, Indian centers and bars provided social contact and a means for interaction among Native participants.

While the first landing on Alcatraz had occurred on November 9, 1969, a second, larger group disembarked on November 20. They included ninety students who began the arduous job of creating an infrastructure to support a long-term occupation. The *San Francisco Examiner* took a matter-of-fact approach to the occupation in its November 20 front-page story:

Four parties of Indians returned to Alcatraz Island today in pre-dawn landings amid indications they planned to stay for a while.

Officials of the General Services Administration, the island's federal landlord, paid them a brief visit, parleyed, and then retreated.

Regional GSA Administrator Thomas Hannon said later he had no plans to return to the island today, or to seek arrest warrants.

But he added that he had received word that phone lines linking Alcatraz to the mainland had been tampered with. That, he said, "might" cause him to alter his plans.

Hannon described the Indians as "reasonable people with a cause," and said he advised them to work through the Department of the Interior and the Bureau of Indian Affairs.

The Indians, about 90 strong and with supplies for two days, were staging a repeat of their Nov. 9 "raid."

This time, however, they were better organized.

While the invaders were settling down on the island, Dean Chavers, speaking for an organization named Indians of All Tribes which sponsored the move, held a mainland press conference.

He said the action was taken to further negotiations to turn the island into a center for Native American Studies.

In addition, the group hopes to form an American Indian Spiritual Center to teach the ancient religions of their people, and to found an Indian Center of Ecology to fight pollution.

Indians, Chavers said, have been aware of their involvement with the total environment for thousands of years.

Their right to the island, he explained, was that of discovery and superior to that of "rich men like H. Lamar Hunt," the Texas millionaire who has proposed immediate intention of leaving.

"We believe we have squatters rights under the 1868 treaty with the United States government," Oakes was quoted as saying.

Hannon left shortly to confer with other officials of the General Service Administration and perhaps to seek guidance from Washington.

Oakes stayed to direct the Indians, who were making themselves comfortable in some of the abandoned structures on the island.

They had crackers, bread, potato salad, meat and sugar. Oakes told reporters that they found the island's water reservoir freshly filled.

The landing party, according to Chavers, included 34 women, 41 men and three children. Reporters saw at least four youngsters, ranging from 2 to 6, however.

Mrs. Marie Hart, wife of John Hart, chief caretaker of the island, was concerned about the youngsters.

She, herself the mother of five, asked Hannon before he left whether she would be permitted to feed the children. He told her, she reported, to "use your own judgment."

There were at least two dogs on the island. One was Duke, a mongrel belonging to Hart, which barked the alarm of the landing during the night, and which was kept secured in his doghouse near the water.

The other was a poodle owned by one of the invaders, Jody Beulieu, 20, a coed at the University of California at Davis.

While they awaited the government's next step, the Indians settled down in the houses that formerly belonged to the island doctor and warden.

The earlier Alcatraz invasion, a week and a half ago, was short-lived. Four Indians swam to the island from a Canadian clipper ship, staying only a few hours.

Another 14, including three young women, went to the island that night, claiming squatters' rights. The GSA removed them by Coast Guard cutter, but made no attempt to file any charges against them.[16]

Not coincidentally, the island prison had been shuttered and virtually abandoned several years earlier. Living conditions on the island were less than desirable, with no electricity, running water, or sewage. In the long run, that proved less of a hardship than it seemed at first, since occupiers were quick to point out that similar conditions existed on many reservations throughout the country.

The island occupants had arranged for their supplies to be carried across the bay past Coast Guard blockades, while on the island, the women worked on the day-to-day operations that comprised running the community kitchen, school, and health center. The men, including Richard Oakes (Mohawk), head of the San Francisco State Native American student group, and twenty-three-year-old John Trudell (Santee Lakota), a bartender who ran the radio broadcast from Alcatraz, received most of the media attention and on-air time, as well as personal publicity.

In all, some one hundred persons occupied the island continuously, while thousands of others from across the nation visited Alcatraz, which had become a symbol of renewed cultural pride and a more-militant stance regarding self-determination. In total, more than fifty-six thousand Native Americans took part in the occupation.[17]

The two most prominent leaders of the student occupiers included Oakes and LaNada Boyer Means (Shoshone Bannock), head of the Native American Student Organization at the University of California, Berkeley. Oakes occupied the island for a few short months in the beginning, but Means, at age twenty-two, was in the first landing party and remained on the island from beginning to end. She had been the first Indian student admitted to the University of California, Berkeley, in January 1968. She later wrote a $300,000 grant proposal that sought to turn Alcatraz into a cultural education center for Native Americans. Accompanying Oakes and Means were Madonna Gilbert/Thunder Hawk (Cheyenne River Lakota) and John Trudell, both of whom would eventually become leaders of AIM.

The protesters used humor and symbolism to drive their political messages home, among them the establishment of a mock "Bureau of Caucasian Affairs" in ridiculing the BIA, whose policies had been criticized universally by Indian leaders for more than a century. Occupiers also used toy bow and arrows to shoot at Coast Guard boats.

Among the original student group of occupiers were two government informers, a condition that plagued Indian groups throughout the history of their protests. The student occupiers of Alcatraz were not armed, in contrast to those who later took center stage at Wounded Knee, South Dakota. The Alcatraz occupiers were also fortunate to be working within the ultra-liberal environment of the Bay Area, as opposed to the Wounded Knee activists who descended upon rural, conservative South Dakotan America.

Although students were the original vigilante occupants of Alcatraz, various community organizers provided stateside logistical and moral support, among them Adam Nordwall/Fortunate Eagle (Anishinabe) and Grace Thorpe (Sac Fox), daughter of Olympic athlete Jim Thorpe. Thorpe procured a generator, water barge, and ambulance service for the island while providing coordinated publicity, including visits by Hollywood luminaries such as Jane Fonda, Marlon Brando, Anthony Quinn, and Candice Bergen. She also handled public relations on Alcatraz and at the later Fort Lawton occupation and helped to acquire the physical property for the future site of Deganawidah-Quetzalcoatl (DQ) University, the first university of American Indian and Chicano students, founded near Davis, California.

But Grace Thorpe's long history of activism began with Alcatraz: "Alcatraz made me put my furniture into storage and spend my life savings."[18] She went on to work as a lobbyist with the NCAI, where she toiled at getting factories to commit to relocating on reservation land so Native people would be able to have jobs nearer to their homes. She returned to her reservation in 1980 and served as a tribal judge and health commissioner. Thorpe remained an activist throughout her life. In her sixties, with only her Social Security checks to rely upon financially, she started a fight against what she called "radioactive racism" in her own tribal government, which was considering storing nuclear waste. She founded the National Environmental Coalition of Native Americans in 1993.[19]

Another community member, fifty-year-old nurse Stella Leach (Colville), ran the health clinic and became one of the occupation's last leaders. Dr. Dorothy Lonewolf Miller (Blackfoot), director of Scientific Analysis Corporation, used her office as the headquarters for Indians of All Tribes and obtained an education grant to found Rock School on the island, as well as to set up the island's health clinic. She also printed the island's newsletter.

Numerous other community members supported the effort, not least of whom was Wilma Mankiller, who years later wrote of the experience, "It gave me the sense that anything was possible. Who I am and how I governed was influenced by Alcatraz."[20]

To resolve the standoff, the government offered the occupiers a cultural center located at Fort Mason next to Fisherman's Wharf, but the protesters wanted to hold out for title to the island itself. Stella Leach warned the government that they would create another Wounded Knee Massacre if federal agents tried removing the protesters by force.

The federal government, though, was able to wait out the islanders' occupation until they finally removed the last of the protestors on June 11, 1971. But the landmark uprising had left its mark on the nation. Many more occupations were to follow in areas across the country during the next several years, including a three-month takeover in March 1970 at Fort Lawton in Washington State, resulting in the formation of the Daybreak Star Cultural Center; an occupation near Davis, California, helping to establish DQ University in 1971; an occupation of Ellis Island in 1970; a 1970 Thanksgiving Day occupation of the *Mayflower* by AIM; and numerous occupations of BIA offices, including the headquarters in Washington, DC—all adding to awakening public awareness of the Indians' plight.

Alcatraz helped to shape public opinion and influence public policy. A top aide to President Nixon later cited at least nine major policy changes as a result of the island occupation. The most far-reaching benefit to spring from the Alcatraz occupation, though, was the raising of America's political consciousness. John Trudell noted: "Alcatraz made it easier for us to remember who we are."[21] Before that, whatever Indian activism had existed manifested itself locally, from one tribe or region to the next, often focusing on specific treaty issues. Alcatraz focused a nationwide problem on the entire country and remains the most prolonged occupation of a federal site by Native Americans to date.

Meanwhile, in Washington State, the so-called Fish-in protests began as a response to that state's policy of tying state laws to restrictions of Indian fishing rights that had been guaranteed by several federal treaties. The 1854 Medicine Creek Treaty, for example, guaranteed Northwest Indian tribes unrestricted use of natural resources, an essential right since fish traditionally formed the basis of Native American diets, culture, and spirituality. With skyrocketing poverty rates, the unrestricted ability to fish provided for family survival. The Fish-ins protested the routine arrest of Indians for fishing off-reservation. Following a decade of demonstrations, in 1975 *United States v. Washington*, known more commonly as the Boldt decision, recognized the treaty fishing rights of state tribes. The landmark decision allocated half the salmon harvest to local tribes.

Begun as nonviolent civil disobedience, the Fish-ins eventually grew to a potential powder keg of violence. After various unlawful acts by state and city law enforcement officers, game wardens, and white vigilantes, including the use of teargas, clubs, beatings, and shootings, Indians responded in self-defense. Many tribal women began carrying arms to protect themselves during the protests. Local news media ran photos of older women with rifles, quoting one as saying, "No one is going to touch my son or I'm going to shoot them."[22] Coastal tribes had a strong sense of sovereignty and demonstrated it by routinely escorting IRS staff and officers off their reservations at gunpoint. In the fall of 1970, at the Puyallup Fish-in camp, spokesperson Ramona Bennett was quoted as saying, "We are armed and prepared to defend our rights with our lives. If anyone lays a hand on that net, they are going to get shot . . . we're serious. There are no blanks in our guns."[23]

Not surprisingly, shoot-outs and fire bombings did occur at some Fish-ins, with the most serious of injuries suffered by the protesters. Both Hank Adams (Anishinabe) from the NIYC and Tribal Chair Ramona Bennett, spokesperson for the Puyallup Fish-ins, were shot by white vigilantes, Ramona while seven months pregnant. Statements from public officials such as Governor Dan Evans, who declared that Indian treaties were worthless, only fueled the incidents of violence by state officials and vigilantes. State attorneys even challenged the legal status of the small tribes. The BIA did not defend Indian fishing rights, even though it was founded for the stated purpose of assisting tribes in claims against the state. Organizers had pursued civil protest because doing so seemed more effective than meetings with bureaucrats to negotiate government policy.[24]

Janet McCloud (Tulalip) was one of the key leaders in the Fish-in movement, having been goaded into activism when state game wardens broke into her home searching for "illegally harvested" deer meat. Although male leaders of the Yakama and other large tribes made fun of McCloud because she was a woman and a half-blood, she never let that bother her. "Now," she said, "you hear them talk and they act macho, they act belligerent, they act rough, but when it comes right down to the bottom line, they couldn't fight their way out of a paper bag. The only people I've ever seen them fight are Indian women and children. And yet they're controlling everything now." McCloud acknowledged that her most consistent sources of support were female elders.[25]

In 1964, Janet McCloud and Ramona Bennett founded the Survival of American Indians Association to raise bail and secure supporters of national prominence, such as Hollywood film star and celebrity Marlon Brando and civil rights protestor Dick Gregory, both of whom lent their support and, in turn, were arrested themselves at Fish-ins. The movement also drew increasing support from college students, one of whom was Hank Adams of the NIYC.

The Fish-ins helped to unite the small fishing tribes in Washington State around a common goal. These included the Makah, Nisqually, Puyallup, and Muckleshoot, among others. According to Vine Deloria Jr., the state avoided confrontations with the larger tribes, choosing to concentrate their efforts on the smaller ones with fewer resources with which to defend themselves.[26]

In July 1968, AIM was cofounded by Mary Jane Wilson (Anishinabe), Clyde Bullecourt (Anishinabe), and Dennis Banks (Anishinabe) in Minneapolis. The group initially chose the name Concerned Indian Americans, but they eventually rejected it when they realized the acronym spelled out CIA. Roberta Downwind suggested the name AIM since "you say you aim to do this and that."[27] Pat Ballinger, universally regarded as the mother of AIM, chaired the St. Paul chapter. The parent group, modeled after the early Black Panthers organization, provided red jackets to members patrolling the Twin Cities community to monitor police harassment. AIM rhetoric was often couched in spiritual terms, since many members saw the organization as primarily religious.

By 1971, the group had become a national phenomenon with seventy-five chapters. Its official symbol was an American flag flown upside down to symbolize an America gone astray. Members staged media events that carried powerful symbolic messages, such as the 1970 takeover of the *Mayflower* on Thanksgiving Day, during which they buried Plymouth Rock beneath a pile of sand, generating their first national publicity. That June, they threatened to hold the Statue of Liberty hostage, providing the sort of sensationalism that appealed more to the white establishment media and those who watched it than to their own Native members.

In 1972, AIM was one of eight groups that organized the Trail of Broken Treaties cross-country march, which they patterned after the 1963 March on Washington by the African American civil rights movement. Marchers planned to arrive in DC during the final weeks of the presidential campaign and present their grievances to both candidates. Three groups—Alcatraz, Pacific Northwest, and Oklahoma—were led by spiritual leaders, with stops at historical sites such as Sand Creek and Wounded Knee. AIM representatives joked that they planned to retake the United States from west to east like a wagon train running in reverse. Not everyone thought the joke was funny.

When the group reached the Capitol, AIM members quickly grabbed control of the BIA office. Although not initially planned, the occupation came when up to one thousand marchers arrived at BIA headquarters in November 1972 and found that "anticipated accommodations" had not been made.[28]

Although their numbers were small compared to the quarter-million antiwar demonstrators who had shown up at the Capitol earlier, the AIM demonstrators were sincere. They generated little notoriety until Capitol police tried to remove protesters from the building and demonstrators pushed them back into the streets and blockaded the office doors. A human barricade of multiracial supporters kept police at bay for three days, when AIM leaders were provided with $66,000 in travel money to leave town. Madonna Gilbert/Thunder Hawk and Russell Means oversaw the collection of one and a half tons of documents that they loaded onto U-Haul trucks to carry away. The documents in time revealed the widespread practice of sterilization abuse and other exploitative practices the government had used on the Native population.

Among its more mundane duties, AIM served as a mobile response unit in the Midwest. Whenever injustices committed against Indians went ignored or unpunished, local tribal members called on the group to raise awareness. Murders and sexual assaults of Indians in border towns had seldom been prosecuted in the past, so some tribal members, tired of the lack of justice and responsiveness, called on AIM.

In February 1972, the organization responded to the murder of Raymond Yellow Thunder (Lakota) in Gordon, Nebraska. His family had been unable to get tribal attorneys or the BIA to investigate his death, so one of his nephews called on AIM. The organization demanded a second autopsy, which discovered that the man's cause of death hadn't been exposure, as initially claimed, but rather a brain hemorrhage from a blunt trauma injury: He'd been beaten to death. A thousand AIM members arrived in Gordon for a two-day protest at City Hall. They called for a boycott of stores and businesses, and before long, city officials reopened an investigation into Yellow Thunder's death.

AIM members were called in to investigate a similar situation by Sarah Bad Heart Bull (Lakota) when her son Wesley was knifed to death by a white man who, shortly after his questioning, had been released without charge. One hundred AIM members showed up en masse at the courthouse in Ouster, South Dakota, to protest. When Bad Heart Bull attempted to get past the crowd and into the courthouse, police officers pushed her back down the steps, using a nightstick against her throat.[29] Watching such brutality against a tribal elder quickly incited a riot. The police responded with teargas grenades; AIM responded by setting fire to the courthouse and the chamber of commerce.

Dennis Banks and Russell Means were brought up on riot charges, even though they were inside the courthouse when the incident occurred. Sarah Bad Heart Bull got a three- to five-year sentence for rioting and served five months. Her son's murderer, in ironic contrast, received a mere two months of probation and served no time. Such incidents drew attention to the injustice Indians had suffered for over a century, propelling AIM into the public eye.

Russell Means characterized South Dakota at the time as being "the Mississippi of the North."[30] There was more than a little truth to the statement. The Pine Ridge Reservation in South Dakota was run by a tribal chair, Dick Wilson, an allegedly corrupt politician overseeing a community with a murder rate seven hundred times greater than that of Detroit.[31] Wilson's private army, called "goons," created an atmosphere where arson, beating, and murder were common.[32] Half of the BIA police moonlighted as goons to enforce Wilson's ban on all AIM activities on the reservation, declaring open war against supporters.[33]

The most radical support to remove Dick Wilson came from female elders, including Gladys Bissonette and Ellen Moves Camp. As Bissonette recalled, "When we marched there were nothing but us women."[34] They joined other women from the Pine Ridge Reservation and picketed Wilson before calling on AIM to mediate the situation. A group led by Dennis Banks and Russell Means arrived in February 1973. Mostly older women, many of whom had lost children or grandchildren during Wilson's regime, packed the meeting in Calico. Means and Mary Crow Dog/Brave Bird remembered that the Wounded Knee Occupation was the idea of older women such as Bissonette, who argued, "Let's make our stand at Wounded Knee, because that place has meaning for us, because so many of our people were massacred there."[35]

The occupiers might have intended well, but the results were anything but fruitful. Federal forces were dispatched surreptitiously without the necessary presidential proclamation and executive order. Phantom jets made daily overhead runs. One occupier and former Vietnam veteran noted that they took more bullets in seventy-one days at Wounded Knee than he had seen in two years in Vietnam.[36]

Public sentiment was overwhelmingly pro–Native American. A 1973 Harris Poll revealed that 98 percent of the public had heard of Wounded Knee, and 51 percent sympathized with the Indians.[37] The ten-week siege was spearheaded primarily by women, many of them armed, all of them devoted to the cause. One photo of Anna Mae Aquash (Mimac) shows her digging a bunker with a golf club. Women also ran the medical clinic and negotiated with the government, led by Bissonette and Moves Camp.

Five hundred sixty-five people were arrested after Wounded Knee, including nearly every AIM member, and 185 federal indictments were issued. The men faced more serious charges because government prosecutors felt women might not be taken seriously in court as dangerous terrorists. A reign of terror followed on the reservation, with Dick Wilson's goons serving as a death squad. Within the next two years, 250 mostly traditionalists were killed on the reservation along with 69 AIM supporters, one-third of them women. Gladys Bissonette lost her son, Pedro, the president of the Oglala Sioux Civil Rights Organization, when BIA police killed him in October 1973. Her daughter, Jeanette Bissonette, was shot dead on the way home from Pedro's funeral. No indictments against the goons were ever handed down.[38]

By the time the legal wrangling was over, AIM had been bankrupted. Although the organization excelled at bringing media attention to national problems, its leadership was often fractious. Some of the division was likely caused by undercover FBI agents: Numerous government infiltrators were uncovered at both Wounded Knee and the Washington, DC, occupation of the BIA offices and at various other events.[39]

The issue of sexism was raised at Wounded Knee amid criticism of male dominance and opportunism. One response was the founding of Women of All Red Nations (WARN) in 1974. While the media remained fascinated with the stereotype of male warriors, many of the male leaders, such as Dennis Banks, acknowledged that women were the real warriors. John Trudell reflected on the times, saying, "We got lost in our manhood."[40]

Mary Crow Dog/Brave Bird noted that women were honored for having children and doing "good beading." But, as she also recalled, "It is to AIM's everlasting credit that it tried to change men's attitudes toward women. In the movement we were all equal."[41] Also, Indian women had an interesting way of accusing men of sexism that was not open to white women. They argued that acting sexist was a sign of being assimilated. Acting sexist was a way of exhibiting ignorance of Indian traditions. It was one of the most humiliating accusations a male tribal member could endure.

Indian women also skirmished with white women, most of whom exhibited a wholesome dose of paternalism but very little fraternalism with Native women. That led to serious problems in communication, since white women assumed a significant degree of superiority in their way of thinking and acting. Yet, for all their smugness, white females were slow to the table where equal rights were concerned. As Bea Medicine (Lakota) observed, "Indian women do not need liberation, they have always been liberated within their tribal structure."[42] White women anticipated that Indian women would take up the mantle on issues with which they assumed all women identified, but that rarely turned out to be the case. As Laura Waterman Wittstock (Seneca) noted, "Tribalism, not feminism, is the correct route."[43]

Wilma Mankiller noted the deterioration of the matriarchal society herself, as author Devon Abbott Mihesuah revealed:

Traditional gender roles eroded from the impact of patriarchal thought, and those ideologies still affect Native women's positions within their tribes and the respect given to them by men. As former Cherokee chief Wilma Mankiller observes, "Our tribe and others which were matriarchal have become assimilated and have adopted the cultural value of the larger society, and, in so doing, we've adopted sexism. We're going forward and backward at the same time. As we see a dilution of the original values, we see more sexism.... The thinking that people come to in a patriarchal society is crazy."

Most tribes were egalitarian, that is, Native women did have religious, political, and economic power—not more than the men, but at least equal to men's. Women's and men's roles may have been different, but neither was less important than the other. Females toiled hard at their various "jobs," but they received recognition and compensation, often in the form of controlling the economic output; in addition, they were secure knowing they would always have food, shelter, and support from their extended families and clans.

Prior to contact [with white society], men and women performed tasks specific to gender. Perhaps men hunted while women farmed, or men performed heavy labor while women cared for the children. Although the duties were different, none was inferior to the others. All work was necessary, and the tribe needed the hands of both men and women. The influence of Europeans' social beliefs, however, changed the way Natives interpreted the world, themselves, and gender roles.[44]

Similarly, the distinction between the goals and the means of achieving equality in white versus Native women was a notion lost on most of the American public but not, coincidentally, on the federal government in its approach to solving its "Indian problem." Wilma identified as a feminist of color for good reason. Rather than a fight for civil rights for Indian women battling in a man's word, Wilma's was a fight to identify with women of all races everywhere in their ongoing battle against federal bureaucracy, bias, and bigotry. As such, she was a prominent voice in speaking out in women's groups everywhere, beginning with those formed in the early 1970s.

A civil rights–oriented group founded in 1977 grew out of the International Women's Year conference and was funded by the Women's Educational Equity Program. Ohoyo, the Choctaw word for "woman," was geared toward Native American women. It lasted only two years, but it generated numerous conferences for professional women. A split had divided the organization's D.C. staff, which was, not surprisingly, more closely aligned with white feminist interests than with Indian matters. The D.C. breakaway group disbanded in 1985.

WARN, on the other hand, developed a more radical focus. Made up of three hundred women from thirty Indian nations who attended the founding conference, it shared a similar philosophy to that of AIM in that many of its efforts focused on struggles over energy resources and sterilization abuse uncovered in the documents that had been confiscated from the BIA. But some people felt that WARN attracted young, urban, college-educated women more than others, which led to the founding in 1981 of the Northwest Indian Women's Circle (NIWC) by Janet McCloud. NIWC attacked issues connected primarily to Indian women and children. Among those issues, sterilization abuse was the most frightening. According to author Donna Hightower Langston:

From those files, AIM members learned that forty-two percent of Indian women had been sterilized, the majority without their consent. Another issue for Indian women's groups was that of adoption. In earlier times, children had been taken away from Indian families at young ages and shipped to boarding schools at great distances. Today, Indian children are placed in foster care and adoption at higher than average rates. Sometimes the reasons children are removed from homes are based in cultural differences and differing family models that value extended families among Indians. Indian women's groups have also raised awareness of their high infant mortality rates and the fact that Indians have the highest school dropout rate of any group in the United States. Indian women's groups also organized around land and resource struggles.[45]

While some white feminists view motherhood with suspicion, believing it to be a key reason for female oppression, many Native American women have long felt that role empowering. The high status of motherhood results in less stigma for unmarried Indian mothers than it does for women in the dominant society. As a result, many Native women have been skeptical of family planning services.[46] Being a mother or grandmother increases a woman's stature in Indian society. Also, white women are more likely to view aging as something that decreases a woman's status. But aging in the traditional connotation within typical Indian communities is more a symbol of power and status, something for women to look forward to and appreciate.[47]

Native American women are also more likely to organize around issues that impact children as well as themselves. They likewise tend to organize around issues of tribal rights. Organizing among different generations of Indian women is more likely than in white women's groups. Many Native females find that their status as elders increases their respect within future generations. Due to lower life expectancies, Indian women may be perceived as elders at a younger age than the population at large, but, according to Langston, "The women who participated in political events of the 1960s and 1970s are now our revered elders. Elders do not last forever in any community. It is important that their contributions receive recognition in their lifetime and in generations to follow."[48]

In September 1993, Wilma Mankiller cited one Native prophecy foretelling that "this is the 'time of the women,' a time when women's leadership skills are needed." As a woman, she had long recognized the differences in how the sexes approach their problems and go about achieving their goals: "Women, by and large, bring to leadership a greater sense of collaboration, an ability to view social, political and personal concerns in a uniquely interconnected, female way."[49]

That conclusion resulted from Wilma's lifelong observations. She operated within a particular political and social climate, well aware of the undeniable fact that she was, first and foremost, a woman. Her public persona was that of Wilma Mankiller, the first *female* chief of a dominant Native American tribe. It was her very status as a female that enabled the public to identify with her. She was not a national leader who just happened to be female. She was a leader of national notoriety *because* she was female. Her femaleness set her apart from all others at the time and paved the way for her success.

Wilma sprang to the forefront of the nation's awareness in part by the way she confronted various gender-related issues. Just as white liberal feminists emphasized their distinct power of "women" as an excuse for political involvement, Wilma and other indigenous women challenged gender-oriented concepts in the name of Native American tradition.

Wilma employed engendered imagery throughout her Cherokee Nation leadership role: She was a woman, and she was good at solving problems. She differed from others who had come before her in that she played upon media interest in such a cultural iteration. She was a female chief, and that made her unique. As Langston concluded, she was a woman named Mankiller who became chief of the second-largest and best-known tribe in the country during a period of renewed interest in Indian culture, and that made her story the stuff of which romance novels are made. Her real talent in achieving notoriety, though, was in the fact that she denied that her gender was an issue, all the while expressing surprise that gender was a serious concern. She used the ploy of pointing to traditional Cherokee history to "solidify the legitimacy of her tribal leadership when, in fact, her election to chief was anything but conventional."[50]

In those regards, Wilma's election didn't depart all that much from the traditional arguments made by nineteenth-century white female reformers to justify their political action. They justified their politicization as traditional when, in reality, it was just the opposite. Advocating for temperance, child-labor laws, and the banning of prostitution lent a commonsense air of legitimacy to female activism, which was quite normal. In the case of Wilma Mankiller, the power of femininity was real;

in the case of the nineteenth-century reformers, traditional concepts of femininity were carefully crafted and remolded to legitimize a new, very *untraditional*, form of behavior.[51]

One of the things that Wilma understood so well was that for the Cherokees to acculturate, according to author Maureen O'Dea Caragliano, "it was necessary to undermine the role of women in Cherokee society." She explained, "This bias against women was something the white man brought to Cherokee culture."[52] Several published works stress the power of Indian women within their tribes and the significance their roles played throughout history. Although the source of that power may be political, it is not always so. Sometimes, the power needs to be considered in light of the broader scope of a social group. Issues such as marriage rights, religious influence, and community involvement all come into play and must be taken into consideration.

Female power within traditional gender boundaries has traditionally been defined by women's historians to show how Indian women are more similar to than different from their European counterparts. Women historically have sought and found ways to express their power. Society can't deny sex-based oppression and discrimination against women, but author Clara Sue Kidwell points out that "the power of women in matrilineal societies included that of selecting men for positions of leadership." Although that's not the case with European women who came to North America, it's true that just as white men dominated public life, Indian men "played the public roles in Native American societies"[53] if not in everyday life, where women were more often than not the real force behind the family.

Sexism simply didn't exist among the Cherokee before contact with European settlers. As a political move, Wilma solidified her own role in tribal government by explaining it as an extension of the powerful role women have played throughout Cherokee tribal history. According to Janda, Wilma followed "in the path of other Beloved Women" in the Cherokee tribe. Yet, the very essence of the Cherokee having "Beloved Women" delineates the differences in status and, sometimes, power between some women and men.

Wilma's astute political maneuvering by characterizing her leadership as a traditional act rather than a contradictory one in Native society, according to Janda, set her apart:

> *Nevertheless, the tendency to characterize Mankiller's tenure as chief as a return to tradition speaks to a larger problem in the area of Native American women's history, which is the fallacy promulgated by romanticized depictions of a distant past prior to the arrival of Europeans in North America in which all Indian women exercised a great deal of power. This is not to dismiss the fact that some groups of Native American women did exercise a greater degree of autonomy than white women, but rather to suggest there existed more similarities between the two groups in terms of the acceptable arena for expressions of power than has been indicated by many scholars. Certainly one could argue, for example, that Abigail Adams, the wife of President John Adams and mother of President John Quincy Adams, occupied something akin to "beloved woman" status. But just as it would be erroneous to take the status and respect afforded to Adams and apply that to an analysis of the roles of other women in the eighteenth century, so too is it inaccurate to take the experience of a small minority of beloved women and argue that all Cherokee women achieved a status of power equal to that of men. Scholarship that overemphasizes the power of Native American women prior to the influence of white culture ignores the diversity of tribal societies and the dynamic nature of human interaction. The larger point, however, is not to dwell on precontact manifestations of female power, but instead to explore how belief in that power shaped the image, as well as identity, of both [LaDonna] Harris and Mankiller.[54]*

Wilma developed two beliefs over her years in a leadership role, during which she met and exchanged ideas with numerous other indigenous women. The first was that sexism didn't exist within Native cultures until colonial occupation introduced it from European cultures. The second was that both sexes contributed equally (although in different arenas) to their cultures. According to Devon Mihesuah, "Many modern

Native women leaders point to their tribal religions and traditions as inspiration and justification for their position as leaders,"[55] which Wilma's own philosophy of leadership bore out.

In describing Mankiller as a "role model for all Americans," New York Republican congresswoman Susan Molinari invited her to speak at the "Women as Leaders" seminar in Washington, DC., in 1996. Molinari expressed confidence that Wilma's "inspirational words" would "impart wisdom and hope" to symposium participants. Wilma rose to the challenge when she voiced her concern over the confirmation of Clarence Thomas to the US Supreme Court after University of Oklahoma law professor Anita Hill accused him of sexual harassment. As she complained to Senator David Boren, "If a Yale educated law professor will not be believed when she complains about sexual harassment, what woman or girl can be encouraged to come forward with complaints about sexual harassment?" She went on to justify her concerns by saying that a Thomas confirmation would discourage females across the country from exposing sexual exploitation and harassment in the future.[56] Neither that contention nor the generalization about Yale-educated law professors turned out to be true, although her assumptions were unarguably popular at the time.

Where Wilma's intellect combined with her intuition to yield a universal truism was in her bemoaning the fact that not enough women had been appointed as judges. She suggested to Boren that he back Jane Wiseman for a federal judgeship in Tulsa, Oklahoma. Wilma wrote, "I don't understand how we can continue to have gender inequity in judgeships when we have so many women qualified to serve in these positions." She added that she had solved a similar problem in the Cherokee Nation "pretty quickly by appointing two women judges in the tribal courts." Boren responded that he agreed about Wiseman, who also wrote Wilma to thank her for her support.[57]

In her work as a woman advocate, Wilma paralleled another Native activist, LaDonna Harris. Janda wrote of the two in her book *Beloved Women*:

That Harris and Mankiller developed a profound sense of themselves as Indian women and, at times, used it to band together is clear in any examination of their interaction with each other and with other Native American women. When Mankiller ran for chief in 1987, for example, a prominent Native American activist, Ada Deer, sent a letter to Harris and other members of the Women of Indian Nations Political Action Committee (WINPAC) board about the election. This organization encouraged the participation of Native Americans in all levels of politics but did not affiliate itself with any political entity or group. In regards to the pending election, Deer explained that Mankiller was "facing three male opponents" and urged the board members to make a personal donation to her campaign. When Mankiller won the election Harris sent her a congratulatory telegram. Harris and another friend, Ella Mae Horse, wrote, "Your sisters across the country are so extremely proud of you" and "Please know we are thinking of you and stand ready to help assure you a successful and productive term." The letter closed with an extension of their "most heartfelt congratulations" and "best wishes." As evidenced here, gender was a central component of the political identity and image of these women and also served as a basis for unity and mutual support. Such support proved a tremendous asset among the network of Native American women involved in politics.[58]

Deer, according to Janda, was also a critical cog in unwinding the workings of Native American women in politics. As Janda said, her relationship to both Harris and Mankiller provided insight into "the centrality of the gender-based support network" forged by these women. As with Harris and Mankiller, Deer urged women to play a larger role in politics, saying, "It is a man's world unless women vote." She encouraged women to support political candidates who "are striving to eliminate oppressions of all kinds."[59]

Harris was a longtime supporter and mentor to Deer—so much so that the two often joked that whenever Harris was appointed to one board or another, she soon brought Deer on board. It was no coincidence. Both LaDonna and her husband, Fred, provided Deer with assistance and hosted her at their Washington home several times. They also provided critical support in Deer's quest to regain federal recognition for her tribe, the upper Midwest's Menominee. Their Native status was terminated during the 1950s. Deer subsequently wrote LaDonna to thank her and Fred for their support. "Your encouragement, consultation, and advice really bolstered my work," she said. "I always marvel at your vision and foresight." Deer concluded the letter by calling Harris an inspiration for all Indian people: "You've won my perpetual Woman-Of-The-Year Award!"[60]

By the mid-1970s, following the restoration of her tribe's status, Deer continued working as an activist for Native American rights and was eventually made head of Native American Studies at the University of Wisconsin–Madison. She unsuccessfully ran as a Democrat for the office of Wisconsin Secretary of State in 1978 and 1982 but lost. In 1993, she was named the first female Native American Assistant Secretary of the Interior for Indian Affairs. When Deer had run for Secretary of State, the Harrises threw their support behind her, writing letters of praise and sponsoring fund-raising events. "We have known and admired her for many years," they wrote, and "we respect her abilities as a leader." They described Deer as an American Indian woman who "has accomplished many firsts in her career." Quoted on the back of a pamphlet promoting her candidacy, a passage from *Ms.* magazine described Deer as representing the "re-emergence of the Indian woman, who historically has filled positions of equal responsibility in a tribal society which operates on qualifications." Native women such as Deer and Mankiller became positive symbols of gender-positive candidates for public office as well as effective tribal leaders.[61]

Deer and Mankiller met in the early 1980s. They worked on projects together while seeking advice from one another. Mankiller testified in support of Deer's confirmation hearing as Assistant Secretary of the Interior for Indian Affairs in July 1993, describing Deer as a "courageous and tireless advocate of Native people" and as "always in tune to the needs of people." Mankiller said that, in her opinion, Deer's greatest contribution was the leadership she exhibited in the restoration efforts of her Menominee tribe and called Deer a "superior choice" for the position. After receiving confirmation for her new job, Wilma continued her support for Deer.[62]

The following year, Wilma advised Deer on suggestions for her priorities for 1994. She warned her cohort of Oklahoma-based opposition to her because of her previous efforts to combine the Oklahoma Bureau of Indian Affairs offices. Wilma said that Senator Boren was "so angry he has threatened taking you personally to federal court." She added that the other US senator from Oklahoma, Don Nickles, was also "pretty pissed off." Wilma suggested that Deer "always question the agenda and recommendations" of the BIA while recalling that even as she "worked for the common good," there existed some people who wanted to see her fail and be removed from Indian Affairs.[63]

To Deer, Wilma was a trusted compatriot and a reliable sounding board, as she said several months later when she praised the chief for her efforts at the 1994 White House Listening Conference, where several Indian leaders met with members of the Clinton administration to discuss policy. Deer told Wilma, "I trust your judgment and am in awe of your intelligence and common sense." She added, "You have already achieved so much in your life and I am counting on you to help me achieve our goals for Indian country."[64]

When LaDonna Harris received the Lucy Covington Award for her lifetime contributions to bettering the condition of Native Americans, both Wilma and Deer joined in the ceremonies. Along with them was feminist/activist Gloria Steinem, reinforcing the concept of the feminist support network. Through their gender, the women represented a central bond that forged the tools for change. Harris thanked Wilma for her presentation at the ceremony: "I know we will always be supportive of each other." Harris described Mankiller as someone other Indian leaders view "with great admiration, maybe sometimes with envy that she can do what she does," while Wilma described Harris as a "remarkable stateswoman and national leader who has enriched the lives of thousands." She called Harris a "consistent and ardent advocate on behalf of indigenous people."[65]

The support complex of women such as Mankiller, Deer, Harris, and others caught the eye of a nation awakening to the values it created within society. It was nothing new—only newly defined and enunciated. In 1993, Clara Nomee, madam chairman of the Crow Tribal Council, wrote to Wilma about the role of Indian women leaders and the responsibilities they shouldered within their respective tribal governments. They "must stand and support each other in the area of tribal sovereignty," she said.[66] She wasn't alone. A growing number of support organizations for Indian women echoed a common sentiment: Native American women were key to Native culture and existence.

One source of support, Women of All Red Nations, stressed the roles women played within Native tribal traditions. Winona LaDuke, one of WARN's founders, described the growth of the organization out of a need for more women to become involved with the American Indian Movement. One of WARN's goals, she said, was to "bring back the traditional role of women in the Indian nations and in the leadership and guidance" of the movement. The goal of reasserting "traditional roles" of Indian women echoed the sentiments of Wilma and other indigenous feminist leaders behind a growing number of Native women elected to tribal offices.

As Native organizations aligned against prejudice and bigotry grew, they developed along notably distinct paths from those of white middle- and upper-class America and college-educated women who dominated the feminist movement. While these women defined "female issues" too narrowly to appeal to poor women and those of color, they nonetheless joined the Native movement in their attempts to appeal to all women of all classes and socioeconomic strata. They advanced rhetoric to help shape the definitions of femininity and increase the options available to women in society. The feminist movement created for women such as Wilma Mankiller and LaDonna Harris a framework within which "they could challenge assumptions about the appropriate place of women in society," writes Janda, who went on to say:

In fact, the feminist movement created a host of new possibilities for women. By the mid-1990s, women still earned less money than men and remained underrepresented in every branch of the government. It is also true, however, that increasing numbers of women go to

*college, pursue advanced degrees, run companies, and do a number of
other things that, prior to the feminist movement, were considered
unusual.*[67]

The friendship between Wilma and Gloria Steinem displays a
connection between white and Native American feminists. The two
developed a camaraderie through their work with the Ms. Foundation,
and Mankiller later credited Steinem for encouraging her to write her
autobiography. In her acknowledgments, Mankiller extended her "love
and appreciation" to Steinem for her support. Janda said that Wilma's
relationship with Steinem brought the Native chief even more publicity.
"What better irony than for feminists and critics alike to see Steinem, the
best-known spokesperson of the movement, linked to a woman named
Mankiller? The name, alone, brought substantial interest, and, in fact,
even the *Wall Street Journal* quipped about her name."[68] Commenting
that their favorite moniker on the list of those in attendance at Clinton's
economic summit was Chief Mankiller, they added their hope that she
represented only the Cherokee Nation and not "a feminist economic priority." Mankiller also used humor about her name, often telling people
that she had earned the name fairly.[69]

Today, women are no more united in their perceptions of the problems they face and their solutions. Still, it is because of the persistence
of women such as Wilma Mankiller, Gloria Steinem, Ada Deer, and
LaDonna Harris that the role of women in politics has evolved dra-
matically while the involvement of women in mainstream politics grows
with each passing year. That fact has an easy alliance to thank: the public
and private support these women have given one another that contributed to the changing role of women in politics. What was appropriately
labeled as radical back in the 1960s is today considered mainstream, at
least regarding the number of opportunities available to women entering
politics and their evolving gender roles. As opportunities for women
continue to increase, stories about women in politics who defeat sexism to rise to accomplish remarkable and remarkably distinctive female
firsts will become increasingly commonplace. Until then, women such as
Wilma and LaDonna continue to remind the world of what needs to be

done to eradicate centuries-old wrongs and to set humanity on the path to decency and survival.

Such opportunities did not come easily—not even for a woman named Wilma Mankiller, who always shunned the thought of being a role model for others, lest she fail in her work and only succeed in letting others down. Despite her discomfort with the limelight, she went on to receive numerous awards—or, perhaps, she did so because of it.[70]

Mankiller's image—her name, her prominence, and her support for women's issues—can never be distinguished from her use of gender. Although claiming that gender had nothing to do with leadership, it had, in reality, *everything* to do with her public image as a strong, assured, and resourceful leader.

The collision of feminism and Indianness that helped to shape both the identity and the image of Wilma Mankiller came from the acts and the sacrifices of dozens if not hundreds or even thousands of long-suffering people before her. It resulted from years of wanting, longing, missing, yearning, loving, hating, fearing, and creating. As author Janda wrote, "Mankiller drew on elements of feminist ideals and Cherokee tradition to create a new modern concept of the beloved woman who is politicized yet traditional. Taken together, Harris and Mankiller are the two most important Native American women in the second half of the twentieth century, both for their accomplishments and for their use of gendered imagery to justify and effect change."[71]

The Race between the Crane and the Hummingbird

The Hummingbird and the Crane were both in love with a pretty woman. The woman preferred the Hummingbird, who was as handsome as the Crane was awkward, but the Crane was so persistent that to get rid of him, she finally told him he must challenge the other to a race, and she would marry the winner. The Hummingbird was so swift—almost like a flash of lightning—and the Crane so slow and lumbering that she felt sure the Hummingbird would win. She did not know the Crane could fly all night.

They agreed to start from her house and fly around the circle of the world to the beginning. The one who came in first would marry the woman. At the word, the Hummingbird darted off like an arrow and was out of sight in a moment. His rival was far behind.

After flying all day, the Hummingbird stopped to roost for the night, knowing he was far ahead. But the Crane flew steadily all night long, passing the Hummingbird soon after midnight and going on until he came to a creek and stopped to rest about daylight. The Hummingbird woke up in the morning and flew on again, thinking how easily he would win the race until he reached the creek and there found the Crane spearing tadpoles, with his long bill, for breakfast. He was very much surprised and wondered how this could have happened, but he flew swiftly by and soon left the Crane out of sight again.

The Crane finished his breakfast and started on, and when evening came, he kept on as before. This time it was hardly midnight when he passed the Hummingbird asleep on a limb, and in the morning, he had finished his breakfast before the other came up. The next day he gained a little more, and on the fourth day, he was spearing tadpoles for dinner when the Hummingbird passed him.

On the fifth and sixth days, it was late in the afternoon before the Hummingbird came up, and on the morning of the seventh day, the Crane was a whole night's travel ahead. He took his time at breakfast and then fixed himself up as nicely as he could at the creek and came in at the starting place where the woman lived early in the morning.

When the Hummingbird arrived in the afternoon, he found he had lost the race, but the woman declared she would never have such an ugly fellow as the Crane for a husband, so she stayed single.

Seven

The Life Spirit

In the 1995 Cherokee election for principal chief, Joe Byrd was elected to succeed Wilma Mankiller following George Bearpaw's disqualification. Wilma, confronted with a dilemma over whether or not to support Byrd, finally decided to decline an invitation to attend his inauguration. She feared that his rival's disqualification, due to an expunged conviction of assault, had been illegal.

Fearing that Byrd would fire in retribution the staff she had hired, the outgoing chief authorized severance packages for the workers in her final days in office. Byrd quickly filed a lawsuit on behalf of the Cherokee Nation to block the severance pay, charging Wilma with embezzlement of tribal funds of $300,000 paid out to tribal officials and department heads who left at the end of her term in 1995. The suit, *Cherokee Nation v. Mankiller*, was subsequently withdrawn by a vote of the tribal council.

Later, reflecting on her years as chief, Wilma said, "We've had daunting problems in many critical areas, but I believe in the old Cherokee injunction to 'be of a good mind.' Today it's called positive thinking."[1]

By the time Mankiller left office, the population of the Cherokee Nation had increased from 68,000 to 170,000 citizens. Mostly, these were certifiable Cherokee Natives who had never bothered to be counted before. By instilling within her people a newfound pride in their indigenous heritage, she encouraged them to come forward to create a more accurate tally of the number of Cherokees living in the country. Wilma also increased annual tribe revenue to nearly $25 million from a variety of sources, including proceeds from manufactured goods, retail-store sales, restaurants, and bingo operations. She had secured federal assistance of $125 million annually to promote numerous education, health, housing, and employment programs. After obtaining the tribe's grant for "self-governance," she minimized the amount of federal oversight of tribal funds, granting more autonomy to the people.

Meanwhile, Byrd's administration became embroiled in a constitutional crisis that he attempted to blame on Wilma, charging that her failure to attend his inauguration and lack of mentoring had divided the tribe and left him without experienced advisors. His supporters also alleged that Mankiller was behind attempts to remove him from office, a contention that she flatly denied.

For the most part, despite flying allegations, Wilma remained silent on Byrd's administration in the name of tribal unity. Even after several months of his indignities, she was determined to allow the Cherokee Nation to sort through its problems on its own. In response to calls for federal intervention, Wilma and Swimmer traveled to Washington to ask that federal authorities keep a hands-off policy toward Native affairs. They wanted Washington to allow the tribe to sort out its own problems. Despite calls from US Secretary of the Interior Bruce Babbitt for congressional intervention and from Oklahoma Senator Jim Inhofe for presidential intercession, Wilma insisted that the problem was one of inexperienced leadership, in which she was determined to remain removed.

When an independent group of legal analysts, known as the Massad Commission, was assembled in 1997 to evaluate the problems in Byrd's administration, Mankiller, despite her ongoing health concerns, was called upon and appeared before the commission to testify. She repeated at the hearings that she believed the problems stemmed from poor advisors and the new chief's lack of political experience. Determined to force Byrd to resolve his own issues within the tribe, she may have turned the other cheek a little too soon.

In January 1996, Byrd agreed to hire a law firm in which his brother-in-law, Terry Barker, was one of the partners. The firm was enlisted to work on an hourly basis, representing Cherokee Nation Industries (CNI) in a dispute with a defense contractor, Stewart & Stevenson Industries,

Inc. (S&S) of Houston, Texas. In May 1996, Barker's law firm filed a federal suit against S&S for breach of contract. By October, the Byrd-affiliated law firm had accrued $54,000 in unpaid hourly fees to CNI and $59,000 more to the Cherokee Nation. On October 24, the CNI leadership signed a contingency agreement with Barker's law firm that granted the firm 37.5 percent of any proceeds from the S&S litigation settlement. Later that same evening, CNI and S&S reached an agreement, with S&S agreeing to pay CNI $1.86 million. Later court filings suggest that Terry Barker, and possibly Joe Byrd himself, knew about the probable settlement with S&S *before* CNI signed the contingency agreement to the Nation's detriment. Despite the agreement limiting Barker's law firm to 37.5 percent of the settlement, the firm juggled the books to receive $894,000, or nearly half of the total settlement.

The less-than-ordinary activities and business dealings of Byrd disturbed many tribal council members. Throughout the summer of 1996, the newly elected chief ignored requests and directives from the tribal council for financial statements and documents. That same summer, Pat Ragsdale, director of the Cherokee Nation Marshal Service, was directed to investigate allegations of corruption against Joel Thompson, Byrd's friend, confidant, and election campaign manager. Several other members of Byrd's administration also came under investigation. The allegations ranged from illegal wiretapping activities on Cherokee Nation premises to diversion of tribal funds and illegal campaign-fund tampering.

Tensions between Byrd and the tribal council increased over Byrd's continued refusal to comply with directives to disclose critical contracts and documents related to Cherokee Nation funds. In August 1996, the tribal council petitioned the Cherokee Nation Justice Appeals Tribunal (JAT) for access to the requested materials from Byrd. The JAT ruled that all of Byrd's documents detailing any Cherokee Nation dealings were subject to review by the tribal council and by any Cherokee Nation citizen as per the Cherokee Nation Constitution. Despite the ruling, Byrd failed to produce the documents.

Faced with his refusal to cooperate, tribal prosecutor Diane Blalock obtained a search warrant for Byrd's headquarters, and on February 25, 1997, tribal marshals raided Byrd's offices, making copies of several documents and seizing others. In retaliation, Byrd fired Director Pat Ragsdale and Sharon Wright of the Cherokee Nation Marshal Service. One hour later, Cherokee Nation Justice Dwight Birdwell ordered their immediate reinstatement. Justice Birdwell also issued a standing order stating that any subsequent firings by Byrd would be considered contempt of court and obstruction of justice.

Byrd then fired Ragsdale, Wright, and the entire Cherokee Nation Marshal Service. He later fired Prosecutor Blalock, who had by then filed obstruction of justice and misappropriation of funds charges against Byrd. As a replacement for the now "fired" marshals, Byrd requested that the Bureau of Indian Affairs (BIA) assume all law-enforcement duties for the Cherokee Nation. He also established a new security force made up of individuals who had signified their loyalty to him.

Byrd announced that he had requested an FBI investigation of Cherokee Nation Tribal Council members, marshals, and justices because they were plotting to overthrow his administration. He also hired criminal defense attorneys who filed appeal briefs with the Cherokee Nation courts in defense of Byrd. The briefs sought a stay of the warrants, stating that the tribal council was "plundering and pilfering" the evidence seized in the search warrants. Byrd also directed his criminal defense attorneys to file motions demanding the suppression of his financial dealings, which had been seized as evidence. Byrd stated to the Cherokee Nation court that he and his associates had been conducting wiretaps of Cherokee Nation employees, government officials, and the courts that provided concrete evidence of the Cherokee Nation justices' plots, information he purported to have sent to the FBI.

The Cherokee Nation court found Byrd in contempt and cautioned him against attempting to fire the Cherokee Nation marshals during an ongoing investigation. Byrd responded by attempting to shut off power and water to the Cherokee Nation Marshals Complex but was stopped by order of Justice Birdwell.

On March 7, 1997, US Attorney John Raley, in conjunction with the FBI, announced an investigation into Byrd's activities and the events that had occurred at the Cherokee Nation Tribal Complex. The FBI seized the tapes that were produced as the result of Byrd's illegal wiretaps. After reviewing the recordings and interviewing numerous Cherokee Nation officials at the tribal complex, the FBI concluded that Byrd's allegations were without merit and closed the case. The matter of Byrd's diversion of funds was turned over to the Cherokee Nation Justice Courts for resolution, although the US Attorney's office, working with the BIA, continued investigating Byrd's activities.

On April 15, 1997, after Byrd was indicted by the Cherokee Nation Justice Courts for obstruction of justice and misuse of funds, he drafted articles of impeachment of the Cherokee Nation court justices before proceeding to the tribal council chambers, where eight of the total fifteen council members were assembled. Although the council was without a quorum, Byrd ordered the councilors to approve the impeachment of the Cherokee Nation court justices. He also ordered the councilors to vote for ratification and relinquishment of sovereign authority to the BIA for purposes of law enforcement within the Cherokee Nation. On April 24, 1997, the BIA ordered its law-enforcement personnel to assume control of law enforcement responsibilities within the Cherokee Nation.

On May 21, 1997, Byrd shut off power and other utilities to the Cherokee Nation Justice Complex, fired the justices, and ordered his security forces to board up the courthouse. In response, the Cherokee Nation justices issued warrants for his arrest. The Cherokee Nation petitioned the federal courts for BIA officers to confiscate the weapons of Byrd's security force. The federal judge declined to rule, stating that the Cherokee Nation would be required to relinquish total sovereignty before federal troops could be sent into the Nation to confiscate weapons. Byrd subsequently ordered the shutdown of the Cherokee Nation courts. His security forces, along with those of the BIA, forcibly evicted the justices from the courthouse.

In August 1997, Byrd was summoned to Washington, DC, for a meeting with Attorney General Janet Reno and Secretary of the Interior Bruce Babbitt. After several days of negotiations, Byrd signed an agreement relinquishing control of the Cherokee Nation law enforcement system to the Bureau of Indian Affairs. By late September, the Cherokee Nation courts were reopened, and the Cherokee Nation Marshal Service was reinstated.

During the Cherokee National Holiday (Labor Day weekend) 1997, Oklahoma SWAT teams with high-powered rifles and BIA helicopters patrolled tribal lands. These actions were later characterized by Joe Byrd's administration in court filings to be necessary to quell an "uprising" of the Cherokee people.

The remaining years of Byrd's term were marked with heightened scrutiny by the BIA. By late 1998, eleven active cases remained open against him, including two criminal charges regarding diversion of federal funds. In early 1998, Byrd moved the district court out of the tribal courthouse. In reaction, six members of the tribal council began boycotting scheduled council meetings, thus leaving the council without a quorum and therefore unable to act. After a yearlong standoff, Byrd capitulated and moved the district court back to the courthouse.

Byrd's 1996–97 actions also had a significant impact on the Cherokee Nation's 1999 Constitutional Convention. During public hearings, there was a strong push for procedures allowing for the recall of elected officials, a call for open financial records of the Nation's government, and a desire to strengthen the power and independence of the judiciary.

When Byrd ran for reelection in 1999, he was defeated by Chad "Corntassel" Smith in the Cherokee Nation elections. After the election, more than four years of transition were required to restore the Cherokee Nation government and remove BIA intervention from the affairs of the Nation.

Meanwhile, after her term as chief had ended in 1996, Wilma Mankiller became a visiting professor at Dartmouth College, where she taught in the Native American Studies program, being honored with the Elizabeth Blackwell Award from Hobart and William Smith Colleges for her exemplary service to humanity. An article in the *New York Times* summarized the appointment on January 3, 1996.

Wilma Mankiller, the former Principal Chief of the Cherokee Nation, arrives at Dartmouth College in Hanover, N.H., today to begin a nine-week appointment as a scholar in residence. In addition to teaching women's studies, Native American studies and law, she plans to hold informal dinner discussions and will give a public address, "Will

Native Americans Enter the 21st Century on Our Own Terms?," on Jan. 23. This schedule may provide something of a respite for her.

Last year, Ms. Mankiller, 50, declined to run for a third term as chief, a position that also required her to be the chief executive of Cherokee Nation Industries, which owns factories, a motel, a ranch and a lumber company.

"I felt it was time for a change for me and for the tribe, and part of the change is to spend time reflecting on the past 25 years," Ms. Mankiller said. "Either I've been an activist, community developer or elected official. I've never had a period of reflection, and it's an opportunity for me to share with other folks."

At Dartmouth, she will explore aspects of her culture, from the history of the Cherokee Nation to maintaining ancient spiritual values within a modern tribal corporation. "It's a little esoteric," she said. "As the Iroquois say, when leaders make decisions they should think of seven generations in front of them, and seven generations in back of them—and the impact of their decisions."

Her law classes will focus on the history of "government to government relations between the United States Government and tribes," from the Trail of Tears in the 1830's, when the Cherokees were forced to move hundreds of miles west from their homeland in what is now the Carolinas and Georgia, to the development of casinos on Indian lands.

Following her year at Dartmouth, Wilma embarked upon a national lecture circuit, speaking on health care, tribal sovereignty, women's rights, and cancer awareness. She addressed various civic organizations, spoke at tribal gatherings and universities, and talked to several women's groups. But amid her tour, life once again took a sharp detour for the former Cherokee Nation chief. The *Daily Oklahoman* detailed the detour in a February 29, 1996, article:

Wilma Mankiller said Wednesday from a Boston hospital that she has lymphoma and is undergoing tests to determine how far the cancer has spread and what type of treatment will be required.

"I have been undergoing tests. There is a form of lymphoma staging. We are doing tests to determine where it is at and how extensive it is," Mankiller, former Principal Chief of the Cherokee Nation, told the Tulsa World *for a story in Thursday's editions.*

Mankiller said her family would issue a statement on her condition Friday. Mankiller was admitted to Deaconess Hospital in Boston last weekend when she failed to improve from a recent bout with pneumonia, said Linda Welch, academic assistant for Native American Studies at Dartmouth College in Hanover, N.H., where Mankiller is teaching.

"We're all quite concerned for her," Welch said. "She had a severe case of pneumonia and a kidney infection earlier this month, and she was feeling weaker, so she decided she should see a doctor she has confidence in."

Mankiller said her husband, Charlie Soap, and two daughters have left Oklahoma to be at her bedside.

"We want to be together when we find out" the extent of the cancer, Mankiller said.

She described herself as being "in a good frame of mind. I feel real strong spiritually, and I am going to be optimistic."

Mankiller served as chief from 1985 to 1995, when she chose not to seek re-election.

She said last summer that her health was a factor in that decision.[2]

Test results came back days later. The news was not good. Doctors found inoperable cancer in her colon and nearby lymph nodes. In a press release, Mankiller said from her hospital room in Boston that the lymphoma was a complication from her 1990 kidney transplant.

"While it wasn't the best possible news from a patient's perspective," she said, "I feel positive. I feel fine, but the past week certainly has been a roller coaster ride. My priority right now is to live, and I intend to do just that." Mankiller, 50, said the cancer was inoperable because of its location and growth into the muscle tissue. A statement released by Mankiller and her former press liaison, Lynn Howard of Tahlequah,

Sequoyah, inventor of the
Cherokee alphabet

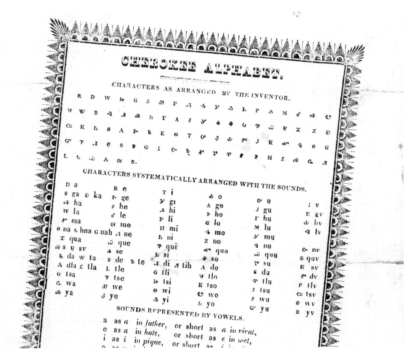

A copy of the Cherokee alphabet, devised by Sequoyah to enable the Cherokee to communicate in writing as well as orally

Cherokee boy practicing Native alphabet

First elected Cherokee principal chief John Ross

The Cherokee Female Seminary, one of several facilities for Native American use near Wilma Mankiller's Oklahoma birthplace

The Cherokee Nation capitol building in Tahlequah, Oklahoma, where official Cherokee governmental business is conducted

Building housing the Cherokee Supreme Court, the top judiciary authority in the Cherokee Nation

The Cherokee Heritage Center serves as a meeting and gathering place for the dissemination of information of interest to members of the Cherokee Nation.

Informal portrait of Clara Irene Sitton Mankiller, Wilma's mother

Wilma Mankiller and her husband, Charlie Soap, at her swearing-in ceremony as principal chief of the Cherokee Nation

WILMA MANKILLER FOUNDATION

View of Alcatraz Island facilities from the mainland around San Francisco

Edited Alcatraz Island sign reflecting Indian sentiments regarding the island's reversion back to Native Americans

Alcatraz Island, former federal penitentiary and, later, site of two Native American take-overs, one of which lasted for more than eighteen months
INTERNATIONAL FEATURES SYNDICATE

Dennis Banks and Russell Means, two "militant" Native American activists who participated in the Alcatraz takeover and protests at Wounded Knee, South Dakota
NATIONAL PORTRAIT GALLERY, SMITHSONIAN INSTITUTION

Gruesome photo of the "Bureal [*sic*] of the Dead at the Battle of Wounded Knee S.D." depicting mass grave for Native Americans killed there

Painted portrait of Native American activist Russell Means by artist Bob Coronato

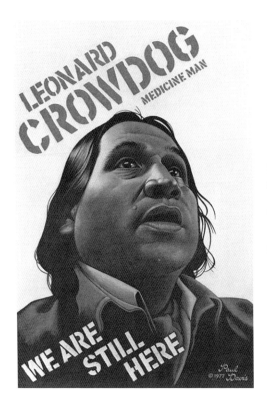

Leonard Crow Dog, medicine man and spiritualist best known for his participation in the takeover of Wounded Knee, South Dakota
NATIONAL PORTRAIT GALLERY, SMITHSONIAN INSTITUTION

John Trudell, Native American activist and close friend and advisor to Wilma Mankiller.
PHOTO BY AUTHOR

Gloria Steinem, activist/author and one of Wilma Mankiller's strongest supporters throughout her political lifetime.
PUBLIC DOMAIN

Gloria Steinem and Dorothy Pitman Hughes, social activists and co-founders of *Ms.* magazine
NATIONAL PORTRAIT GALLERY, SMITHSONIAN INSTITUTION

Native American activist
Ada Deer

Ada Deer, Native American activist named Assistant Secretary of the Interior in charge
of the BIA

President Bill Clinton awards Wilma Mankiller the Presidential Medal of Freedom, the highest US civilian award available.

Wilma Mankiller, who once made the "most watched" list of the Federal Bureau of
Investigation (FBI)

Felicia Olaya-Mankiller during the filming of a documentary about her mother titled *Mankiller* by Gale Anne Hurd and Valerie Red-Horse Mohl

WILMA MANKILLER FOUNDATION

The headstone marking the grave of Wilma Mankiller
INTERNATIONAL FEATURES SYNDICATE

said Mankiller would begin treatments that included radiation and chemotherapy at Deaconess Hospital in Boston.[3]

The paper went on to say that the diagnosis of lymphoma, a tumor-related disease of the lymphatic system, forced doctors to take Mankiller off a medication that helps keep her body from rejecting her previously transplanted kidney. Although she'd been advised in 1990 that transplant patients often develop that type of lymphoma because of their compromised immune system, she felt she had little recourse. "But you're given a set of choices, and you make the best possible decision for the time and the place. That's what I did," she said. "I don't regret for a moment the course I chose in 1990."

Wilma went on to admit that her failing health had played a decision in her choosing not to seek reelection to the office of chief the previous term. It had also kept her out of the fray between Byrd and his Cherokee constituents.[4]

Following treatment over the next several months, Wilma was back on the trail in 1996, speaking to students at Northeastern State University in Tahlequah to join in her quest to preserve the heritage, language, and traditions of Native Americans. She spoke during an observance of American Indian heritage, giving her first speech since her return to Oklahoma.

"We need a country full of young, educated Native American people," she said. "Be proud of who you are as a native person." She added that she saw her job evolve into one to "warn people about our heritage, language and background. I need help from you all."

She said that after returning to her rural Adair County home following treatment out East, "I feel good. Actually, I feel as well as I could be." She alluded to her past as a leader of the Cherokees and to her ongoing battles with various health issues, including her recovery from a near-fatal automobile accident and her diagnosis of a muscular disorder called myasthenia gravis and later lymphoma.

But those, she said, are only temporary barriers in life that should be seen as challenges to overcome. "I've managed to survive cancer. I've managed to survive a kidney transplant. I've managed to get elected as a female chief of our tribe three times . . . but I've never looked at the things that didn't work as failures."[5]

She had said at a Tulsa news conference in September that she was weak but was free of lymphoma symptoms. The former chief urged her audience to have a sense of community and to care for others.

Never content with resting upon her laurels, Wilma was soon back at work, again, promoting a better lifestyle for her people. Her work did not go unnoticed. In 1998, President Clinton, who had admired Mankiller for years, awarded her the Presidential Medal of Freedom. At the ceremony at the White House on January 15, 1998, Wilma arrived wearing a green blazer, black slacks and blouse, and feather-shaped earrings. She stepped onto a small stage in the East Room to ringing applause. The president put the medal around her neck after a citation was read praising her for bringing "opportunity, a higher standard of living, improved health care and quality education to Native Americans."

Wilma, visibly touched, said later, "To be recognized by the United States for my work is just an unbelievable honor." She accepted the medal, she said, "not only for myself, but for all Native Americans. I loved every single day of my work. It's kind of interesting to receive an award for something you love doing. It's like giving a bird an award for singing or an artist an award for painting."

She acknowledged in a thinly disguised reference to Chief Joe Byrd and his corruption-riddled administration that the problems plaguing the tribe's leadership in the past year "have diverted people from the real work, which is providing services to Cherokee people and for people acting as an advocate for Cherokee citizens as well. It's an unfortunate period of time."

Afterward, she added that following "a lot of radiation and chemotherapy," she believed her cancer was in remission. Asked if she was working, she said at first she wasn't. "Yeah, I guess I am busy, but not at the pace I was earlier." She acknowledged that despite the achievements for which she was honored, American Indians continued to face a daunting set of problems: "There's still a lot of needs in health care and housing and education and, in many cases, just basic amenities that I think every

American should have. So, while we've made some progress, I think we still have an awful long way to go."[6]

Also in 1998, Wilma was invited to be the keynote speaker at the American Indian Law Review Annual Conference. But her failing health precluded her attendance, so she sent an open letter to the conference in her place. Titled "Tribal Sovereignty Is a Sacred Trust," it expressed her feelings about her work and life in general:

Dear Friends:

I deeply regret my inability to join you for this important conference. My health is precarious and unpredictable. Yet I remain hopeful that I will ultimately regain reasonably good health again.

I have looked forward to this conference for months. I have been involved in tribal rights and sovereignty issues for almost 30 years and have observed enormous changes in both the public perception of tribal sovereignty and changes in how the judicial system views tribal sovereignty. The only constant I have seen during the past thirty years is a continual attempt to erode the strength of tribal governments by the legislature and by the courts. Tribal communities and govern-ments were under siege at the turn of the century and they remain under siege as we approach the millennium.

When I began working on tribal sovereignty, we were mostly concerned with issues involving land, water rights and fishing rights. When visionaries like Richard Oakes, Oren Lyons and Tom Porter spoke of sovereignty, they always reminded us that our ancestors had fought very hard for us to remain together as distinct tribal groups, as Indian Nations. Protecting tribal sovereignty then became a sacred trust of each generation.

The tribe that I worked for in the late 1960s took the position that they did not need federal recognition because they did not recognize the United States. They were a part of the international community of governments. Therefore, many of us were surprised when various Indian lawyers initiated litigation conceding that the US Congress had plenary power over Indian nations. Now, unfortunately the notion that Congress has plenary power over tribes is accepted as conventional wisdom. And we find ourselves facing a Congress that is increasingly hostile to tribal governments.

It is imperative that Indian nations collectively develop a proactive strategy to protect tribal governments. It is not enough to wait to see where the next attack will come from. Indian nations have to initiate measures that will strengthen and support tribal governments.

Finally, let me repeat what I was told decades ago: "tribal sovereignty is a sacred trust." Our ancestors who spoke so eloquently of our history and culture are gone now. Their voices have been lost in time. They can no longer speak for themselves or the people. It then is our duty as Indian people to always remember our responsibility to speak for those who cannot speak for themselves. We have given up way too much . . . from this day forward we must pledge not to allow any more of our rights to be eroded, we must not be moved a single inch, not a single inch.

Wado.

Wilma P. Mankiller[7]

The letter was widely praised, expressing the sentiments of the vast majority of Native American representatives at the conference. Not long afterward, Wilma had a second kidney failure and received a second transplant—this time from her niece Virlee Williamson. As before, she immediately returned to work, resuming her lecture tours while continuing her writing and editing four books. In 1999, she was diagnosed with breast cancer and underwent a double-lumpectomy followed by radiation treatment. That same year, *The Reader's Companion to US Women's History*, which Mankiller coedited, was published.

In 2002, Wilma contributed to the book *That Takes Ovaries! Bold Females and Their Brazen Acts*, and in 2004, she coauthored *Every Day Is a Good Day: Reflections by Contemporary Indigenous Women*. The following year, she worked with the Oklahoma Breast Cancer Summit to encourage early screening and raise awareness of the disease.

In 2006, when, along with other Native American leaders, Wilma was asked to send a pair of shoes to the Heard Museum for the exhibit

Sole Stories: American Indian Footwear, she provided a simple pair of walking shoes. She chose the shoes because she had worn them all over the world, including trips from Brazil to China, and because they conveyed the normalcy of her life, her durability, steadfastness, and determination. Other tribal members were firebrands and rebels and protestors; for Wilma Mankiller, the "slow-and-steady" approach was the one that would win the race.

In 2007, Wilma gave the Centennial Lecture in the Humanities for Oklahoma's 100th anniversary of statehood. Following that, she was honored with the inaugural Oklahoma Humanities Award by the Oklahoma Humanities Council. She continued her lecture tours and scholarship, and in September 2009, accepted the title of first Sequoyah Institute Fellow at Northeastern State University.

Things were going well, and they would continue to do so for the girl named Wilma Pearl from the small, rural community of Mankiller Flats. At least they would until the bottom fell out. The following year, on Wednesday, March 2, 2010, staff reporter Shannon Muchmore wrote in an article in the *Tulsa World* newspaper:

> *Wilma Mankiller, the first female chief of the Cherokee Nation and a Presidential Medal of Freedom winner, is gravely ill with stage IV pancreatic cancer, her husband confirmed Tuesday.*
>
> *Mankiller, 64, was principal chief from 1985 until 1995, when she did not seek re-election because of health problems. She issued a statement from the Cherokee Nation and husband Charlie Soap on Tuesday evening: "I want my family and friends to know that I am mentally and spiritually prepared for this journey; a journey that all human beings will take at one time or another. I learned a long time ago that I can't control the challenges the Creator sends my way but I can control the way I think about them and deal with them. On balance, I have been blessed with an extraordinarily rich and wonderful life, filled with incredible experiences."*[8]

Among those experiences was an awakening within a dozing Native American community to the fact that America's indigenous people didn't have to accept the crumbs thrown out to the dregs of society. They were far from dregs, as they proved time and again at Wilma's gentle prodding, and they deserved—in fact, *demanded*—far more than crumbs. They were an independent people, separate from those people who traversed the ocean to populate a newly discovered land—at *any* cost. These Native people were, in fact, the first owner-occupants of the lands that the Europeans stumbled upon to claim as their own. Unskilled in organized governments, unwise in the workings of Manifest Destiny, unaware of the sinister nature of these visitors from a faraway place, America's Native American population believed, as they had always believed, that there was room for everyone to coexist.

They saw no sudden infiltration of people. They witnessed no violent takeovers of large swaths of land. They knew no reason to begrudge a few strangers from a distant place beyond the rise of the moon a peaceful coexistence. In turn, they expected nothing less from the visitors, their guests. And thus, they feared no one, and they begrudged nothing.

They were mistaken in doing so. By the time the Indians awakened to their relegation to a position of second-class citizenry—or, worse, no citizenry at all—they were too late to change things.

Almost.

When Wilma Pearl Mankiller, that most unassuming and unprepossessing advocate of equal rights for all human beings everywhere, was awakened from her own hibernation toward the end of a long, cold, bitter winter, she roared. When she realized that the yearnings within her were not hers uniquely but shared by countless other Native Americans, in fact by downtrodden classes of people everywhere, she was elated. She was rejuvenated. She was enlightened and empowered and emboldened.

Would humankind have been awakened to progress down a different path had it not been for the first woman to be elected principal chief of a major tribal nation? Perhaps, but again perhaps not.

The fact that Wilma Mankiller wore the mantle of her power so gracefully and unobtrusively is a lesson for us all. The fact that she held no grudges, hated no one or nothing short of bigotry and abuse of power, and never acted out of malice or spite is inspirational. Could she have accomplished more if she'd had the radicalism inside her of an Ada Deer or a Vine Deloria Jr.? Or a John Trudell or a LaNada Boyer Means? Or perhaps even a Russell Means or a Dennis Banks? Is it fair even to ask?

After all, how much can one person be expected to do? How much is enough without being too much? How high is the mountain, and how deep is the sea?

For Wilma Pearl Mankiller, the mountain was just high enough to climb and the sea, just deep enough to traverse. No more, no less.

Activist/feminist/author Gloria Steinem once wrote, "Wilma Mankiller became the best kind of leader: one who creates independence, not dependence, who helps people go back to a collective broken place and begin to heal themselves. Though there is a long way to go before the Cherokee Nation restores in a new form the dignity and self-sufficiency it knew 500 years ago, before the terrible centuries of genocide and the banning of even the Cherokee language and religion, now there is a way of making progress that is their own."[9]

The Mankiller approach to problem-solving, as to life itself, has been evident for generations. Wilma's father possessed it and practiced it, as did his father and, most likely, his father before him. Steinem recognized it in Wilma's book *Every Day Is a Good Day: Reflections by Contemporary Indigenous Women*, writing of it in an introduction to the volume titled "Wheels over Indian Trails":

> *Wilma Mankiller has brought together wise voices in a conversation about the things for which we long the most: Community, a sense of belonging in the universal scheme of things, support from kin and friends, feeling valued as we are. Balance, between people and nature, women and men, youth and age, people of different skills and colors, past and present and future. Peaceful ways of resolving differences, sitting in a circle, listening and talking, a consensus that is more important than the time it takes. Being of good mind, a positive out-look that energizes positive words and actions. Circle as paradigm, a full range of human qualities in each of us, equal value of different tasks, reciprocity, a way of thinking that goes beyond either/or and hierarchy. Spirituality, the mystery in all living things, the greatest*

and smallest, and therefore, the origin of balance, a good mind, peace, community.

I suspect we are all drawn to these lifeways. They may be in our DNA from the 95 percent of human history in which they were common, before patriarchy made hierarchy seem natural. I know we are suffering without them. Kids deprived of community create gangs, adults without talking circles create conflict, people without balance "conquer" nature and so defeat themselves, and cultures without spirituality consign it to life after death.[10]

Wilma recognized this view of life, too. As if the young, displaced girl from the middle of nowhere thrust into the big-city life of San Francisco with no warning, no preparation, and no understanding of what was happening to her could have failed. As if she might have accomplished more under different circumstances. That's a notion that begs the questions: How much more? And would it have made a difference? And, in particular, why Wilma? After all, numerous Native American women feel conflicted. How is it that she succeeded where others had failed or even refused to recognize their conflict?

She answered that herself, when she said:

Feeling firmly rooted in my own sense of tribalism and my own culture keeps me strong and able to share with women no matter what their racial, cultural, or economic background. Because I feel very Cherokee and have a strong sense of self and history, I'm more able to interact with other tribes and women of other races. Now, at my home at Mankiller Flats, surrounded by my books, my art, my grandchildren, and the natural world, I realize that my journey has indeed brought me to the place where I was destined to be. As I sit by a winter fire or walk to the spring where my family has gone for generations or rest on the porch where the walkingsticks like to come to munch on redbud leaves, I often think about my past and the history of my people.[11]

Prejudice, insecurity, bigotry, and confusion may well be part of society until society itself comes to an end and no more people exist to exercise their biases and aggrandize their fears. Who can say? But one thing is certain: Wilma Pearl Mankiller walked the face of this earth for too short a time and accomplished more than any other indigenous person of Native American ancestry before or since. And she reinstated the independence and dignity of the first local governments ever convened in North America long before others showed up, intent upon supplanting them.

And today, Native Americans everywhere are better off for what she brought to them.

Her gift?

Their very right to life.

Two Wolves

An old Cherokee is teaching his grandson about life. "A fight is going on inside me," he said to the boy. "It is a terrible fight, and it is between two wolves. One is evil—he has anger, envy, sorrow, regret, greed, arrogance, self-pity, guilt, resentment, inferiority, lies, false pride, superiority, and ego." He continued, "The other is good—he has joy, peace, love, hope, serenity, humility, kindness, benevolence, empathy, generosity, truth, compassion, and faith. The same fight is going on inside you—and inside every other person, too."

The grandson thought about it for a minute and then asked his grandfather, "Which wolf will win?"

The old Cherokee replied simply, "The one you feed."

EIGHT

A God Named Forever

On March 2, 2010, Charlie Soap confirmed that the first female chief of the Cherokee Nation was "gravely ill with Stage IV pancreatic cancer."[1]

Those were the last words issued on the stoic warrior and civil rights battler Wilma Pearl Mankiller. Little more than one month later, on April 6, 2010, Charlie announced with tears in his eyes that his wife, with whom he had worked and for whom he had cared so profoundly for more than thirty years, had passed on to another place.

Worldwide reaction flooded the media. Brian Williams on *NBC Nightly News* led off his April 6 report: "A genuine American trailblazer has died. Wilma Mankiller was the first woman to lead the Cherokee Native American tribe. Under her leadership, the tribe grew. Many of its members prospered with jobs, health care, and programs for their children. She received the Medal of Freedom, the highest civilian honor, back in 1998. Wilma Mankiller had pancreatic cancer. She was sixty-four years old."

Michael Martin on NPR's *Tell Me More* broke the story to his audience: "Some sad news. Wilma Mankiller, the former principal chief of the Cherokee Nation, passed away yesterday after a battle with pancreatic cancer. She was sixty-four. Mankiller made history in 1985 when she became the Cherokee Nation's first female chief. She went on to become one of the country's most high-profile Native American leaders."

In addition, hundreds of other luminaries who had known Wilma over the years offered their thoughts on her life, her times, her work:

"Wilma Mankiller broke down all barriers as the first female Cherokee chief, and her legacy will continue for generations to come. She overcame many obstacles and never backed down to a challenge, which serves as a lesson to all of us as we seek to make our state a better place for all its people. My thoughts and prayers are with her friends and family during this difficult time."—Oklahoma Speaker of the House Chris Benge, R-Tulsa

"Chief Wilma Mankiller brought honor to Oklahoma and the Cherokee tribe through her leadership, not only within our state and among tribal leaders, but certainly her influence was felt across our nation. She leaves a legacy of service that will be sorely missed by all."—Oklahoma State Senate President Pro Tempore Glenn Coffee, R-Oklahoma City

"She was a pioneer for her generation, and for the generations of women to follow. It would be hard to overstate what a great role model she was, not only as a woman and a Cherokee, but as a leader and a public servant. Her death is a loss for all Oklahomans."—Oklahoma State House Leader Danny Morgan, D-Prague

"All Oklahomans and every Native American who knew her mourn the passing of Wilma Mankiller. Chief Mankiller was not only the first woman to serve as principal chief of the Cherokee Nation, she was a national icon and role model for women and Native Americans everywhere. Her strong, visionary and principled leadership set a standard seldom equaled and never to be surpassed. She was tough, shrewd and dedicated to the well-being of the Cherokee Nation and all Native Americans. No one more fiercely defended the concept of tribal sovereignty, yet no one was more willing to partner with others of different backgrounds and points of view than Wilma Mankiller. My deepest sympathies go out to her family, the people of the Cherokee Nation, and all her many friends and admirers. We'll not soon see her like again."—US Representative Tom Cole, R-Moore

"She was a unique force for change and progress, not only in the Native American community in Oklahoma, but in the whole country. All Oklahomans should be proud of her accomplishments."—US Representative Frank Lucas, R-Cheyenne

"Chief Wilma Mankiller was a legendary figure in the Cherokee Tribe and the state of Oklahoma. Her desire to serve her tribe both broke barriers and was a shining example of compassion and dedication. As her family and those closest to her bear the tragedy of her passing, Andrea and my thoughts and prayers are with them during this time of loss."—US Representative Dan Boren, D-Muskogee

"Oklahoma has lost a legend. Chief Mankiller was a true trailblazer in our state's history, as well as an esteemed and revered leader of her tribe. Her leadership is an inspiration to us all, reminding us to challenge the status quo and overcome barriers for the betterment of our neighbors, our communities and our nation as a whole. My thoughts and prayers are with her family and many, many friends."—US Representative Mary Fallin, R-Oklahoma City

"She was a good friend and a really good leader . . . a neat lady."—US Senator Tom Coburn, R-Oklahoma

"On behalf of all Interior employees, and especially those in Indian Affairs who knew and worked with Wilma, I want to extend our heartfelt sympathy and prayers to her family for their comfort and peace. Throughout her long career of advocating the best for her people, and all of Indian Country, Wilma was a shining example of courage and leadership for all Americans. We will miss her dearly, but we know that her spirit and example live on, encouraging all American Indians to stand up for what they believe in and to step up and accept the challenge of serving in leadership roles."—US Interior Secretary Ken Salazar

"The news of Wilma's passing has deeply touched all of us here at Interior and throughout Indian Country who knew her as a leader, friend or colleague. She willingly reached out beyond her tribal community and Indian Country in search of solutions to the social and economic challenges facing the Cherokee people, while sharing her knowledge and insights with anyone who needed them. We honor her with our gratitude for all she has contributed in service to her people and to Indian Country."—Larry Echo Hawk, Assistant Secretary for Indian Affairs

"Wilma Mankiller was a role model for women and for Native Americans. When speaking, she could hold an audience mesmerized for hours because she knew her community well, knew politics and ultimately knew humanity. She was a very wise person."—Lee Hester, Director of American Indian Studies at the University of Science and Arts of Oklahoma, Chickasha

"She was an inspirational leader. She was one of only a small number of women who were tribal leaders at the time. It made it more acceptable to a larger number of people, helping show the powerful position women hold in American Indian society."—Michael Darrow, Tribal Historian for the Fort Sill Apache Tribe

"We have lost a great leader and inspiration. Much of what we have is part of Chief Mankiller's legacy."—Quapaw Chairman John Berrey

"We are so blessed to have had the privilege to work alongside Wilma Mankiller as part of the NSU community. Her contributions as an advocate for Native American and indigenous peoples worldwide, and her commitment to the role of women in leadership, will continue to inspire individuals in all walks of life and have impact beyond our lifetimes."—Don Betz, President of Northeastern State University, Tahlequah[2]

On April 7, 2010, the day following Wilma's death, the *Oklahoman*, Wilma's adopted hometown paper, ran a tribute to the Cherokee leader:

More than a month before her death Tuesday morning at age 64, Wilma Pearl Mankiller issued a remarkable public statement. Time was running out for Mankiller, the first woman to serve as principal chief of the Cherokee Nation. Pancreatic cancer, an implacable killer, was eating away at her body, but it had not claimed her formidable mind. That much was evident in her March 2 remarks, aimed at comforting the many who loved her. "I want my family and friends to know that I am mentally and spiritually prepared for this journey; a journey that all human beings will take at one time or another," she said in the statement. "I learned a long time ago that I can't control the challenges the Creator sends my way but I can control the way I think about them and deal with them.

"On balance, I have been blessed with an extraordinarily rich and wonderful life, filled with incredible experiences. . . . It's been my privilege to meet and be touched by thousands of people in my life and

I regret not being able to deliver this message personally to so many of you."

In a statement Tuesday, April 6, 2010, President Barack Obama said he was "deeply saddened" by Mankiller's death. "As the Cherokee Nation's first female chief, she transformed the nation-to-nation relationship between the Cherokee Nation and the federal government, and served as an inspiration to women in Indian Country and across America," Obama said. "A recipient of the Presidential Medal of Freedom, she was recognized for her vision and commitment to a brighter future for all Americans. Her legacy will continue to encourage and motivate all who carry on her work."

Gov. Brad Henry called her "an inspirational leader and a great American, someone who was truly a legend in her own time.

"As a leader and a person," Henry said, "Chief Wilma Mankiller continually defied the odds and overcame seemingly insurmountable obstacles to better her tribe, her state and her nation. Oklahoma, the Cherokee Nation and the United States will dearly miss Wilma and her visionary leadership, but her words and deeds will live on forever to benefit future generations."

Chad Smith, principal chief of the Cherokee Nation, expressed sadness. "We feel overwhelmed and lost when we realize she has left us but we should reflect on what legacy she leaves us. We are better people and a stronger tribal nation because of her example of Cherokee leadership, statesmanship, humility, grace, determination and decisiveness."

Ross Swimmer, whom Mankiller succeeded as principal chief when Swimmer was named to head the Bureau of Indian Affairs in 1985, said in an interview Tuesday that he visited Mankiller at her home two weeks ago. He said she was "in very good spirits" and that she felt like her work had made an impact. "She leaves a tremendous legacy, not just for the Cherokee Nation but for Indian women and women generally across the land," Swimmer said. "We're going to truly miss her."

She was a leader in women's rights and Indian rights and served on the boards of numerous humanitarian groups and foundations.

Mankiller counted feminist icon Gloria Steinem as a friend. Steinem was married in Mankiller's home.

Mankiller was born in Tahlequah and moved to California as a child. She returned to Oklahoma in 1977 and was the founding director of the Cherokee Nation Community Development Department before being elected deputy chief. She met with Presidents Ronald Reagan, George H. W. Bush and Bill Clinton to discuss tribal issues and helped facilitate the establishment of an Office of Indian Justice within the US Department of Justice.

Mankiller received numerous awards and was presented with the Medal of Freedom by President Clinton in January 1998. She was named Ms. *magazine's Woman of the Year and* ABC News *Person of the Week, both in 1987, and was named one of the "100 Most Important Women in America" by* Ladies' Home Journal *in 1987. At the time of her death, she held 14 honorary doctorates, including ones from Yale University and Dartmouth College.*

"Mankiller was a leader at a critical time in American history," said Bob Blackburn, executive director of the Oklahoma Historical Society. "For much of the early 20th Century, the government's policy was to disperse our Indian populations, putting them in cities . . . away from the land and away from their history. . . . When she burst onto the scene as principal chief, she understood the pressures of being the victim of misguided policy and trying to find her way back home and was determined to bring prosperity and an improved way of life to the Cherokee people. She set an example that was inspirational to America."

Mankiller donated letters and other papers dating from 1977 to 1995 to the University of Oklahoma in 1998. They are housed in the school's Western History library. "Wilma Mankiller made a lasting mark on our state and nation," OU President David Boren said in a written statement. "She helped all Americans understand the need to preserve the basic values of community and stewardship which are central to Native American culture. Above all, through her example she taught us the power of kindness and how to live and die with dignity."

Following the announcement of her death Tuesday, April 6, the Oklahoma Senate observed a moment of silence in her honor. It was a fitting testament to a woman who encouraged the world to listen. "In a quiet way . . . she could hold an audience just in the palm of her hands, everyone waiting for the next idea," said the Historical Society's Bob Blackburn. "And the love and compassion that came through her words just moved people. . . . I think that's how she lived her life: one word, one sentence at a time and built on the best principles of caring about other people."[3]

On Saturday, April 11, five days after her passing, the rolling thunder of a Kiowa drum rained down upon the Cherokee Nation Cultural Grounds at a small field near Tahlequah, where Wilma had been born. It was the only sound that could be heard that day, drowning out even the birds overhead and the squirrels skittering around in the distance. A crowd of nearly 1,200 people who had gathered to pay their last respects to the Cherokees' former principal chief fell silent for the woman they had come to see off on her final journey. The two-and-a-half-hour memorial service unfolded just as Wilma, in life, would have wanted it. Traditional tribal songs accompanied ceremonies and remembrances by those who knew Wilma best and loved her the most. The Clintons arrived to offer their statements, as did President Barack Obama and others.

The event was attended by government dignitaries, including Governor Brad Henry, Lieutenant Governor Jari Askins, and US Representative Dan Boren; feminist author and icon Gloria Steinem; and tribal leaders from across the state and country. The Cherokee Nation's principal chief, Chad Smith, recalled a letter that he had received from Wilma only weeks before her death, stating that she was emotionally prepared for the journey that lay ahead. The letter, he said, showed Mankiller to be a strong yet humble leader and a "patriot of the Cherokee Nation who gave her all for her nation."[4]

Smith and Deputy Chief Joe Grayson presented Wilma's family with the tribe's Medal of Patriotism in her honor, the first time a nonmilitary member had been given the award.

Former principal chief Ross Swimmer recalled her service with him as deputy chief, and how he, a Republican, and she, a Democrat, worked together for the tribe. Wilma's daughter Gina Olaya and her husband, Charlie, recalled some of the more personal moments of her life.

Her daughter Felicia Olaya read a statement that her mom had written four days before her death. In it, Wilma acknowledged that she'd led a fulfilling life, and she hoped people would be encouraged by it: "When I was 7 or 8 and living here, no one would have ever guessed what the future would bring. I hope people will learn from that about themselves and about others. Don't turn away from people because of how they look or what they have because you never know what they'll contribute to the world."[5]

After Felicia finished reading her mother's words, she whispered, "Rest in peace, Mom . . . you will forever be in our hearts."[6] Her mother was interred in Echota Cemetery in rural Stilwell, Oklahoma.

Symbolic of Wilma's never-ending quest for accomplishment, she had been scheduled to address Northeastern State University's 38th Annual Symposium of the American Indian on April 15, as she had done the previous year. Advocating, as always, for the rights and freedoms of indigenous people everywhere, she hoped to reach an entirely new generation of young Native Americans.

But she never made it.

Reporter Clifton Adcock of the *Tulsa World* staff wrote in an article about the symposium, titled "Symposium Lacking Its Star," the following day:

> *The chair sat empty.*
>
> *Modestly, yet respectfully, draped with a brown cloth bordered by yellow tassels and set stage right of the podium, the empty seat was a reminder that Wilma Mankiller would not be arriving that day.*
>
> *On Thursday, April 15, only nine days following Wilma Mankiller's death, the four people who composed the speakers' panel . . . remembered Mankiller's burning passion of the subject for the gathering.*

Mankiller, the former Cherokee Nation principal chief, and the other panelists last saw each other in November as she laid out a rough draft of the discussion on Indigenous Studies in the 21st Century.

She had planned to attend the event and moderate the panel, but she died April 6 of pancreatic cancer. She was 64.[7]

The NSU symposium that year was to feature a variety of events ranging from a powwow and American Indian–issue academic discussions to cornstalk shoots and stickball. The event had been dedicated in Wilma's honor.

But word spread quickly throughout the NSU campus. Before the panel took the stage, the audience fell hushed as university organizers dimmed the lights to reveal a short video tribute showing the former principal chief delivering NSU's 2009 commencement address only a year before. Portraits of symposium supporters who had died during the previous year, including Wilma and former Cherokee Nation deputy chief Hastings Shade, adorned the stage in stoic silence.

As the evening's discussion began, the panelists spoke about what they hoped would become of the college's indigenous studies programs, a term that Wilma liked to use to show solidarity with Native populations in countries around the world. Richard Allen, a policy analyst for the Cherokee Nation and the panel's moderator, said that he hoped to see NSU offer an advanced-degree program for American Indian studies. Wilma Mankiller, he emphasized, shared that vision.

"She was very concerned about the future of Indian students. It was her idea that Northeastern would become the premier university for American Indian studies" in the world, Allen said.[8]

Another panelist, Phyllis Fife, director of the Center for Tribal Studies at NSU, explained how advances in technology enabled American Indians to employ new ways to look at their past and revitalize their traditional languages.

"Students have always motivated the movements that have taken place on campus," Fife said. "We depend on that, and we would like to encourage that. With new technology, a wide range of resources and our abilities to communicate with one another, I see a great future for indigenous studies at NSU."[9]

Panelist Les Hannah, chairman of NSU's Department of Languages and Literature, said he hoped to see NSU unite with tribes across the state to create the Wilma P. Mankiller School of Indigenous Studies at NSU. Hannah recalled how he was often asked in his travels what good a degree in tribal studies was and what a person could do with it. Then, as if echoing the sentiments of Wilma Mankiller, he asked the rhetorical question, "What can you do with a native studies degree from Northeastern State University?" His response was as pointed as hers would have been: "Anything you want."[10]

* * *

And so it was that the coming and the going of one Native American woman by the name of Wilma Pearl Mankiller left its mark on humanity. She had stumbled into, contributed to, and departed the physical realm of the earth's boundaries forever. Battling a life-endangering automobile accident, polycystic kidney disease, myasthenia gravis, lymphoma, breast cancer, and two kidney transplants, she finally succumbed to pancreatic cancer. Throughout all the adversity, she never lost her good spirits, her mindfulness of the needs and wants of others, her motherly instincts both to her own two daughters and to the universe. She never lost her courage.

For that, Wilma could thank her father, a full-blooded Cherokee named Charlie Mankiller, and her mother, a sturdy woman of Dutch-Irish stock named Irene. They possessed similar traits, and they taught them to their daughter well. But most of all, Wilma could thank her own sense of survival, of upheaval and resettlement that was anything but settling, and of renewal of a spirit so anxious and set upon surviving. That young girl who refused to succumb to the pain and fear of desolation and isolation but instead rejected them. That young girl who refused to accept the adversity dealt to her as the new norm. She was the same young girl who grew into the older, wiser woman who refused to surrender to negativity, disparity, and failure. She is the one for whom her legacy lives on—not only in what she did to change the Cherokee Nation, but also in how she worked to alter the world view of the history and future of all Native Americans everywhere.

As principal chief, she is the one who rebuilt and remolded the Cherokee Nation Industries to include factories, motels, ranches, and a lumber company. She founded various community self-help programs and taught people ways out of poverty. She brought about significant strides for her people, including improved health care, education, utilities management, and tribal government. She played a pivotal role in attracting higher-paying industry to the area, improving adult literacy, and supporting women returning to school.

But she also lived in a much larger world, where she was active in civil rights issues, lobbying for government protection, and supporting women's issues and activities. She said, "We've had daunting problems in many critical areas, but I believe in the old Cherokee injunction to 'be of a good mind.' Today it's called positive thinking."[11] Mankiller was instrumental in establishing an international relationship between the Cherokee Nation and the federal government.

For her efforts, Wilma Mankiller received numerous awards on her travels through life, including *Ms.* magazine's Woman of the Year in 1987, the Oklahoma Women's Hall of Fame Woman of the Year, the Elizabeth Blackwell Award, and the John W. Gardner Leadership Award. She was inducted into the National Women's Hall of Fame in 1993, the same year in which she received the American Association of University Women's Achievement Award. Twenty years later, a 2013 feature film, *The Cherokee Word for Water*, was released, documenting the story of Wilma's tireless spearheading of the Bell waterline project that helped launch her political career.

In the end, Wilma Mankiller was not a child of the world but a woman *for* the world. She lived not to take what she could from life's offerings but, rather, to offer to life whatever she was capable of giving. After all, that's what she had intended to do from her earliest days as a civil rights advocate.

And that's what she did.

The Coyote and Death

In the beginning, death did not exist. Everyone stayed alive until there were so many people that there wasn't room for anyone else. The chiefs held a council to determine what to do.

One man rose and said that it would be good to have the people die and be gone for a little while and then to return. As soon as he sat down, Coyote jumped up and said that people ought to die forever because there was not enough food or room for everyone to live forever. The other men objected, saying that there would be no more happiness in the world if all their loved ones died.

All except Coyote voted to have the people die and be gone for a little while and then to come back to life.

Following the council, the medicine men built a large grass house facing east. They gathered the men of the tribe and told them that the people who died would come to the medicine house and then be restored to life. The chief medicine man said that he would put a large white and black eagle feather on top of the grass house. When the feather became bloody and fell over, the people would know that someone had died. Then all of the medicine men would come to the grass house and sing a song that would call the spirit of the dead to the grass house. When the spirit came to the house, they would restore the person to life again. All of the people were glad about these rules regarding death, for they were frightened for the dead.

After a time, the people saw the eagle feather turn bloody and fall, and they knew that someone had died. The medicine men assembled in the grass house and sang for the spirit of the dead to come to them. In about ten days, a whirlwind blew from the west, circled the grass house, and finally entered through the entrance in the east. From the whirlwind appeared a handsome young man who had been murdered by another tribe. All of the people saw him and rejoiced except Coyote, who was displeased because his wishes had been ignored.

In a short time, the feather became bloody and fell again. Coyote saw it and at once went to the grass house. He took his seat near the door and sat with the singers for many days. When at last he heard the whirlwind coming, he hurried to close the door before the whirlwind could enter. The spirit in the whirlwind passed on by. Coyote thus introduced the idea of permanent death, and people from that time on grieved over the dead and were unhappy.

Now, whenever anyone meets a whirlwind or hears the wind whistle, he says: "There is some one wandering about." Ever since Coyote closed the door, the spirits of the dead have wandered over the earth, trying to find some place to go, until at last they find the road to spirit land.

After that day, Coyote ran away and never came back, for he was afraid of what he had done. He always looked over his shoulder, fearful that someone was pursuing him. He has been starving ever since because no one will give him anything to eat.

Looking Ahead

In the 2008 run-up to the election for the office of president of the United States, upstart Democrat Party nominee Senator Barack Obama of Illinois found himself pitted against populist Republican senator John McCain of Arizona. For McCain's running mate, he chose sitting Alaska governor Sarah Palin, a feisty firebrand who never failed to draw large crowds and even larger controversies. In one of her more famous quips, she asked a gathering of enthusiastic supporters what the difference was between a hockey mom and a pit bull. After several seconds, she responded, "Lipstick."

Wilma Mankiller, no slouch herself when it came to quotable quips, appeared for a speech at the Heard Museum in Phoenix, Arizona, in October 2008. It was her last public appearance. The talk was titled "Challenges Facing 21st Century Indigenous People," and it coincidentally fell on the same evening as one of Sarah Palin's political rallies.

As Mankiller took the stage following an introduction by Native American activist and longtime friend Simon Ortiz, she stepped behind the microphone, looked out over the crowd, and said, "Let me begin by thanking all of you who came out tonight. I know it was a difficult decision." She held her hands out at her sides. "Sarah Palin, Wilma Mankiller. Sarah Palin, Wilma Mankiller. What should we do tonight?"

She followed up by describing her longtime relationship with Ortiz, saying that she had known him for, "Well, this is how long ago it was. He had black hair, and I was skinny. That was a long time ago."[1]

Why the people had decided to gather in the hall that night was obvious. It was nearly as apparent as the subject of Wilma's talk. In it, she hit upon the highlights of Native American accomplishments throughout her lifetime and targeted those challenges indigenous people throughout North America (and, indeed, the world) had to face.

She emphasized how water and water rights are critical to indigenous people—that controlling their access to life-giving, life-sustaining water literally meant the difference between life and death. All twenty tribal entities calling Arizona home have fought for and succeeded in reclaiming Native rights to their water. She pointed out, in particular, the Gila River Water Settlement in 2004, which came about only after decades of contracted litigation. The Gila River people, she said, never gave up the fight for their water rights, which were the very lifeblood of the tribe. "The Gila River Water Settlement is an example for all tribal people," she said.

More than 300 million indigenous people exist throughout the world, all with their own culture, language, history, and unique ways of life. Yet, all share several common traits, including one that dictates their lives are part of and inseparable from the natural world around them. Wilma quoted Onandaga (Iroquois) spiritual leader Oren Lyons:

> *Our knowledge is profound and comes from living in one place for untold generations. It comes from watching the sun rise in the east and set in the west from the same place over great sections of time. We are as familiar with the lands, rivers, and great seas that surround us as we are with the faces of our mothers. Indeed we call the earth Etenoha, our mother, from whence all life springs.*[2]

Throughout Native America, many prophecies exist. Stories are told, ranging from the meaning of life to the prophesizing of the end of the world, which will come about only when the people are no longer capable of protecting nature or restoring its balance. Wilma acknowledged the many thousands of people from different ethnic groups who care deeply about the environment and fight every day to protect the earth. "The difference between indigenous people and non-indigenous people who are engaged in that fight," she said, "is that indigenous people have the benefit of being regularly reminded of their responsibilities to the land by the [Native] stories and by ceremonies. That's the difference. They remain close to the land not only in their hearts but in the way they view the world."

She emphasized that when indigenous people talk about saving the land, they don't mean for the benefit of human beings only but, rather, for the profit of all living things, including plants and animals. Human beings are relatively insignificant beings when observed through the microcosm of time. She pointed to feminist activist/author Gloria Steinem, who said,

> *For 95% of the time that human beings walked the earth, you and I would have been living very differently, in small bands raising our children together as if each child were our own and migrating with the seasons. The whole idea of a settled life is about two minutes old in human history. There were no nations, no lines were drawn in the sand. Instead, there were migratory paths and watering places with trade and culture blossoming wherever the paths came together in patterns that spread over the continents like lace. This was far from a primitive way of life. Inner space was as explored by the many as outer space is now explored by the few. The ways of nature and animals, of creating language and art, of healing illness and preserving food, of governing and resolving conflicts had already been perfected over millennia.*[3]

It may seem ironic to those who didn't know her that Wilma summarized in a few words the difference between indigenous and non-indigenous people and laid down the gauntlet for human beings of *all* races inhabiting planet Earth. Many of the world's indigenous people share a fragmented but still omnipresent sense of responsibility for one another. Cooperation has always been necessary for the survival of tribal people, and even today, working together is more conducive to success than competing with one another. As Wilma observed, it's impressive to see how a sense of sharing and reciprocity continues in Native American communities into the twenty-first century given the "staggering amount of adversity indigenous people have had to face."

> *There is evidence of this sense of reciprocity in Cherokee communities. My husband, Charlie Soap, leads a widespread self-help movement among the Cherokee in which low-income volunteers work together to build walking trails, community centers, sports complexes, water lines, and houses. The self-help movement taps into the traditional value of cooperation for the sake of the common good.*

Despite such charitable philosophies among Native people—or perhaps because of them—North American tribal communities suffered at the hands of colonials who had infiltrated their lands, often by force, leading to the loss of an "incalculable number of lives and millions and millions of acres of land."

Subject to the will and authority of these invaders, Native people were forced to assimilate into colonial society or die. For those who chose to assimilate, the results were always the same: poverty, high infant mortality, rampant unemployment, and substance abuse with all its precipitant problems. Mankiller pointed out that in her studies of indigenous people around the world, their stories sounded "all too familiar." Except for the different tribal names and places, they were the same storied tales as those of Native Americans, and their outcomes were identical.

In one African culture, for example, the colonial interlopers methodically worked to gain control: "Take the land, discredit the leaders, ridicule the traditional healers and medicine men, take the children and send them off to boarding schools." As Wilma recalled, it was "a very familiar story." The same scenario played out in Australia with its aboriginal population, in the Amazon rain forest, as well as on every other continent throughout the world. She said, "It's important to remember that many of the world's social, political, and economic problems can be found in colonial policies, and these policies continue today across the globe."

Even environmentalists, assumed to be in the vanguard of the rush to save the planet from exploitation, often get things askew. They find themselves so focused on the land and the animals that inhabit it that they often overlook the local people who are being killed or forcibly removed for the sake of big business and corporate profits. Yet, these very people are the keepers of the gate, the ones who know the local lands best and understand how best to care for and preserve them for future generations.

Such a lack of information about indigenous people by those outside their cultures creates a void that simply can't be filled by outside influences. Instead of attempting to understand indigenous people and their worlds, colonials attempt to fill the void by either vilifying the Natives as the "bad guys" who are savage descendants of other demonic forces throughout history or romanticizing them as innocent children of nature, spiritual but incapable of higher thought or commendable action. Whether vilified or romanticized, these stereotypes are equally damaging, said Mankiller, "to our children, to our families, and to our people."

Public stereotypes about indigenous people, she warned, must change in the future. Indigenous leaders are beginning to realize the direct tie between public perception and public policies created toward them. These are the very same leaders who must frame their issues before the public; if they don't, other non-indigenous individuals will. History shows that indigenous leaders throughout North America had signed several treaties with world leaders before the first permanent settlements were ever established in North America. They met with the French, English, and Spanish and often traveled overseas to confer with their monarchs, carrying along various documents and painstakingly hand-drawn maps showing their traditional lands in the belief that they were being taken seriously, as would any modern-day representative head of state. It was only years later that historical records revealed just how poorly they were regarded and how they were taken simply for objects of curiosity or even disdain—savages in a refined world.

Sadly, few non-indigenous people in the United States today understand the workings of the indigenous people whose traditional homes and villages some colonials have occupied now for upwards of hundreds of years. Few of them understand, as Wilma emphasized, how indigenous people have their own judicial system, operate their own police force, run their own schools, administer their own clinics, own more than a dozen tribal colleges, and operate a wide range of businesses and enterprises.

Yet, she said, each indigenous community is unique, and each has its specific needs and requirements to meet in order to ensure its survival. Instead of being viewed through a single homogeneous prism, indigenous people need to be seen through a more sharply focused lens, exposing them as complex, multicultural human beings who cannot be lumped into a single group and labeled accordingly. "And we're certainly not getting that from the media," she said.

> Without question, the combined efforts of government and various religious groups to eradicate traditional knowledge systems had had a profoundly negative impact on the culture as well as the social and economic systems of indigenous people. But despite all that, we can still hear the languages being spoken. There are still many cultural processes that continue. We've held onto our values and our sense of community and responsibility for one another. . . .
>
> It makes you optimistic about where we're going in the future. And although some of the original languages, ceremonies, and knowledge systems have been irretrievably lost, the ceremonial fires of many indigenous people across the globe have survived the upheaval. Sometimes indigenous communities have almost had to reinvent themselves as a people. But they have never, ever given up their sense of responsibility to one another and to the land. It is the sense of interdependence and the values that have sustained tribal people thus far, and I believe it will sustain them well into the future.

It's true that the world is changing, but indigenous people understand all about change, having proven time and again that they're quite capable of adopting and adapting. One of the greatest of these changes today involves the challenges for indigenous people to figure out a way to develop practical models to capture, maintain, and pass on traditional tribal systems to future generations. "There is nothing in the world, *nothing*, that can replace the sense of continuity in knowing that a genuine understanding of tribal knowledge brings," Wilma said, "so we've got to figure out a way to preserve that."

Perhaps one day, indigenous people who believe intrinsically that all living things are related and interdependent can help policymakers understand how counterproductive destroying the very nature that sustains us is. In 2007, following thirty years of advocacy by indigenous people around the globe, the United Nations passed a resolution supporting the universal rights of Native people. The resolution passed over the objections of the United States and Australia. The challenge that followed remains today: How can we be certain that the provisions of the resolution are honored and the rights of indigenous people all over the world are upheld?

When the Cherokee people had control of their lives, they built schools and hospitals, places of worship and governmental centers that rivaled any in the world. They developed their own alphabet, wrote books, produced poetry, and created fine art. Following the US government's attempts to assimilate the Cherokee into the larger society, educational levels among indigenous people plummeted. Unemployment skyrocketed. Living conditions dropped to subhuman. Since the 1970s, when the government was forced to reevaluate its programs and recognize the Cherokee people as a unified social entity entitled to equal rights and protections under US law, Native people have once again lifted themselves up to a higher standard of living, showing the world that when allowed to govern themselves, these people have enormous potential. It's only when the federal government steps in to mediate that the systems fall apart.

As Wilma stressed, "I am an indigenous woman of the twenty-first century [and being so means] my life has literally played itself out within a set of reciprocal relationships with members of my community and also with members of my family."

One of the advantages of being born an indigenous person is in knowing that no matter what happens in your life, someone will always be there for you and you'll be there for that person. It's a reciprocal relationship. No matter where in the world you go, someone will be around to remind you: You belong. As Wilma explained,

Being an indigenous person in the twenty-first century means being part of a group of people with the most valuable and ancient knowl-edge on the planet, a people who still have a direct relationship and a responsibility to the land and to other people.

Being indigenous also means enjoying family life while growing personally through Native stories, languages, and ceremonial rituals despite an incredible history of oppression. It means you can trust your thought processes, believe in yourself, and envision the future while being able to turn to your community for the skill sets and leadership abilities to turn those visions into reality. It means being able to dream of a future in which people everywhere support indigenous human rights and self-determination. It means that while land and resources can be colonized, hopes and dreams cannot be.

Being indigenous means sharing traditional knowledge and practices with indigenous communities the world over as never before possible via cell phones and the Internet. It means becoming a physician or a scientist or an astronaut who leaves her footprints on the moon and then returns home to participate in ceremonies her people have embraced since the beginning of time. It means putting your anger aside and forgetting past injustices capable of paralyzing your future actions. As Wilma said,

We've always been advised to keep our eyes fixed firmly on the future. One of my favorite proverbs . . . is a Mohawk proverb, and they tell their people not to be angry about the past and not to be paralyzed by what's going on in their community today but to continually move forward, pick yourself up and keep moving forward, and their prov-erb is it's hard to see the future with tears in your eyes. I love that proverb. I think it speaks for all our nations and certainly speaks for me personally. So let me leave you with that proverb: It's hard to see the future with tears in your eyes.

And with those simple words, Wilma Pearl Mankiller concluded her talk at the Heard Museum in Phoenix, sponsored by Arizona State University. No one outside of her immediate family knew how seriously ill she was when she stood up behind the podium that night. During her remaining eighteen months on earth, she would only get worse. As her physical strength drained from her body and she was no longer able to keep pace with her mental acuity, she began turning down additional requests for talks, awards, and various other appearances and remained close to hearth and home. She was not uncomfortable there, for home to Wilma Mankiller meant being near her friends and family, near nature in its most glorious finery, near where she had been born and raised before being yanked away by a vindictive and thoughtless program of the federal government bent upon destroying her and all like her who came before or would soon come after.

It's difficult to say whether or not the government would have succeeded in destroying America's indigenous culture but for Wilma Mankiller's innate resistance. That seems something of a stretch. But it's no stretch in saying that through that resistance—as well as through her endless bravery and bravado, her quick wits and quicker action—she made the task that much more difficult for Uncle Sam. And she eventually forced him to recognize the error of his ways. And to capitulate.

It is perhaps cruelly ironic that of all US presidents throughout the nation's long and vaunted history, it was Eisenhower who first embarked upon the ill-fated and ill-advised program of resettlement bent upon the eventual destruction of the tribal unit in America. Dwight D. Eisenhower, the World War II general and multi-decorated war hero who returned to the States following the armistice to the resounding cheers of all Americans everywhere. Not surprisingly, those cheers included those of Native Americans, many of whom had served in that conflict and would go on to serve—and some, to die—in the Korean War a few short years later.

And ending the resettlement program, ironically enough again, was Nixon, who quietly, beneath the glare of the spotlights and beyond the gaze of the political rallies, said, *Enough!* That's the same Richard M. Nixon who lied incessantly to the American public, broke his word innumerable times along the bumpy trail to the Oval Office, was caught red-handed playing "dirty tricks" on political opponents, approved a cover-up of the Watergate office break-in, lied to Congress under oath, and ultimately resigned the presidency in disgrace under threat of an impeachment vote in the US Senate that would have stripped him of all power and forcibly removed him from office.

Who is to know, sometimes, who will do what in politics and who will do something else? Who is to anticipate who will be lauded and who will be crucified? Who will be the hero and who the goat?

Certainly, Wilma Mankiller couldn't have known when the resettlement act was issued quietly into existence, and she hadn't known when it was just as quietly phased out. But one thing is certain.

She knew what was right and what was wrong. Thanks to her parents and their parents and their parents before them, she never once had to stop to contemplate the difference. And she never stopped working for the benefit of her beloved people. The Cherokee Nation? Yes, of course. But also the oppressed minorities. The downtrodden women of America. And the indigenous people of the entire world.

Wilma Mankiller was a fighter for freedom and justice. There is simply no other, no better, way to describe her. And for that, she will always be appreciated, lauded, and revered.

And remembered.

Endnotes

One: Pure Pearl

1. Wilma Mankiller and Michael Wallis, *Mankiller: A Chief and Her People* (New York: St. Martin's Press, 1993), 8.
2. Ibid., 9.
3. Ibid., 10.
4. Ibid.
5. Ibid., 11.
6. Gerald Hausman, *Turtle Island Alphabet: A Lexicon of Native American Symbols and Culture* (New York: St. Martin's Press, 1992), 131.
7. Mankiller and Wallis, *Mankiller*, 13.
8. Ibid.
9. Ibid., 31–32.
10. Ibid., 32.
11. Ibid.
12. Ibid., 33.
13. Ibid.
14. Ibid., 34.
15. Ibid., 34–35.
16. Ibid.
17. Ibid., 35.
18. Ibid., 36.
19. Ibid.
20. Ibid., 36–37.
21. Ibid., 37.
22. Ibid.
23. Ibid.
24. Ibid., 37–38.
25. Ibid., 38.
26. Ibid., 39.
27. Ibid., 40.
28. Ibid., 40–41.
29. Ibid., 42.
30. Ibid.

31. U.S. Department of the Interior, Bureau of Indian Affairs, accessed February 11, 2019, https://www.bia.gov/sites/bia.gov/files/assets/public/press_release/pdf/idc016139 .pdf.

32. "Trail of Tears," History.com, last modified July 7, 2020, https://www.history.com /topics/native-american-history/trail-of-tears.

33. "A Brief History of the Trail of Tears," Cherokee Nation (website), accessed February 11, 2019, https://www.cherokee.org/About-The-Nation/History/Trail-of -Tears/A-Brief-History-of-the-Trail-of-Tears.

34. Ibid.

35. Mankiller and Wallis, *Mankiller*, 69.

36. Ibid.

37. Ibid.

38. Ibid., 70.

39. Ibid., 70–71.

40. Ibid., 71.

41. Ibid.

42. Ibid., 72.

43. Connie Griffin, "Relearning to Trust Ourselves: Interview with Wilma Mankiller," *Women of Power* 7, 256.

44. Mankiller and Wallis, *Mankiller*, 72.

45. Ibid.

46. Ibid., 73.

47. Ibid.

48. Ibid., 62.

49. Sarah Eppler Janda, *Beloved Women: The Political Lives of LaDonna Harris and Wilma Mankiller* (DeKalb: Northern Illinois University Press, 2007), 82.

50. Mankiller and Wallis, *Mankiller*, 76.

51. Ibid.

52. Ibid., 102–3.

53. Ibid., 104.

54. Ibid.

55. Ibid., 105.

56. Ibid.

57. Ibid., 106.

58. Ibid., 108.

59. Ibid., 109.

60. Ibid., 110.

61. Ibid.

Two: Every Inch a Mankiller

1. Wilma Mankiller and Michael Wallis, *Mankiller: A Chief and Her People* (New York: St. Martin's Press, 1993), 106–7.

2. Ibid., 107.

3. Sarah Eppler Janda, *Beloved Women: The Political Lives of LaDonna Harris and Wilma Mankiller* (DeKalb: Northern Illinois University Press, 2007), 83.

4. Mankiller and Wallis, *Mankiller*, 111.

5. Ibid., 112.

6. Ibid., 113–14.

7. Ibid., 114.

8. Ibid.

9. Ibid.

10. Ibid., 114–15.

11. Wilma Mankiller, "Rebuilding the Cherokee Nation," Gifts of Speech, Sweet Briar College, April 2, 1993, http://gos.sbc.edu/m/mankiller.html.

12. Mankiller and Wallis, *Mankiller*, xxiii.

13. Ben Winton, "The Occupation of Alcatraz," Native Press, May 1, 2010, https://thenativepress.com/rezpolitics/the-occupation-of-alcatraz.

14. Mankiller and Wallis, *Mankiller*, 192.

15. Winton, "Occupation of Alcatraz."

16. Ibid.

17. Mankiller and Wallis, *Mankiller*, 193.

18. Winton, "Occupation of Alcatraz."

19. Ibid.

20. Ibid.

21. Ibid.

22. Ibid.

23. Ibid.

24. Ibid.

25. Ibid.

26. Ibid.

27. Ibid.

28. Ibid.

29. Ibid.

30. Mankiller and Wallis, *Mankiller*, 158.

31. Ibid., 193.

32. Troy R. Johnson, *The Occupation of Alcatraz Island* (Carbondale: University of Illinois Press, 1996), 101.

33. Mankiller and Wallis, *Mankiller*, 194.

34. Ibid., 195.

35. Ibid.

36. Ibid., 196.

37. Ibid., 197.

38. Ibid.

39. Ibid., 198.

40. Ibid., 199.

41. Ibid., 200.

42. Ibid.

43. Ibid., 201.
44. Ibid., 202.
45. Ibid., 202–3.
46. Ibid., 203.
47. Ibid., 204.
48. Ibid.
49. Ibid., 205.

THREE: TRAIL OF TRAGEDY

1. Wilma Mankiller and Michael Wallis, *Mankiller: A Chief and Her People* (New York: St. Martin's Press, 1993), 208.
2. Ibid.
3. Ibid., 208–9.
4. Ibid., 210.
5. Devon Abbott Mihesuah, *Indigenous American Women: Decolonization, Empowerment, Activism* (Lincoln: University of Nebraska Press, 2003), xix.
6. Mankiller and Wallis, *Mankiller*, 211.
7. Ibid.
8. Ibid., 211–12.
9. Ibid., 212.
10. Ibid., 212–14.
11. Ibid., 214–15.
12. Ibid., 216.
13. Ibid., 217.
14. Ibid., 220.
15. Ibid., 121.
16. Ibid., 221.
17. Ibid., 221–22.
18. Ibid., 223.
19. Ibid., 223–24.
20. *Daily Oklahoman* (Oklahoma City), November 9, 1979.
21. Mankiller and Wallis, *Mankiller*, 225–26.
22. Ibid., 226–27.
23. Ibid., 227.
24. Ibid., 228.
25. Ibid., 228–29.

FOUR: THE LONG WAY HOME

1. Wilma Mankiller, "Keeping Pace with the Rest of the World," *Southern Exposure* 13, no. 6 (January 1985).
2. Wilma Mankiller and Michael Wallis, *Mankiller: A Chief and Her People* (New York: St. Martin's Press, 1993), 233.

3. Ibid.

4. Gloria Steinem, *Revolution from Within: A Book of Self-Esteem* (New York: Open Road Media, 2012), 94–95.

5. Charlie Soap and Thomas Muskrat to Applicants, March 24, 1983, folder 3, box 37, Wilma Mankiller Collection (WMC), Western History Collection (WHC), University of Oklahoma (OU); Wilma Mankiller to Housing Participants, October 6, 1983, folder 3, box 37, WMC, WHC, OU.

6. Steinem, *Revolution from Within*, 96.

7. Sarah Eppler Janda, *Beloved Women: The Political Lives of LaDonna Harris and Wilma Mankiller* (DeKalb: Northern Illinois University Press, 2007), 89.

8. Steinem, *Revolution from Within*, 96.

9. Ibid.

10. Ibid., 97.

11. Mankiller and Wallis, *Mankiller*, 235.

12. Ibid., 236.

13. Ibid., 237–38.

14. Ibid., 238.

15. Ibid.

16. Ibid.

17. Ibid., 239.

18. Ibid.

19. Ibid.

20. Ibid., 240–41.

21. Ibid., 241.

22. Ibid.

23. Ibid., 241–42.

24. *Daily Oklahoman* (Oklahoma City), August 14, 1983.

25. "Wilma Mankiller: The Legacy of Wisdom," Corporation for Public Broadcasting, accessed February 23, 2020, https://www.cpb.org/files/wilma-mankiller-legacy-wisdom.

26. Ibid.

27. Mankiller and Wallis, *Mankiller*, 242.

28. Ibid., 243.

29. Ibid., 244.

30. "Woman to Take Over as Chief of Cherokees," *Salina Journal*, November 18, 1985.

31. Steinem, *Revolution from Within*, 97.

32. Mankiller and Wallis, *Mankiller*, 245.

33. Ibid.

34. Ibid., 246.

35. Ibid.

36. William T. Hagan, "Full Blood, Mixed Blood, Generic, and Ersatz: The Problem with Indian Identity," *Arizona and the West* 27, no. 4 (Winter 1985): 317–18.

37. Devon Abbott Mihesuah, *Indigenous American Women: Decolonization, Empowerment, Activism* (Lincoln: University of Nebraska Press, 2003), 103.

38. Gloria Gaynor, *I Will Survive* (New York: St. Martin's Press, 1997), 21.

39. Mankiller and Wallis, *Mankiller*, 246–47.

40. Ibid., 247.

41. Ibid., 248.

42. Ibid., 248–49.

43. Ibid., 249.

44. Steinem, *Revolution from Within*, 98.

45. Mankiller and Wallis, *Mankiller*, 250.

46. Jo Carillo, *Readings in American Indian Law* (Philadelphia: Temple University Press, 1998), 251.

47. Mankiller and Wallis, *Mankiller*, 251.

48. Ibid., 252.

49. Ibid., 253–54.

50. Ibid., 254.

51. Ibid., 255.

52. Ibid.

53. Ibid., 256.

54. Ibid., 256–57.

55. Ibid., 257.

FIVE: IN CONTROL OF CHANGE

1. Wilma Mankiller and Michael Wallis, *Mankiller: A Chief and Her People* (New York: St. Martin's Press, 1993), 259.

2. Ibid.

3. Ibid., 259–60.

4. Ibid., 261.

5. Ibid.

6. Ibid., 270.

7. Ibid.

8. Ibid.

9. Ibid., 271.

10. Ibid., 271–72.

11. Ibid.

12. "Mankiller Gets Kidney from Niece," *Daily Oklahoman* (Oklahoma City), July 23, 1998.

13. Mankiller and Wallis, *Mankiller*, 273.

14. Ibid., 274.

15. Ibid.

16. Ibid.

17. Ibid., 274–75.

SIX: WHERE ACTIVISM AND FEMINISM COLLIDE

1. Wilma Mankiller/Michael Wallis interview, January 27, 1992, p. 9, folder 7, box 43, WMC, WHC, OU.

2. Robert Hill Winfrey, "Civil Rights and the American Indian: Through the 1960s" (PhD diss., Department of History, University of Oklahoma, 1986), 145.

3. Karen Ziegelman, "Generational Politics and American Indian Youth Movements of the 1960s and 1970s" (master's thesis, University of Arizona, 1985), 4.

4. Ibid., 13.

5. Donna Hightower Langston, "American Indian Women's Activism in the 1960s and 1970s," *Hypatia* 18, no. 2 (2003): 115, www.jstor.org/stable/3811016.

6. Ibid.

7. Winfrey, "Civil Rights," 86.

8. Kathryn Sinclair, "Maka Sitomniya Teca Ukiye Oyate Ukiye: The American Indian Movement," *Political Expressions* 1, no. 2 (1996): 33–52.

9. Langston, "American Indian Women's Activism," 116.

10. Troy Johnson, *Alcatraz Indian Land Forever* (Los Angeles: UCLA American Indian Studies Center, 1994), 29.

11. Ward Churchill and Jim Vander Wall, *Agents of Repression: The FBI's Secret Wars against the Black Panther Party and the American Indian Movement* (Boston: South End Press, 1990), 118.

12. Winfrey, "Civil Rights," 237.

13. Ibid., 238.

14. Langston, "American Indian Women's Activism," 124.

15. Ibid.

16. Mary Crawford, "Indians Back on Alcatraz 'For 2 Days,'" *San Francisco Examiner*, November 20, 1969.

17. Ben Winton, "Alcatraz Changed Everything," *News from Indian Country* 8, no. 20 (November 1999): 8–11.

18. Troy Johnson, Diane Nagel, and Duane Champagne, *American Indian Activism: Alcatraz to the Longest Walk* (Champaign: University of Illinois Press, 1997), 30.

19. Langston, "American Indian Women's Activism," 120.

20. Winton, "Alcatraz Changed Everything," 10.

21. Ibid., 9.

22. Annette Jaimes, "American Indian Women: Center of Indigenous Resistance," in *The State of Native America*, ed. Annette Jaimes (Boston: South End Press, 1992), 312.

23. Ziegelman, "Generational Politics," 27.

24. Langston, "American Indian Women's Activism," 122.

25. Diane Payne, "Each of My Generation," *Indian Truth* 239 (May-June 1994): 5–7.

26. Langston, "American Indian Women's Activism," 123.

27. Timothy Baylor, "Modern Warriors: Mobilization and Decline of the American Indian Movement (AIM), 1968–1979" (PhD diss., Department of History, University of North Carolina at Chapel Hill, 1994), 74.

28. Ziegelman, "Generational Politics," 73.

29. Russell Means, *Where White Men Fear to Tread* (New York: St. Martin's Press, 1995), 244.

30. Johnson, Nagel, and Champagne, *American Indian Activism*, 248.

31. Baylor, "Modern Warriors," 191.

32. James Olson, *Native Americans in the Twentieth Century* (Champaign: University of Illinois Press, 1984), 171.

33. Peter Matthiessen, *In the Spirit of Crazy Horse* (New York: Viking, 1983), 60.

34. Rex Weyler, *Blood of the Land* (Philadelphia: New Society Publishers, 1992), 73.

35. Mary Brave Bird, *Ohitika Woman* (New York: Grove Press, 1994), 196.

36. Weyler, *Blood*, 83.

37. Matthiessen, *Crazy Horse*, 69.

38. Ibid., 132.

39. Baylor, "Modern Warriors," 202.

40. John William Sayer, *Ghost Dancing the Law* (Cambridge, MA: Harvard University Press, 1997), 224.

41. Mary Crow Dog, *Lakota Woman* (New York: Harper, 1990), 206.

42. Frederica Daly, "Perspectives of Native American Women on Race and Gender," in *Challenging Racism and Sexism: Alternatives to Genetic Explanations*, ed. Ethel Tobach and Betty Rosoff (New York: Feminist Press, 1994), 138.

43. Bea Medicine, *The Native American Woman: A Perspective* (Las Cruces, NM: National Educational Laboratory Publishers, 1983), 334.

44. Devon Abbott Mihesuah, *Indigenous American Women: Decolonization, Empowerment, Activism* (Lincoln: University of Nebraska Press, 2003), 42.

45. Langston, "American Indian Women's Activism, " 129.

46. Rayne Green, "Native American Women: A Review Essay," *Signs* 6, no. 2 (1980): 248–68.

47. Ibid.

48. Langston, "American Indian Women's Activism," 130.

49. Sarah Eppler Janda, *Beloved Women: The Political Lives of LaDonna Harris and Wilma Mankiller* (DeKalb: Northern Illinois University Press, 2007), 167.

50. Nancy Burns, Kay Lehman Schlozman, and Sidney Verba, *The Private Roots of Public Action: Gender, Equality, and Political Participation* (Cambridge, MA: Harvard University Press, 2001), 155.

51. Ibid.

52. Maureen O'Dea Caragliano, "Beyond Princess and Squaw: Wilma Mankiller and the Cherokee Gynocentric System" (master's thesis, Department of Social Sciences, San Jose State University, 1997).

53. Clara Sue Kidwell, "The Power of Native American Women in Traditional Societies," April 1, 1982, Department of Special Collections and University Archives, California State University, https://archive.org/details/css_000021.

54. Janda, *Beloved Women*, 171–72.

55. Mihesuah. *Indigenous*, 143.

56. Wilma Mankiller to "Dear Friends," September 1, 1993, folder 6, box 1, WMC, WHC, OU; United States Representative Susan Molinari to Wilma Mankiller, March 5, 1993, folder 19, box 10, WMC, WHC, OU; Wilma Mankiller to United States Senator David Boren, October 15, 1991, folder 3, box 6, WMC, WHC, OU.

57. Wilma Mankiller to United States Senator David Boren, November 1, 1993, folder 2, box 2, WMC, WHC, OU; United States Senator David Boren to Wilma Mankiller,

November 12, 1993; Jane P. Wiseman, district judge, to Wilma Mankiller, August 26, 1993, folder 2, box 2, WMC, WHC, OU.

58. Janda, *Beloved Women*, 175.

59. Ibid.

60. Correspondence from Ada Deer to LaDonna Harris, July 26, 1974, series 1, box 6, LaDonna Harris Collection, NAES College, Chicago.

61. Clara Sue Kidwell, "Ada Deer," in *The New Warriors*, ed. R. David Edmunds (Lincoln: University of Nebraska Press, 2004), 239–60.

62. "Testimony of Principal Chief Wilma P. Mankiller, Cherokee Nation of Oklahoma, in support of Ada E. Deer for confirmation as assistant secretary of interior for Indian affairs, Senate Committee on Indian Affairs," July 15, 1993, p. 2, folder 13, box 19, WMC, WHC, OU.

63. Wilma Mankiller to Ada Deer, February 22, 1994, folder 1, folder 15, box 13, WMC, WHC, OU.

64. Ada Deer to Wilma Mankiller, June 27, 1994, folder 15, box 3, WMC, WHC, OU.

65. LaDonna Harris to Wilma Mankiller, October 10, 1994, folder 17, box 2, WMC, WHC, OU.

66. Clara Nomee, madam chairman, Crow Tribal Council, to Wilma Mankiller, August 4, 1993, folder 1, box 10, WMC, WHC, OU.

67. Janda, *Beloved Women*, 177.

68. Ibid., 179.

69. Wilma Mankiller and Michael Wallis, *Mankiller: A Chief and Her People* (New York: St. Martin's Press, 1993), x.

70. Wilma Mankiller/Michael Wallis interview, January 27, 1992, p. 9, folder 7, box 43, WMC, WHC, OU.

71. LaDonna Harris biographical profile, p. 1, folder 1, box 2, WMC, WHC, OU.

Seven: The Life Spirit

1. "Wilma Mankiller," National Women's Hall of Fame, accessed February 12, 2020, https://www.womenofthehall.org/inductee/wilma-mankiller.

2. "Mankiller Undergoes Cancer Testing at Boston Hospital," *Daily Oklahoman* (Oklahoma City), February 29, 1996.

3. "Mankiller's Tests Show Inoperable Colon Cancer," *Daily Oklahoman*, March 6, 1996.

4. Ibid.

5. "Mankiller Tells Students to Embrace Heritage," *Daily Oklahoman*, November 15, 1996.

6. "Clinton Gives Mankiller Highest US Honor," *Daily Oklahoman*, January 16, 1998.

7. Wilma P. Mankiller, "'Tribal Sovereignty Is a Sacred Trust': An Open Letter to the Conference," *American Indian Law Review* 23, no. 2 (1998): 479–80.

8. Shannon Muchmore, "Former Cherokee Chief Wilma Mankiller Gravely Ill, Husband Says," *Tulsa World*, March 2, 2010.

9. Gloria Steinem, *Revolution from Within: A Book of Self-Esteem* (Boston: Little, Brown and Co., 1992), 98.

10. Wilma Mankiller, *Every Day Is a Good Day* (Golden, CO: Fulcrum Publishing, 2004), xiii-xiv.

11. Devon Abbott Mihesuah, *Indigenous American Women: Decolonization, Empowerment, Activism* (Lincoln: University of Nebraska Press, 2003), 82.

EIGHT: A GOD NAMED FOREVER

1. Shannon Muchmore, "Former Cherokee Chief Wilma Mankiller Gravely Ill, Husband Says," *Tulsa World*, March 2, 2010.

2. "She Was a Pioneer for Her Generation," *Oklahoman* (Oklahoma City), April 7, 2010.

3. Ken Raymond, "A Legend in Her Own Time," *Oklahoman*, April 7, 2010.

4. Clifton Adcock, "Family, Leaders Honor Former Cherokee Chief," *Tulsa World*, April 11, 2010.

5. Ibid.

6. Ibid.

7. Clifton Adcock, "Symposium Lacking Its Star," *Tulsa World*, April 16, 2010.

8. Ibid.

9. Ibid.

10. Ibid.

11. "Wilma Mankiller," National Women's Hall of Fame, accessed February 16, 2020, https://www.womenofthehall.org/inductee/wilma-mankiller.

EPILOGUE

1. Unless otherwise noted, all quotes in the epilogue are taken from "Wilma Mankiller—Challenges Facing 21st Century Indigenous People" (video), Arizona State University Libraries, October 2, 2008, https://archive.org/details/WilmaMankiller -ChallengesFacing21stCenturyIndigenousPeopleVideo/MankillerWilma_ASULibraries _20081002.mp4.

2. "Our knowledge is profound and comes from living in one place for untold generations," Wilma Mankiller, "Being Indigenous in the 21st Century," Cultural Survival, March 1, 2009. Accessed March 4, 2020, https://www.culturalsurvival.org/publications/ cultural-survival-quarterly/being-indigenous-21st-century.

3. "Transgressing Distinctions of Gender and Race" (plenary session, American Sociological Association, 101st Annual Meeting, Montreal, Quebec, August 14, 2006), https://www.asanet.org/sites/default/files/awards_ceremony_transcript_2006.pdf.

About the Author

Born and raised in Chicago, **D. J. Herda** worked for years at the *Chicago Tribune*, the *Chicago Sun-Times*, and at numerous other Chicago-area newspapers and magazines before becoming an internationally syndicated columnist. During its decade-long run, Herda's column, *In Focus*, appeared in more than 1,100 newspapers with a combined circulation of nearly twenty million readers. He also taught Creative Writing Workshop and analytic grammar at the college level for more than a decade. He has worked as a book, magazine, and newspaper editor and has ghostwritten or book-doctored numerous authors' works. His photographs have appeared in publications and galleries around the world.

Herda's interest in Western Americana goes back to his childhood. He has published books and articles on the subjects of Calamity Jane, Doc Holliday, Frank and Jesse James, Billy the Kid, Butch Cassidy and the Wild Bunch, Wyatt Earp, Etta Place, and other Western legends. He wrote "Forts of the American West" and other articles for *American West*, *Arizona Highways*, and other Western magazines. Herda lived in the Rocky Mountains of the southwestern United States for nearly three decades before moving to Oklahoma to complete work on his tribute to a remarkable woman.